# THE
# INQUISITION

# THE
# INQUISITION

John A. O'Brien, Ph.D., LL.D.

UNIVERSITY OF NOTRE DAME

*Macmillan Publishing Co., Inc.*
NEW YORK

*Collier Macmillan Publishers*
LONDON

Macmillan Publishing Co., Inc.
866 Third Avenue
New York, New York 10022
Collier-Macmillan Canada Ltd., Toronto, Ontario

Library of Congress Catalog Number: 73-1962

FIRST PRINTING 1973

Printed in the United States of America

*To*

*The Memory of Pope John XXIII*

*Who Brought a New Era of*

*Understanding, Friendship and Love*

*To the Religious World*

*This Volume is Dedicated*

*With the Author's Esteem and Gratitude*

Every step of progress the world has made has been from scaffold to scaffold and from stake to stake.

WENDELL PHILLIPS

I have sworn eternal hostility to every form of tyranny over the mind of man.

THOMAS JEFFERSON

# Contents

|  | FOREWORD | xi |
| I | UNDERSTANDING THE INQUISITION | 1 |
| II | ESTABLISHMENT OF THE INQUISITION | 9 |
| III | THE INQUISITION IN OPERATION | 17 |
| IV | EXTORTION OF CONFESSION | 26 |
| V | THE USE OF TORTURE | 38 |
| VI | THE CATHAR THREAT | 55 |
| VII | THE CONFISCATION POLICY | 73 |
| VIII | THE SPANISH INQUISITION | 88 |
| IX | EXPULSIONS FROM SPAIN | 100 |
| X | THE WITCH-HUNT MANIA | 112 |
| XI | THE SABBAT: HEART OF WITCHCRAFT | 129 |
| XII | JOAN OF ARC | 143 |

x                              *Contents*

XIII   SAVONAROLA: A HERETIC?                        159

XIV    GALILEO FACES THE INQUISITION                 183

 XV    A NEW ERA                                     210

       NOTES                                         219

       BIBLIOGRAPHY                                  223

       INDEX                                         227

# Foreword

For many years the Inquisition has been a subject of deep interest and fascination to me. I find in this unique institution of the Middle Ages a strange combination of remarkable faith and zeal, on the one hand, and of incredible cruelty and savagery, on the other.

To answer the questions most frequently asked by university students and other thoughtful people, I wrote a 64-page booklet, *The Truth about the Inquisition,* published by the Paulist Press of New York in 1950. Each chapter had a list of questions designed to stimulate class discussion and further study. The booklet evidently met, at least in part, a widespread need, for it went through a number of printings.

Despite its popularity, however, I was conscious that limitations of space rendered it impossible to do anything remotely approaching full justice to such a vast theme stretching, in one form or another, over approximately six centuries (1231-1834). For many years I have hoped to find time to treat this engrossing subject at much greater length and with greater thoroughness. This book is the realization of that hope.

Unlike most books which treat the Inquisition in a cold, abstract and distant manner, I have endeavored to relate many incidents which bring the subject to life and thus enable the reader to feel as a participant. Neither have I failed to let my moral indignation come to the surface when narrating the cruel and inhuman actions of the Inquisitors.

For a historian to relate such incidents with icy indifference and no feeling of repugnance would be to strip history of moral values and undertones and put it on par with wrestling with a problem in mathematics.

Running as a *leitmotiv* through the volume is the principle of freedom of thought and conscience against the violence and coercive measures of the Inquisitors who generally regarded a day's work wasted if it brought no victim to the jail, dungeon or stake.

Instead of ending with the cries of the victim in the reader's ear, I am fortunate in being able to end realistically on a blended note of optimism and joy by citing the revolutionary changes in the relations of the great religious bodies toward one another. The ecumenical movement has gone a long way toward replacing aloofness, suspicion and animosity with understanding, good will and love. Not since the foundation of Christianity nineteen centuries ago has there been such a change in the religious climate. It is my hope that this volume will give further impetus to that movement wherein lies the hope for peace and a better world.

I have not undertaken to document every statement of fact, not wishing to inflict upon the general reader the burdensome critical apparatus of a doctoral dissertation. I have, however, provided references for those items which might seem disputable or which some reader with a good library might wish to pursue further.

I am grateful to the students who, over the years, have bombarded me with questions, to the many scholars who have treated this theme and provided helpful data. I appreciate the privilege of having several enlightening discussions with Professor Astrik Gabriel, Director of the Medieval Institute at Notre Dame.

I am especially indebted to Dr. James A. Corbett, Professor of Medieval History at Notre Dame, who read the entire manuscript with meticulous care and favored me with numerous suggestions which have greatly enriched the volume. As the author, however, I accept full and sole responsibility for every statement contained therein.

I acknowledge with thanks the kindness of David E. Sparks, the Director of the University Library, in providing me with the services of a research librarian, Linda Hildebrand. Lastly my thanks are due to my secretary, Loretta Budzinski, who has helped to put this and several other manuscripts of mine through the press.

I wish to express my deep gratitude for permission to quote from the following: G. G. Coulton, *Inquisition and Liberty*, published in Boston by Beacon Press, copyright 1938; Lynn Thorndike, "Magic, Witchcraft, Astronomy and Alchemy" in *The Close of the Middle Ages, Cambridge Medieval History*, New York, Macmillan Company, 1936, through the courtesy of Columbia University Press; Pierre Van Paassen, *A Crown of Fire*, published in New York by Charles Scribner's Sons, copyright 1960; *Calvin: Institutes of the Christian Religion*, Vol. XX, The Library of Christian Classics, edited by John T. McNeill and translated by Ford Lewis Battles, published in the U.S.A. by The Westminister Press, copyright MCMLX by W. L. Jenkins (used by permission).

JOHN A. O'BRIEN

# THE
# INQUISITION

## CHAPTER I

# Understanding the Inquisition

The equal toleration of all religions . . . is the same thing as atheism.

POPE LEO XIII, 1885

THERE IS PROBABLY no other activity in the long history of the Roman Catholic Church which has aroused such intense bitterness, hostility and lasting hatred as that associated with the Inquisition. The agents of this institution pursued persons suspected of heresy with an implacable relentlessness and a zeal worthy of a better cause.

They made use of tortures which ranged from flogging to burning at the stake. Inquisitors fastened iron collars around the necks of individuals accused of heresy and condemned to life imprisonment even repentent heretics.

When death at times apparently removed accused heretics from the greedy grasp of Inquisitors, the latter would at times dig up their remains to heap indignities upon their bones. Incredible as it seems, they perpetrated these outrages in the name of the gentle Christ whose Gospel exalts the virtues of compassion, forgiveness and love.

It is all the more difficult to understand how officials of the Church, both high and low, did not perceive the incongruity of their behavior with the teachings and actions of Christ. The Evangelist Luke relates the following memorable incident.

Having determined to go to Jerusalem, Jesus sent messengers

before him. "And they went and entered a Samaritan town to make ready for him; and they did not receive him, because his face was set for Jerusalem. But when his disciples James and John saw this, they said: 'Wilt thou that we bid fire come down from heaven and consume them?' But he turned and rebuked them, saying, 'You do not know of what manner of spirit you are; for the Son of Man did not come to destroy men's lives, but to save them'" (Luke 9:52-56).

The Evangelist Matthew relates a similar incident. Publicans and sinners came to the table with Jesus and his disciples. Professing to be scandalized, the Pharisees said to his disciples: "Why does your Master eat with publicans and sinners?" Jesus happened to hear the question and replied: "It is not the healthy who need a physician, but they who are sick. But go and learn what this means: 'I desire mercy and not sacrifice.' For I have come to call sinners, not the just" (Matt. 9: 11-13).

The appraisals of the Inquisition by Catholic encyclopedias are of especial significance, since they reflect the judgment not only of a single writer but of the editorial board as well. Thus the scholarly work *Sacramentum Mundi*, an Encyclopedia of Theology, with an international editorial board, reaches the following conclusion:

As a judicial prosecution of heresy by a special court set up by the Church and acting in its behalf, the Inquisition conflicts sharply with the civil tolerance which has been customary for centuries and was confirmed officially by the Church in the Second Vatican Council (Declaration on Religious Freedom, *Dignitatis humanae*). It is strange that the Inquisition took shape in a Church appealing to the Gospel and enjoining love.[1]

With similar candor the *Catholic Encyclopedia for School and Home* expresses the following judgment of the Inquisition:

Because its procedures often denied elementary justice to the defendant, because it showed hostility to the spirit of scientific inquiry (as in the case of the astronomer Galileo), and finally because it permitted torture and infliction of the death penalty, the Inquisition has come to stand in the judgment of many historians as a symbol of cruelty, intellectual terrorism and religious intolerance. The attempts of certain Catholic apologists to exonerate the medieval Church and Inquisition of those charges have been futile.

Historical evidence forces us to admit that on occasion Inquisitors such as the thirteenth-century Conrad of Marburg and Robert LeBourge (whom the pope subsequently condemned to life imprisonment) committed grave crimes against justice, charity and the human person by summarily condemning large numbers of heretics to death. The Inquisition not only offends modern ideals of justice and spiritual freedom, it also contradicts the teaching of the Fathers and Doctors of the Church such as St. Bernard, who said: "Faith must be the result of conviction and should not be imposed by force."[2]

In short, the judgment of virtually all modern Catholic scholars is that the actions of the Inquisition, judged by modern moral and intellectual standards, were indefensible. The object of scholars today is not to justify the Inquisition but to understand it and the forces which brought it into existence and made it operative for so many centuries. This requires a study of the special context of medieval society, culture and tradition. Only in the light of these conditions, forces and circumstances can one understand that strange and bewildering institution which shaped so largely the religious life and thought of the medieval world. It has been, as the *Encyclopedia Britannica* points out, the stock example cited by those who accuse the Roman Catholic Church of "tyranny and cruelty." [3]

## *Suppression of Heresy during the First Twelve Centuries*

While acknowledging with complete candor the cruelty and intellectual terror of the Inquisition, as judged by our contemporary standards of justice and compassion, it must also be acknowledged with equal frankness that it would be grossly unfair to judge the Church by standards which were in existence in no country at that time. Writers have approached the Inquisition carrying a bucket of paint—black or white—intent upon smearing it or whitewashing it.

Neither is called for. The function of the historian is to present the facts, to render an institution intelligible, to make the past live again and to enable the reader to see it through the eyes of the people of that day. In other words, it is his purpose to enable the reader to enter *inside* the minds of the dwellers of other lands and far-off days and understand how they came to act, think, judge and evaluate as they did, to feel the same currents of thought, aspiration, fear, terror and hope; to enter into the *Zeitgeist* and feel its cultural and spiritual winds beating upon his brow and its music making a melody on his own heartstrings.

Thus only does history become a resurrection of the flesh from the tomb of the past by breathing into it its distinctive spirit and ethos. "The whole art of history," observes Hilaire Belloc, "consists in eliminating the shock of noncomprehension and in making the reader feel as the men of the past felt." [4]

When the historian begins to look for the black paint or the white, he takes his eyes from the target which should be his one concern: the truth. "The first law of history," declared Pope Leo XIII, "is to assert nothing false and to have no fear of telling the truth." [5] The only treatment of the Inquisition that is in accordance with the canons of historical science is to tell the truth and the whole truth without fear or favor. We shall make no effort to whitewash ecclesiastical Inquisitors whose cruelty merits the execration of mankind; neither shall we blacken characters simply to conform to popular legend and unscientific history.

In his *Historical Sketches*, Cardinal Newman speaks of "that endemic perennial fidget which possesses certain historians about giving scandal. Facts are omitted in great histories, or glosses are put upon memorable acts, because they are thought not edifying, whereas of all scandals, such omissions, such glosses, are the greatest." [6] There have been too many treatments of the Inquisition which have aimed to edify by glossing over disagreeable facts rather than to present the unvarnished truth. We shall not consciously add to that list.

The work which has exercised the greatest influence in shaping public opinion among English-speaking people concerning the Inquisition is that of Dr. Henry C. Lea. Published in New York in the '80s of the last century, the work consists of three massive volumes entitled *A History of the Inquisition of the Middle Ages*. It was highly praised by Lord Acton, one of the greatest Catholic scholars of that era. In his introduction to the French edition of the work, Abbé Paul Fredericq acclaimed it as "the most thorough history of the Inquisition which we possess." [7] A German edition also was brought out in 1905.

Despite its vast amount of data, the work manifests a bitter bias against the Church and a lack of objectivity. "Honest he may be," says Abbé E. Vacandard of Lea, "but impartial never. His pen too often gives way to his prejudices and his hatred of the Catholic Church. His critical judgment is sometimes gravely at fault." [8]

Another author who has written extensively and fascinatingly of the Church in the Middle Ages is George G. Coulton of Cambridge University. Like Lea, he was a man of immense erudition and of pronounced prejudice toward the Church. This comes to the surface in virtually all his works on the Middle Ages and particularly in *Inquisition and Liberty*. [9]

During a year of post-doctoral research at Oxford in 1939-40, I became acquainted with him and became aware of his reputation for hostility toward the Church and for constantly challenging Catholic scholars to debate. Dialectics seemed to be the breath of his nostrils.*

Most scholars, we think, would agree with Vacandard that an objective history of the whole Inquisition in Europe is still to be written. [10] We do not attempt, however, such a formidable task. Our purpose is much more modest. We undertake the simple task of showing first how the Inquisition came into being in a society where there was a union of Church and State and then of showing how the Church's notion of coercive power became prevalent in the Middle Ages.

Critical though Lea is of much of the life and activity of the medieval Church, he frankly acknowledges that the growth of such a coercive power was the natural and almost inevitable result of the evolution of the social, religious and cultural forces then at work. "The Inquisition," he says, "was not an organization arbitrarily devised and imposed upon the judicial system of Christendom by the ambition or fanaticism of the Church. It was rather

---

* To illustrate. During the Easter vacation of 1940, Catholic scholars of England held their annual convention that year at Cambridge University. Though uninvited, Dr. Coulton not only came to the convention but was almost constantly attempting to participate in the discussion. Aware of his penchant for interminable controversy, the chairman ignored his raised hand. Taking pity upon him, I requested the chairman to allow the professor to ask his question. "Yes," he said, "provided he limits himself to one question instead of the usual dozen." Later as we walked back to his quarters on the campus, Dr. Coulton thanked me for helping him get at least a brief hearing.

a natural—one may almost say an inevitable—evolution of the forces at work in the thirteenth century, and no one can rightly appreciate the process of its development and the results of its activity, without a somewhat minute consideration of the factors controlling the minds and souls of men during the ages which laid the foundation of modern civilization." [11]

## Five Basic Facts

The difficulty of many moderns in understanding the Inquisition is traceable to their failure to perceive and appreciate the five following important facts which form the key to the understanding of much of the thought and action of medieval Christendom.

1. The Church is a society, perfect and sovereign, with legislative, judicial and executive powers, charged with the supreme task of disseminating in all its purity the body of divinely revealed religious truth.

2. Faith was considered by the people of the Middle Ages (and of today as well) as a gift of God, more precious than all the treasures of the earth. The faith had come down to them in its original integrity because their ancestors had suffered persecution and death rather than modify it or deny it. It was their duty to safeguard its purity so there would be no departure from the teachings of Christ and his Apostles. Since it was the key that would open to them the gates of heaven, no earthly treasure could compensate them for its loss. Hence orthodoxy was to be maintained at all costs.

3. There existed a moral, spiritual and juridical unity of medieval society wherein Church and State constituted a closely knit polity. Theocratic in structure, the State could not be indifferent about the spiritual welfare of its subjects without being guilty of treason to its supreme Lord and Sovereign—almighty God. The spiritual authority was inseparably intertwined with the secular in much the same way as the soul is united with the body. The modern concept of these two authorities operating in separate watertight compartments would have shocked the medieval mind much as a schizophrenic personality dismays the modern.

4. There was a severity of the penal code of those days, in

which the use of torture and the stake was common. Counterfeiters were burned alive; those who gave false weights and measures were scourged or condemned to death; burglars were led to the scaffold; thieves convicted of relapses were put to death. The whole penal code bristled with vengeance for those who transgressed its laws. Even as late as the reigns of Henry VIII and Elizabeth, persons were being drawn, disemboweled and quartered; others were being boiled to death. Still more revolting was the torture of the wheel, on which the victim was left with broken bones and limbs to die a lingering death of excruciating pain. John Calvin experienced no scruples in having his theological opponent, Michael Servetus, burned to death. The penalties inflicted by the Inquisition were simply those in current use in their day.

5. The modern concept of the secular State, neutral toward all religions and guaranteeing to their adherents equal rights and freedom of conscience and of worship, would have shocked the medieval mind. Few people realize how comparatively recent is the development such as we have in the United States. To view the thought and action of the people of the Middle Ages against the background of today is to misunderstand and misjudge them entirely. It would be like viewing the covered wagon in which the early settlers in America trekked to the West against the background of the airplane travel of today.

It is because most moderns have lost sight of these five cardinal facts that they experience such difficulty in understanding the Inquisition. Yet to any Christian living before the religious revolution of the sixteenth century these conceptions were commonplace. Indeed, he would be shocked at the modern conception that religious orthodoxy is a matter of indifference to society and to the State—a mere item of private judgment or individual whim.

If we try to view the Inquisition or any other institution of the Middle Ages through the lens of twentieth-century habits of thought and action, it will appear strange and mystifying—giving us the shock of noncomprehension with all its disturbing emotional repercussions. Hence it is necessary to study the society of that day with its prevailing customs of thought and action to understand how our ancestors behaved as they did. This does not mean that we must agree with their viewpoint or philosophy.

Indeed we may be utterly opposed to both. But we must be able to see them as flesh-and-blood men and women, children of their day, doing what we in all probability would have done if we were their next-door neighbors.

Among the characteristics of the Inquisitors, which shock people today, were their cruelty to heretics and their incredible indifference to the pain and agony of their victims. This is illustrated by the following incident related by G. Pelhisse. It occurred in 1234 on the day on which the news of St. Dominic's canonization reached Toulouse, France.

The bishop, Raymond du Felgar, had just finished celebrating solemn high Mass in the Dominican monastery in honor of the canonization. Along with the brethren he was on his way to the refectory when a messenger arrived from the city with the news that an old woman, sick with the fever, was about to be denounced as a heretic. The bishop, along with the prior of the monastery, immediately went to the woman's home.

Thinking that he was a bishop of the Catharan sect, the woman openly professed her faith to him. Then, when she learned who he was, she persisted in her faith. Thereupon he condemned her as a heretic and handed her to the Count's vicar, who had her transferred to Pré-le-Compte, where she was burned to death in her bed.

After this, the bishop and the Dominicans went to the refectory, where they joyfully ate their dinner, giving thanks to God and to St. Dominic. The condemnation and execution of the poor sick woman did not interfere in the slightest with their festivities in honor of St. Dominic because they all thought they had performed a pious duty. Such light-heartedness is very difficult for people to understand today. But it is typical of the treatment meted out by the Inquisitors to thousands of victims. It illustrates the climate that prevailed during the centuries and in the countries in which this papal institution operated. [12]

## CHAPTER II

# Establishment of the Inquisition

There is no freedom on earth or in any star for those who
deny freedom to others.

ELBERT HUBBARD

W HAT WAS THE INQUISITION and why was it established? It
was an ecclesiastical court of the Middle Ages, established
either by diocesan bishops or by the pope to suppress heresies
which threatened the doctrinal orthodoxy of the Roman Catholic
faith. Its purpose was to detect and identify deviants from the
faith, to secure if possible their return to the Catholic Church, and
finally to arrest and punish those who refused to abandon their
errors.

The Second Lateran Council in 1139 had obliged secular
princes to prosecute deviants from the faith under penalty of
anathema. These decrees were renewed by Pope Alexander III
(1159-81) who also stipulated imprisonment and confiscation of
property for all persisting in heresy. In 1215 the Fourth Lateran
Council threatened negligent prelates with deposition and negligent rulers with forfeiture of office.

Despite all the decrees, the suppression of heresy remained un-
organized. Accordingly Pope Gregory IX in February, 1231,
issued the fundamental constitution, *Excommunicamus*, which set
up courts to hear cases of heresy and mete out punishment. Thus
life imprisonment as a salutary punishment was imposed upon
the repentant heretics and capital punishment upon the obstinate
ones after they were turned over to the secular arm.

9

## Birth of the Inquisition

On October 11, 1231, Pope Gregory entrusted the execution of this decretal in Germany to Conrad of Marburg, a secular priest, who was privileged to select his collaborators. Conrad chose chiefly Dominicans, calling upon the priors of Regensberg, Freisach and Strasbourg. Through the bull *Ille humani generis*, he entrusted to them the mission of ferreting out heretics and punishing them and their abettors. "For the first time," points out Y. Dossat, "there now existed a body of law that, under the initiative of the papacy, placed the punishment of the enemies of the faith under exempt jurisdiction. This marked the birth of the Inquisition." [1]

It is extremely difficult to cite the exact day or the month when the Inquisition was founded, but practically all sources agree that its founder was Pope Gregory IX and the majority will probably agree with George G. Coulton when he says: "In 1233 he [Gregory IX] formally entrusted the work to the recently formed and specially enthusiastic Dominican Order. From among these he named certain Inquisitors, whom he sent to different lands with powers to work with, and in many ways to supersede, the diocesan bishops. It is from this year that we must date, in so far as an exact date may be fixed, the full-blown Inquisition: the *Monastic*, as some call it, in view of the fact that it was mainly worked by Dominicans and Franciscans: or the *Papal*, as it may be more exactly called in virtue of the absolute papal responsibility for its creation." [2]

Abbé E. Vacandard also attributes the establishment of the Inquisition to Gregory IX. "In short," he says, "Gregory IX only pressed upon Christendom the application of already existing laws, and introduced, when no such existed, the most rigorous legislation against heresy. But what belongs specially to him is the procedure to which he had recourse for the prosecution of heretics: that is, his Inquisitorial system. The Inquisition proper, the *Monastic*, is in fact his work." [3]

While at first it was confined chiefly to Germany, it was extended to Aragon in 1232, and it became general in 1233. Tactfully Pope Gregory IX explained to the hierarchy of France and the neighboring territory that he was relieving them of a part of their burdensome task by choosing the Dominicans, who seemed especially equipped to lead the struggle against heresy. Owing to local difficulties the Inquisition was not officially organized in central Italy and Lombardy until 1235 and 1237, respectively.

## The Ideal Inquisitor

Bernard Gui, a distinguished Dominican Inquisitor, thus sets forth the qualities which should characterize the holder of such an office:

He ought to be diligent and fervent in his zeal for religious truth, the salvation of souls, and the extirpation of heresy. He should so conduct himself amid unpleasant and difficult affairs that he never loses control of himself in fits of temper or anger; nor on the other hand should he give way to debilitating sluggishness and languor, for such torpor saps the vigor of an administrator.

The Inquisitor must be constant, persevering amid dangers and adversities even to death. He should be willing to suffer for the sake of justice, neither rashly precipitating danger nor shamefully retreating in fear, for such cowardice weakens moral stability. While remaining adamant to the entreaties and blandishments of sinners, nevertheless he must not so harden his heart as to repel appeals to grant delays or to mitigate penances according as circumstances of place and time may suggest, for such procedure savors rather of cruelty. By the same token he should refrain from too lenient an attitude which degenerates into dissoluteness. . . .

Let him be careful in doubtful cases not to believe too easily everything that appears probable, for such is not always true; nor on the other hand should he stubbornly refuse to believe what may seem improbable, for such is often true. With all diligence, therefore, he should discuss and examine every case and inquire into the truth of the matter . . . So let mercy and truth, which should never be far from the mind of a judge, rule his actions and always shine from his face with the result that his judicial decisions never be marred by irregularity nor blemished by avarice or cruelty.[4]

## The Inquisition Tribunal

In the early period of the institution the Inquisitors rode through the countryside in search of heretics. But soon they acquired the authority to summon suspects from their homes to such places as they considered suitable and safe. Gradually the judges confined their activities to the Inquisition center, among their notaries and official family.

After some experimenting the territorial organization of each tribunal was established in a definite way, varying with the number of heretics in the area. Paris was the headquarters for the Inquisitors of France. Dominicans had jurisdiction throughout the whole kingdom as it existed at the beginning of the fourteenth century. It was gradually extended to Flanders, Lorraine, the Franche-Comte, Aragon, the kingdom of Majorca, Lombardy, Romagna and Tuscany.

Local ecclesiastical authorities were frequently reluctant to cooperate with the Inquisition. Even diocesan bishops at times endeavored to avoid collaboration. This prompted Pope Innocent IV on several occasions to censure them for their lack of zeal. In 1279 Pope Nicholas III scolded the bishop of Padua for impeding the work of the Inquisitors. At Marseilles in 1266 the Dominicans brought false charges through perjured witnesses against the Franciscan Inquisitors, causing the pope to intervene.

Of even greater significance was the hostility of the people themselves toward the Inquisition. In July, 1233, a band of persons, charged with heresy, put to death the fanatical Conrad of Marburg. On May 28, 1242, the Inquisitors of Toulouse, William Arnaud, Stephen of Narbonne and their companions were killed in the chateau of the count of Toulouse at Avignonet. On April 6, 1252, the Inquisitor Peter of Verona was assassinated on the road from Como to Milan.

## The Inquisition Procedure

The procedure of the Inquisition was radically different from the traditional forms of accusation or of denunciation, which were deemed ill suited for the repression of heresy. According to the new procedure, the Inquisitor could bring suit against any person who might even vaguely be the object of public rumor.

When questioned on the charges brought against him, the individual was required to take an oath to tell the truth and thus testify against himself—a radical departure from Roman law. The accused was kept in the dark as to the identity of the witnesses for the prosecution and was thus deprived of any opportunity to challenge or confront them.

Factors which would normally disqualify a witness from testifying were totally disregarded. Testimony from infamous persons, thieves, criminals, the excommunicated and heretics was freely accepted. Blood relationship did not excuse a person from testifying. The accused was denied the services of clerks and lawyers, for the latter would then become accomplices. In the case of definitive sentences, even the right of appeal to the Apostolic See was denied by the constitution *Excommunicamus* of Gregory IX. Judged by the rules governing the operation of our courts today, those of the Inquisitorial procedure were sadly lacking in fairness and justice.

## General Inquests

In some cases the Inquisition undertook general inquests which occasionally extended to the entire populations within their jurisdictions. The Inquisitors would begin by preaching a general discourse in which they set forth their mission to the people assembled for this enquiry. An indulgence of forty days was imparted to all in attendance.

Convocations were also held in every parish by the chaplain. All male parishioners over fourteen and all females over twelve were required to be present on the appointed day. All who did so and made truthful depositions escaped the graver penalties. This was known as the period of grace. But the Council of Beziers in 1246 decreed that this favor could be granted only once.

The Inquisition obliged the parochial clergy to assist the Inquisitors in ferreting out suspected heretics. The pastor was required to serve notice on the suspect to appear before the Inquisitors. This he did by going first to the home of the suspect and by announcing the summons the following Sunday at high Mass.

If the suspect did not appear within the specified time, he incurred provisional excommunication; at the end of the year a definitive sentence of heresy was imposed upon him. As there was no right of appeal for heretics, they not infrequently disappeared to another part of the country where they were unknown.

When the suspect appeared at the Inquisition center, he was notified by the Inquisitor or one of his aides, in the presence of two witnesses, of the charges against him. He was required to take an oath to tell the truth about the allegations against him. A refusal to take an oath constituted a presumption of guilt. The interrogations and the answers were recorded in Latin and translated, if desired by the defendant. Suspects who refused to answer or who were judged to have answered falsely were imprisoned, either in simple detention or in solitary confinement.

## Setting the Trap

While the suspect was in prison, the Inquisitors would frequently use planted spies to trap him into disclosures of guilt. When a confession was not forthcoming, proof of heresy could be achieved by witnesses, two of whom must be in agreement.

Among the results of the revival of Roman law was the reappearance of torture which was foreign to canonical tradition. In the documents concerning the establishment of the Inquisition one searches in vain for any reference to torture. Any judge who resorted to it would have incurred an irregularity and hence would have been disqualified.

Probably the first to use torture were the Italian Inquisitors after the issuance of the bull *Ad extirpanda* (May 15, 1252), in which Innocent IV declared that the podesta, the chief magistrate of a city, would be required to use torture to compel heretics to confess. These regulations do not seem to have been in use outside of Italy. The situation for tribunals elsewhere was altered by the decision of Alexander IV to give judges the faculty to absolve one another from any irregularities which they might have incurred by being present when torture was inflicted (1256-60).

Jean Galand, the Inquisitor of Carcassonne in southern France, was charged with many abuses in this matter. As the use of torture, direct or indirect, by the Inquisition is one of the most shocking charges brought against it, this topic will be discussed at length later on. It can be discussed intelligently only against the background of the system of punishments prevalent in those times.

Prior to rendering a definitive sentence, the Inquisition was required to have the approval of the local bishop and of a certain number of consultors or assessors, both ecclesiastic and lay, selected because of their competence in the case. It is easy, however, to exaggerate the significance of this practice, since it immediately preceded the proclamation of the sentence.

## Pledge Acceptance of Verdict

Even before the verdict was announced, the defendant was required to pledge himself, in the presence of the judges alone, to accept the sentence whatever it might be. Furthermore, Pope Alexander IV dispensed the Inquisitors of Lombardy (January 11, 1257) from convoking the bishops or their representatives if they deemed such convocation unnecessary. After 1260 this arrangement was modified in the light of the gravity of the sentence.

Surrender to the secular arm and life imprisonment could not be pronounced without the intervention of the diocesan authorities, but minor penalties were left to the discretion of the Inquisitors. In 1283 greater weight was accorded the judgment of the assessors. No longer were women to be imprisoned. Instead they were condemned chiefly to wearing crosses (see pages 17-18) and making pilgrimages.

In the fourteenth century the consultations assumed much greater importance, lasting sometimes for days, and the number of consultants was greatly increased. For example, in 1328 at Pamiers they numbered thirty-five, of whom nine were lawyers. Although their recommendations were not legally binding, the Inquisitors customarily followed their advice.

Despite the conviction of Pope Gregory IX that in establishing the Inquisition he was the righteous champion of order against religious anarchy, he could scarcely have been oblivious of the debasement of religious values that would be the inevitable result.

This is illustrated by an incident which occurred just before the battle of Muret when the pope's legate cried out to the soldiers: "Go forward in the name of Christ. I will be your witness and your warranty at the Day of Doom that all who die in this glorious fight shall earn the everlasting reward and glory of martyrdom without any pains of purgatory, provided that he be confessed and contrite, or at least that he have a firm resolve of showing himself to a priest concerning such sins as he has not yet confessed." [5]

The establishment of the papal Inquisition, as we shall see, was destined to lead not only to a debasement of religious values but also to immense cruelty and suffering. So much for the circumstances leading to the founding of the papal Inquisition which was destined to play so large a role in the religious history of Europe in the subsequent five centuries.

## CHAPTER III

# The Inquisition in Operation

He maketh his sun to rise on the evil and on the good, and
sendeth rain on the just and on the unjust.

MATTHEW 5:45

IT IS COMMONLY MAINTAINED that the Inquisition did not inflict
the punishment due, only "salutary penances" for the spiritual
benefit of former heretics who had returned to the faith. Neither
did it have the authority to impose sanctions upon stubborn heretics, and this led to the practice of surrendering them to the secular power. When the Inquisition pronounced sentences it was
before a large concourse of people, in a solemn ceremony, attended by prelates, civil officials, municipal magistrates and nobles,
who took their places on a platform next to the Inquisitors. The
ranking Inquisitor preached a short sermon and announced the
usual indulgence.

He proclaimed the "decrees of mercy," setting forth various
commutations of punishment. He then briefly stated the charges
made against each defendant. Then the defendants, kneeling, abjured heresy, each with his hand on the Gospel, held by the Inquisitor. The verdicts were then proclaimed, first in Latin and
then in the vernacular. The Inquisitor generally grouped together
the minor penances which the judges on their own initiative could
impose, commute or remit.

The penances included scourging, visits to churches, wearing
the cross of infamy, pilgrimages, imposed either separately or in

combination. In the south of France, Inquisitors distinguished between major pilgrimages outside the country and minor pilgrimages to nearby shrines. The penitent might also be obliged, for a specified period, to attend high Mass on Sundays, rod in hand. Between the reading of the Epistle and the Gospel, he would be scourged. Sometimes the Inquisitor would impose fines, either as the principal penalty or as a payment for a dispensation from certain obligations.

Generally regarded as a severe penalty was the wearing of the cross. Crosses of yellow cloth were sewn on the outside clothing, front and back. In the case of perjurers the crosses generally would be double, with a second transverse arm. Crosses were worn continuously, exposing the wearers to humiliating jeers and jibes.

The papal statutes required the presence of assessors, notaries and skilled jurisconsultants during the trials as measures of protection for the accused and to assure a just and fair trial. Rightly or wrongly, the Inquisitors generally preferred to act on the confessions of the accused, for this eliminated the necessity of relying on the testimonies of witnesses and on cross-examinations.

To secure confessions the Inquisitor called on all his persuasive powers, since a confession made voluntarily afforded sufficient proof for conviction. This precluded the necessity of further investigations and judicial processes to substantiate the charges. The accused was assured of a lighter sentence if he freely confessed. If he refused, however, recourse was had to stronger measures: imprisonment in close confinement, reduction of food to a minimum and finally torture.

In the lack of a confession on the part of the accused, proof of heresy had to be established by the testimony of witnesses. In contrast to secular law, however, the testimony of criminals was permitted. It was generally very difficult for the accused to get witnesses to testify in his behalf. The fact that the witness knew the defendant and might even have been a friend of his could easily arouse the suspicion that he himself might well be a heretic also. How could he testify unless he was a witness of the heretical acts or a hearer of statements of the accused?

These would likely be the questions which the Inquisitors would be turning over in their minds. Furthermore, Inquisitors generally frowned upon the accused having a lawyer to defend him. Pope Urban IV issued a decree, dated July 28, 1262, authorizing the Inquisitors to conduct the trial "simply and plainly without the noisy and disputatious wrangling of lawyers."[1]

## A Mockery of Justice

"In other words," observes Abbé Vacandard, "the Inquisitors wished to be perfectly untrammeled in their action. The secrecy of the Inquisition's procedure was one of the chief causes of complaint." [2] After depicting at some length the procedure of the Inquisition, Henry Charles Lea characterizes the Inquisitorial system as "a standing mockery of justice—perhaps the most iniquitous that the arbitrary cruelty of man has ever devised." [3]

Dreadful as the system was, it did not lack defenders whose arguments were incredibly extravagant and farfetched. To illustrate his point, Lea cites the curious line of reasoning used by Louis de Paramo, a defender of the Inquisitor's system of secrecy:

Paramo in the quaint pedantry with which he ingeniously proves that God was the first Inquisitor, and the condemnation of Adam and Eve the first model of the Inquisitorial process, triumphantly points out that he judges them in secret, thus setting the example which the Inquisition is bound to follow, and avoiding the subtleties which the criminals have raised in their own defence, especially at the suggestion of the crafty serpent. That he called no witnesses is explained by the confession of the accused, and ample legal authority is cited to show that these confessions were sufficient to justify conviction and punishment.

If this blasphemous absurdity raises a smile, it has also its melancholy side, for it reveals to us the view which the Inquisitors themselves took of their functions, assimilating themselves to God and wielding an irresponsible power which nothing short of divine wisdom could prevent from being turned by human passions into an engine of the most deadly injustice. [4]

In short, the procedures of the Inquisition offend virtually every requirement for the administration of justice. The dice were loaded against the accused and the chances of his gaining freedom were slim indeed.

## Normal Punishment

The normal punishment for the converted heretic, whose case did not warrant some special indulgence, was imprisonment. As a general rule, it was for life, but commutations were frequent. In 1246 the Inquisitor Bernard de Caux passed sentence upon 207 heretics, but condemned only twenty-three to life imprisonment. Similarly Bernard Gui commuted life imprisonment in 139 out of 246 convictions. [5]

In nine sessions of the Inquisition in Pamiers, in which sixty-four persons were condemned, only five heretics were abandoned to the secular arm. "Taking all in all," says Abbé Vacandard, "the Inquisition in its operation denoted a real progress in the treatment of criminals; for it not only put an end to the summary vengeance of the mob, but it diminished considerably the number of those sentenced to death." [6]

"The bread of sorrow and the water of tribulation" constituted the prisoner's diet, but supplementary food was afforded when it was necessary. The customary imprisonment was at least tolerable, but those in solitary confinement fared miserably and their health was usually undermined. The stern conditions of imprisonment were sometimes mitigated by the negligence or complicity of the guards, which permitted many prisoners to escape.

The responsibility to provide prisons and to supervise their operation rested upon the bishops. But it was a task for which they showed little enthusiasm. The bishops in southern France at the Council of Narbonne (1243 or 1244) bluntly declared that mortar and stone were lacking for prison construction. As a result of the attitude of the bishops, the burden of providing for prison needs generally fell upon the king of France.

Because the infliction of penalties, involving suffering and especially death, was contrary to both ecclesiastical ideals and canon law, the Church could not herself inflict such punishment on the obstinate heretic. When the Inquisitors could not obtain an abjuration, no choice was left except to pronounce the sentence of surrender to the secular court or secular arm. This was required to proceed to the execution, despite the customary formula pleading against mutilation and death.

## Burning at the Stake

Capital punishment generally meant death by fire. The burning at the stake usually took place in a public place outside the building in which the Inquisition had been conducted. Although this was the fate generally reserved for the relapsed heretics, in practice they were frequently spared. Thus in Toulouse in 1256 only a single case of burning at the stake was recorded, compared with twelve sentences to life imprisonment. During his career of seventeen years, in which he heard more than nine hundred cases, Bernard Gui abandoned only forty heretics to the secular arm.

Even death, however, did not stop the course of justice in matters of faith. Depending upon the seriousness of the case, the Inquisitors decided either simply to exhume the remains of the convicted heretic, or to exhume and burn them. What a strange spectacle, found in no other court in the civilized world, is the spectacle of a vengeance which reaches into the grave to exhaust the fury of its vindictiveness against a person whose soul has passed beyond the Inquisitor's reach.

What a strange role for an institution that professes to speak in the name of the gentle and compassionate Christ who said, "I will have mercy and not sacrifice." In cases involving only life imprisonment, the heirs were stamped with the taint of heresy. As a consequence of the imposition of a maximum penalty—death or imprisonment for life—all the property of the condemned person was confiscated.

The operation of the Inquisition was very extensive, but it did not embrace the whole of Christendom, nor even all the Latin countries. Castile and Portugal were free from it until the reign of Ferdinand and Isabella. The Scandinavian countries escaped it almost entirely, while England experienced its distressful activity only in the case of the Templars. It was virtually unknown in France, at least as an established institution, except in the south, in what was known as the county of Toulouse and later on in Languedoc.

In Aragon and in upper Italy, however, the Inquisition was in full swing. The Emperor Frederick II instigated its establishment in the two Sicilies and in many cities of Italy and Germany.

Pope Honorius IV (1285-87) introduced it into Sardinia, and it was active in Flanders and Bohemia in the fifteenth century.

## A Wholesale Execution

The character of the Inquisitors differed greatly. The ideal Inquisitor was sketched beautifully by Bernard Gui and Nicolas Eymeric, but few seemed to have measured up to their prescriptions. Notorious for his fanaticism and cruelty was Conrad of Marburg and even worse in both respects was Robert the Dominican, known as Robert the Bugre. Bishop Moranis had permitted a sizeable community of heretics to grow up about him at Montwimer in Champagne. Robert announced his determination to punish the town severely.

In a single week he managed to try all his prisoners. On May 29, 1239, approximately 180 of them, along with their bishop, were sentenced to the stake to be burned alive. The news of his outrageous action reached Rome, and he was first suspended from his office and subsequently condemned to life imprisonment. [7]

No less odious were other acts of the Inquisition. In 1280 the civic officials of Carcassonne brought to the attention of the pope, the king of France and the episcopal vicars, the outrageous cruelty and injustice of the Inquisitor, Jean Galand, in the use of torture. This fiend had boldly inscribed on the walls of the Inquisition chamber the words: *domunculas ad torquendum et cruciandum homines diversis generibus tormentorum*—chambers for the torturing and punishing of people with differing kinds of torments.

Some of the defendants had been tortured on the rack, and most of them had been so savagely treated that they could not use their arms or legs and were completely helpless. Some even expired in great agony in the midst of their torture. The report of the Carcassonne officials referred repeatedly to the incredible agony the accused were obliged to suffer.

## Ferocity of Inquisitors

On May 13, 1291, Philip the Fair, King of France, addressed to the governor of Carcassonne a letter in which he strongly denounced the Inquisitors for their unrestrained torturing of innocent people, whereby the living and the dead were fraudulently convicted. [8] Deeply disturbed by the reports of these cruelties, Pope Clement V issued a bull intended for Cardinals Taillefer de la Chapelle and Berenger de Fredol, who were appointed to investigate the dungeons and alleged abuses of the Inquisition.

In it he mentions the complaints of the citizens of Carcassonne, Albi and Cordes concerning the cruelty practiced in the prisons of the Inquisition. He mentioned that some of these unfortunates "were so weakened by the rigors of their imprisonment, the lack of food, and the severity of their tortures that they died." [9]

Something of the ferocity and cruelty of the Inquisitors is evidenced by the remorse experienced by one of them. He had inflicted upon a sorceress the torture of the burning coals. A short time later the unfortunate woman died in prison as a result of her torments. Realizing that he had caused her death, the Inquisitor wrote to Pope John XXII for a dispensation from the irregularity which he had thereby incurred.[10]

## Intrusion of Secular Rulers

Probably the greatest excesses and abuses of the Inquisition were traceable to the intrusion of secular rulers. The Inquisition had scarcely been established when Emperor Frederick II sought to use it for political purposes. He was eager to have the prosecution for heresy taken from bishops and monks and placed in the hands of his royal officers. Hence, in 1233, he boasted in a letter to Pope Gregory IX that he had executed a large number of heretics in his kingdom.

The pope replied that he was not at all deceived by this pretended piety and zeal. He was fully aware that the emperor's real purpose was simply to get rid of his personal enemies and that Frederick had executed many who were not involved in heresy in any way. [11]

According to the theory under which the Inquisition operated, the severest penalties it could inflict—apart from such minor penalties of wearing crosses, pilgrimages and the like—were imprisonment, abandonment to the secular arm, and confiscation of property. In the mind of the Inquisitors, imprisonment was not a punishment but a means by which the penitent could secure, "on the bread of tribulation and the water of affliction," forgiveness from God for his sins. At the same time he was closely watched to see that he persevered in the right path and was kept aloof from the rest of the flock to obviate any danger of infection.

Individuals who voluntarily confessed their heresy during the time of grace were sentenced for a short imprisonment. Those who confessed under torture or under threat of death were imprisoned for life. This was the customary punishment for the relapsed during the greater part of the thirteenth century. This was the only punishment which the Inquisitor Bernard de Caux (1244-48) imposed upon them.

## Forms of Punishment

There were two kinds of imprisonment: the mild and the harsh. Under the latter, all the prisoners were on bread and water, and each was confined in a separate cell. It was impossible, however, to enforce this harsh rule strictly, and we find Geoffroi d'Ablis in 1306 complaining about the visits of clergy and the laity of both sexes, allowed to prisoners.

Indeed as far back as 1282, the harsh Inquisitor Jean Galand had issued orders prohibiting the jailer of the prison of Carcassonne to eat or take recreation with the prisoners or to permit them to take recreation or to keep servants. An exception was made, however, for husband and wife if either or both were imprisoned.

In the milder form the prisoners, if well behaved, were allowed to exercise in the corridors, where at times they had opportunities to converse with one another and with visitors. This privilege was extended to the old and infirm as a result of the order given by the two cardinals who investigated the prison of Carcassonne and took measures to alleviate its rigors.

In sharp contrast, under the harsh form of confinement, the convict was thrust into the darkest, smallest and most noisome of cells, with chains on his feet, or in some cases he was chained to the wall. This penance was imposed upon prisoners whose offences had been conspicuous or who had perjured themselves by making incomplete confessions. The latter depended wholly upon the discretion or whim of the Inquisitor.

## Extreme Cruelty

Lea tells of one case, in 1328, of aggravated false witness where the unfortunate victim had chains on both hands and feet. Cases in which the culprits were members of a religious order were usually heard privately in order to avoid scandal, and the confinement would be in monasteries of their own order. [12]

Lea relates a case of 1246, that of Jeanne, widow of B. de la Tour, a nun of Lespenasse, who allegedly was involved in both the Catharan and Waldensian heresies and who had allegedly prevaricated in her confession. She was sentenced to imprisonment in a separate cell in her own order, where no one was to enter or see her. Food was to be pushed in through a small opening arranged for that purpose. Her cell became virtually a living tomb and became known as the *in pace* (in peace).[13]

"The cruelty of the monastic system of imprisonment, known as *in pace* or *vade in pace*," observes Lea, "was such that those subjected to it speedily died in all the agonies of despair." In 1350 the archbishop of Toulouse urged King John to intercede for its mitigation, and he himself issued an order that the superior of the monastery should twice a month visit and comfort a prisoner. Moreover, the prisoner should have the right twice a month to ask for the company of one of the monks. Even this slender mitigation provoked the most bitter resistance of the Dominicans and Franciscans, who appealed to Pope Clement VI, but in vain. [14]

# CHAPTER IV

## Extortion of Confession

Whoever attempts to suppress liberty of conscience finishes
some day by wishing for the Inquisition.

JULES SIMON

T O UNDERSTAND THE PROCEDURE of the Inquisition it is necessary first to know the unique role which the Inquisitor
sought to play. He thought of himself not only as a judge but
also, and perhaps more important, as a father-confessor striving
for the salvation of unfortunate souls perversely headed for perdition. As a judge, he was vindicating the faith and avenging God
for the wrongs inflicted upon him by heretics.

In both roles he acted under the conviction that his authority
transcended that of any earthly judge. If he accomplished his
sacred mission of rescuing the accused from the endless torment
of hell, it mattered little what method of procedure was used.
Although theologians taught that the end does not justify the
means, that abstract principle seemed to be lost sight of in the
frantic and desperate effort to save the unfortunate prisoner's
immortal soul.

That is the reason why the first demand made upon him, when
he appeared before the tribunal, was an oath to observe the man-
dates of the Church, to answer truthfully all questions put to him,
to disclose the names of all heretics known to him and to perform
whatever penance might be imposed upon him. A refusal to take
this oath was tantamount to branding himself a defiant and ob-

stinate heretic. Soon the stake would claim another victim, writhing in the flames. [1]

The task of the Inquisitor was, moreover, vastly more difficult than that of the ordinary judge, because he was assigned the impossible task of ascertaining not the external acts of the defendant but his secret thoughts and opinions, known only to himself and God. External acts were of value to the Inquisitor only as indications of belief, to be accepted or rejected as he might deem them conclusive or illusory. The crime which the Inquisition sought to suppress by imprisonment or torture was purely mental, while deeds, no matter how vicious and horrible, were beyond its jurisdiction and concern.

## An Impossible Task

This is illustrated by the fact that the murderers of St. Peter Martyr were prosecuted not as assassins but as promoters of heresy and obstructors of the Inquisition. Since even doubt was considered heresy, the Inquisitor had the additional duty of ascertaining whether the defendant's faith was fixed and unwavering or tinged by even the shadow of doubt. Outward actions and verbal professions of unwavering faith were far from conclusive.

An individual might be a daily attendant at Mass, a frequent recipient of the sacraments of confession and Holy Communion and generous in his offering when the collection box or its equivalent was passed around, and yet be a heretic at heart. He might profess before the tribunal the strictest adherence to Catholic doctrine, complete submission to the decisions of the Holy See and a readiness to comply with every request of his ecclesiastical superiors and still be secretly a Cathar or a Waldensian. Few indeed were the persons willing to admit their heresy when brought before a tribunal authorized to sentence them to lifelong confinement or to burn them alive at the stake.

On the other hand, the conscientious judge, eager to measure up to the responsibility placed upon him, found the task of exploring the secret heart of the defendant an utterly impossible one. One can readily understand the reason why he speedily freed himself from the "red tape" of the complex and involved judicial procedures which, in safeguarding him from committing injustice, would have frustrated him at every turn.

"Still less," observes Lea, "can we be surprised that fanatic zeal, arbitrary cruelty, and insatiable cupidity rivaled each other in building up a system unspeakably atrocious. Omnipotence alone was capable of solving with justice the problems which were the daily routine of the Inquisitor. Human frailty, resolved to accomplish a predetermined end, inevitably reached the practical conclusion that the sacrifice of a hundred innocent men was better than the escape of one guilty." [2]

## Presumption of Guilt

There were three forms of criminal action: accusation, denunciation and inquisition. In the process of accusation, the accuser pledged himself to prove his case. He submitted to the tribunal a written statement of charges. If he failed to prove his charge, he incurred the same penalty as the defendant would have incurred by guilt. This was called the *poena talionis*: the penalty of retribution. Because this was so hazardous for the accuser, the tribunal discouraged it and it was discontinued at an early period. The method of denunciation, which permitted the tribunal to conduct the case and see if the accused was really guilty, was less objectionable.

But it too gave way to the Inquisition: the search for the guilty with laws to safeguard the rights of the accused. At an early period this became virtually the only one followed. Unfortunately these safeguards were soon withdrawn and the Inquisition became clothed with practically all the authority, and the presumption of guilt was assumed in advance.

Along in 1278 the rule was laid down and generally enforced that, in areas where heretics were thought to abound, every inhabitant was cited to appear. He was then compelled to abjure heresy and to tell the truth. He was next subjected to a detailed interrogation about himself and others, in which any lack of candor would subject him to the frightful penalties of a relapse from the faith.

Such great inquests were held by Inquisitors Bernard de Caux and Jean de Saint-Pierre in 1245 and 1246. They recorded 230 interrogations of inhabitants of the small town of Avignonet, 100 of those of Fanjeaux, and 420 of Mas-Saintes-Puelles. From this sweeping obligation there was no escape for anyone who had reached the age at which the Church held him responsible for his conduct. What this precise age was, however, was a matter of dispute. The Councils of Albi, Béziers and Toulouse placed it at fourteen for males and twelve for females when they prescribed the oath of abjuration to be taken for the entire population.

Failure to appear before the Inquisition was construed as contumacy and increased one's guilt by adding a new and unpardonable offense, besides being tantamount to confession. In his earliest edict, in 1220, following the Lateran Council of 1215, the Emperor Frederick II declared that the suspect who failed to clear himself within a year was to be condemned as a heretic. Enduring excommunication for a year without seeking its removal was deemed evidence of heresy in regard to the sacraments and the power of the keys.

## Death No Escape

The Inquisition generally contented itself with imprisoning for life those against whom no offense was proved except contumacy unless, when caught, they refused to submit and abjure. Death itself did not permit the defendant to escape. Even though he had been summoned to appear before the judgment-seat of God, the faith must be vindicated by his condemnation and the faithful be edified by his punishment.

Even though the individual had incurred only imprisonment or the lighter penalties, his bones were simply dug up and cast out. If his heresy, however, was such as to incur the penalty of being turned over to the secular authority and hence to be burned at the stake, his bones were burned with solemn ceremony to show the malignance of the crime and the inappeasable vengeance and implacable hostility of the Inquisition.

A bit of defense was permitted the heirs and descendants, who suffered the heavy penalties of confiscation and personal disabilities. The fanatical zeal with which these mortuary prosecutions were sometimes carried out is illustrated in the case of Armanno Pongilupo of Ferrara. Over his remains war was waged between the bishop and the Inquisitor of Ferrara for thirty-two years after his death in 1269. The contest ended, as it virtually always did, with the victory of the Inquisition in 1301.

Similarly the heirs and descendants of Gherardo of Florence discovered in 1313 that there was no "statute of limitation" to prevent Frà Grimaldo, the Inquisitor, from commencing a successful prosecution against their ancestors who had died prior to 1250 —some sixty-three years previously.[3]

## Prosecutor and Judge

The uniting of the roles of prosecutor and judge in the Inquisitorial process was hazardous even when ecclesiastical jurisprudence placed careful limitations upon their respective roles. The hazards were doubled when the prosecuting judge was a fanatic zealot who saw in every suspect a heretic to be convicted at any cost. Neither were the dangers lessened when the judge was merely greedy and eager for fines and confiscations.

In the mind of the Church the Inquisitor was an impartial spiritual father whose concern for the salvation of souls should be fettered by no rules. Every doubtful point was decided "in favor of the faith." The Inquisitor was instructed to proceed summarily, to allow no impediments arising from judicial rules, to terminate speedily the wrangling of lawyers, to shorten the proceedings as much as possible by depriving the defendant of the ordinary facilities of defense, and to reject all appeals and dilatory exceptions.

To tip the scales still more heavily against the accused, the proceedings of the Inquisition were shrouded in secrecy until after the verdict was announced and the tribunal was ready to impress the multitude with the fearful solemnities accompanying the pronouncement of judgment and its execution. Not infrequently this was the burning of the convicted persons at the stake by the agents of the secular powers. The whole ceremony was known as the *auto-da-fé*.

The usual course of a trial by the Inquisition was this. The name of the individual would be reported to the Inquisitor as suspected of heresy or his name would occur in the confessions of prisoners. A secret search would be made and all accessible evidence would be collected. The suspect would be secretly ordered to appear at an appointed time, and bail taken to guarantee his appearance. If he were suspected of trying to flee, however, he would be suddenly arrested and imprisoned until the tribunal was ready to try him.

## The Dragnet

The law required three citations, but this was generally circumvented by making the summons "one for three." When the case was based on common report, the witnesses were summoned seemingly at random, making a sort of dragnet. When the mass of surmises and gossip—exaggerated and distorted by the natural fear of the witnesses eager to save themselves from the suspicion of being friends or intimates—became sufficient for action, the blow would fall.

The accused was thus prejudged. He was assumed to be guilty or else he would not have been put on trial. Practically his only mode of escape was by confessing the charges made against him, abjuring heresy, and accepting any penalty that might be imposed on him in the form of penance. If, on the other hand, the defendant persisted in the assertion of his innocence, when there appeared to be some evidence against him, he was judged to be an impenitent, stubborn heretic to be turned over to the secular arm to be burned at the stake.

If a person caught in heresy acknowledged his guilt and remained impenitent, he was to be handed over to the secular arm to be executed. If penitent, he was not let loose on bail but was to be sentenced to life imprisonment.

As has been mentioned previously, the chief goal of every Inquisitor was to secure the confession of the accused. For this purpose he would earnestly exhort the prisoner to acknowledge his guilt and throw himself upon the mercy of the tribunal. Except in rare cases, confession was accompanied by professions of conversion and repentance. Not only was a soul snatched from the fires of hell, but a convert was gained as well, and there was the hope that he would prove his sincerity by denouncing all whom he knew to be suspected of heresy. Thus was a double victory gained.

## Evidence of True Conversion

As early as 1246 the Council of Béziers had stressed the importance of such conversions, for it was generally agreed that the
disclosure of heretical associates was the indispensable evidence of
true conversion. A person's refusal to betray his friends and relatives was usually regarded as a lack of sincerity, which would
mean that he would be delivered to the secular arm for execution
by fire.

The usefulness of such confessions is illustrated in the case of
Saurine Rigaud, whose confession is recorded at Toulouse in 1254,
where it is followed by a list of the names and addresses of 169
persons incriminated by her. Here was enough information to
keep the Inquisition fruitfully occupied for quite some time.

The rigorousness of the duty of the reconciled heretic to
supply such detailed information is evidenced by the fate of
Guillem Sicrede at Toulouse in 1312. He had abjured his heresy
and been reconciled in 1262. Almost fifty years later, in 1311,
he had been present at the deathbed of his brother, where a heretical ceremony had been performed. He had objected to it in
vain, but had failed to report it. When the Inquisitors inquired
why he had failed to disclose it, he explained that he had not
wished to injure his nephew. For this, incredible as it seems, he
was thrust into prison for life.

So important for the success of the Inquisition was the betrayal
of one's friends and relatives, that Bernard Gui reports that those
who betray all their former friends and associates are not only to
be pardoned but are to receive their livelihood at the hands of
princes and prelates. [4]

So vital to the success of the Inquisition's effort to suppress
any deviation from the Roman Catholic faith was the attempt to
secure confessions of such deviation that it became the center of
the whole Inquisitorial process. To secure such confessions, no
effort was too arduous, no means too repulsive. The Inquisition
thus exercised, as Lea points out, "a vast and deplorable influence
for five centuries on the whole judicial system of Continental
Europe." [5]

## A Sharp Contrast

The sharp contrast between the judicial operation of the Inquisition and the social jurisprudence of the thirteenth century is illustrated in the charter granted by Alphonse of Poitiers to the town of Auzon (Auvergne) about 1260. Any person could clear himself by his own oath and that of a single legal advocate, unless there was a legitimate plaintiff. Furthermore, no citizen could be tried by the Inquisitorial process without his own consent. [6] Here were two widely different worlds of judicial action, with the secular process protecting the inherent dignity and rights of a human being and the ecclesiastical procedure denying them, not in theory but in practice.

In preparing for the trial of an accused person, the Inquisitor collected all the adverse evidence that could be procured, while the accused was kept in ignorance of the information against him. A preeminent requisite of the Inquisitor was skill in interrogation. Manuals were prepared by experienced judges for the younger officials who were taught how to lay pitfalls for the incautious and how to take advantage of hesitation, ambiguity and contradiction.

Few spectacles could be more ludicrous than those of the Inquisitors pitting their skill and sophistication against the untutored shrewdness and caution of the peasants in seeking to avoid any incriminating circumstances as they fought not only for their liberty but also frequently for their very lives. An experienced Inquisitor prepared for the guidance of his successors a list of questions with typical answers, showing how they may deal with quibbles and evasions of those who shrank from denying their faith. In testimony of its helpfulness Bernard Gui reproduced it fifty years later in his *Practica*. It affords such a vivid picture of the battle of wits of the learned with the cunning and the mentality of both groups centuries ago that it is worth reproducing. [7]

## A Battle of Wits

When a heretic is first brought up for examination, he assumes a confident air, as though secure in his innocence. I ask him why he has been brought before me. He replies, smiling and courteous, "Sir, I would be glad to learn the cause from you."

INQUISITOR. You are accused as a heretic, and that you believe and teach otherwise than Holy Church believes.

ACCUSED. (*Raising his eyes to heaven, with an air of the greatest faith*) Lord, thou knowest that I am innocent of this, and that I never held any faith other than that of true Christianity.

INQUISITOR. You call your faith Christian, for you consider ours as false and heretical. But I ask whether you have ever believed as true another faith than that which the Roman Church holds to be true?

ACCUSED. I believe the true faith which the Roman Church believes, and which you openly preach to us.

INQUISITOR. Perhaps you have some of your sect at Rome whom you call the Roman Church. I, when I preach, say many things, some of which are common to us both, as that God liveth, and you believe some of what I preach. Nevertheless you may be a heretic in not believing other matters which are to be believed.

ACCUSED. I believe all things that a Christian should believe.

INQUISITOR. I know your tricks. What the members of your sect believe you hold to be that which a Christian should believe. But we waste time in this fencing. Say simply, Do you believe in one God the Father, and the Son, and the Holy Ghost?

ACCUSED. I believe.

INQUISITOR. Do you believe in Christ born of the Virgin, suffered, risen, and ascended to heaven?

ACCUSED. (*Briskly*) I believe.

## "Ought I Not to Believe?"

INQUISITOR. Do you believe the bread and wine in the Mass performed by the priests to be changed into the body and blood of Christ by divine virtue?

ACCUSED. Ought I not to believe this?

INQUISITOR. I don't ask if you ought to believe, but if you do believe.

ACCUSED. I believe whatever you and other good doctors order me to believe.

INQUISITOR. Those good doctors are the masters of your sect; if I accord with them you believe with me; if not, not.

ACCUSED. I willingly believe with you if you teach what is good to me.

INQUISITOR. You consider it good to you if I teach what your other masters teach. Say, then, do you believe the body of our Lord Jesus Christ to be in the altar?

ACCUSED. (*Promptly*) I believe.

INQUISITOR. You know that a body is there, and that all bodies are of our Lord. I ask whether the body there is of the Lord who was born of the Virgin, hung on the cross, arose from the dead, ascended, etc.?

ACCUSED. And you sir, do you not believe it?

INQUISITOR. I believe it wholly.

ACCUSED. I believe likewise.

INQUISITOR. You believe that I believe it, which is not what I ask, but whether you believe it.

ACCUSED. If you wish to interpret all that I say otherwise than simply and plainly, then I don't know what to say. I am a simple and ignorant man. Pray don't catch me in my words.

INQUISITOR. If you are simple, answer simply, without evasions.

ACCUSED. Willingly.

INQUISITOR. Will you then swear that you have never learned anything contrary to the faith which we hold to be true?

ACCUSED. (*Growing pale*) If I ought to swear, I will willingly swear.


## "*Why Should I Swear?*"

INQUISITOR. I don't ask whether you ought, but whether you will swear.

ACCUSED. If you order me to swear, I will swear.

INQUISITOR. I don't force you to swear, because as you believe oaths to be unlawful, you will transfer the sin over to me who forced you; but if you swear, I will hear it.

ACCUSED. Why should I swear if you do not order me to?

INQUISITOR. So that you may remove the suspicion of being a heretic.

ACCUSED. Sir, I do not know how unless you teach me.

INQUISITOR. If I had to swear, I would raise my hand and spread my fingers and say, "So help me God, I have never learned heresy or believed what is contrary to the true faith."

Then trembling as if he cannot repeat the form, he will stumble along as though speaking for himself or for another, so that there is not an absolute form of oath and yet he may be thought to have sworn. If the words are there, they are so turned around that he does not swear and yet appears to have sworn. Or he converts the oath into a form of prayer, as "God help me that I am not a heretic or the like"; and when asked whether he had sworn, he will say: "Did you not hear me swear?"

And when further hard pressed he will appeal, saying, "Sir, if I have done amiss in aught, I will willingly bear the penance, only help me to avoid the infamy of which I am accused through malice and without fault of mine." But a vigorous Inquisitor must not allow himself to be worked upon in this way, but proceed firmly till he makes these people confess their error, or at least publicly abjure heresy, so that if they are subsequently found to have sworn falsely, he can, without further hearing, abandon them to the secular arm.

## The Sorriest Part

If one consents to swear that he is not a heretic, I say to him, "If you wish to swear so as to escape the stake, one oath will not suffice for me, nor ten, nor a hundred, nor a thousand, because you dispense each other for a certain number of oaths taken under necessity, but I will require a countless number. Moreover, if I have, as I presume, adverse witness against you, your oaths will not save you from being burned. You will only stain your conscience without escaping death. But you will simply confess your error, you may find mercy." Under this anxiety, I have seen some confess.

This same nameless Inquisitor cites a case showing how a simple waitress eluded the tricky questions of the examiners for several days running. She would have escaped except for the accidental finding in her chest of a fragment of a bone from a recently burned heretic, which she had preserved as a relic, according to one of her companions who had collected the bones with her.

"But the Inquisitor does not tell us," observes Lea, "how many thousand good Catholics, confused by the awful game which they were playing, mystified with the intricacies of scholastic theology, ignorant how to answer the dangerous questions put to them so searchingly, and terrified with the threats of burning for persistent denial, despairingly confessed the crime of which they were so confidently assumed to be guilty, and ratified their conversion by inventing tales about their neighbors, while expiating the wrong by suffering confiscation and lifelong imprisonment."[8]

This is the sorriest part of the whole tragic story: the un-counted thousands of good and devout Catholics who were caught in the traps meant only for heretics, and were unable to extricate themselves. Through dragging days and sleepless nights these tragic victims eked out their days in the cold dark dungeons as prisoners for life or were burned alive at the stake with crim-inals and murderers. If the cries of both groups of innocent vic-tims were united, what a cry of agony and terror would resound throughout the whole of Christendom. How shocking to think that, for all we know, the vast majority of the victims may well have been good and faithful Catholics.

## CHAPTER V

# The Use of Torture

God almighty . . . has given to all men a natural right to be free, and they have it ordinarily in their power to make themselves so, if they please.

JAMES OTIS

THE MEMBERS OF THE CHURCH in the first three centuries were held together by the bond of love, and the mercy and forgiveness of God were ever foremost in their minds. Echoing in their memories were the words addressed by Peter to Christ: "Lord, how often shall my brother offend against me, and I forgive him? till seven times?" To which Jesus replied: "I say not to thee till seven times, but till seventy times seven times" (Matt. 18:21-22).

Furthermore, Jesus made it clear that his solicitude went out especially to the sheep that had strayed away. "What think you?" he asked. "If a man have an hundred sheep, and one of them should go astray: doth he not leave the ninety-nine in the mountains, and go to seek that which is gone astray? And if it so be that he find it: Amen I say to you, he rejoiceth more for that, than for the ninety-nine that went not astray. Even so it is not the will of your Father, who is in heaven, that one of these little ones shall perish" (Matt. 18: 12-14).

Christ impressed upon his disciples the duty not only of solicitude for the strayed but also of love for one another. "A new commandment I give unto you, that you also love one another." Then he added the memorable words: "By this shall all men know that you are my disciples, if you love one another" (John 13:34-35). "See," said the pagans in Rome, "how these Christians love one another."

To foster such love, the early Christians had love feasts, called agapes, during which they ate together, prayed, read from the Scriptures and sang hymns. The spirit of mutual kindness, understanding and compassion prevailing among the followers of Christ is aptly reflected in the words of the Apostle Paul to the Galatians: "Brethren, if a man be overtaken in any fault, you, who are spiritual, instruct such a one in the spirit of meekness, considering thyself, lest thou also be tempted. Bear ye one another's burdens, and so you shall fulfill the law of Christ" (6:1-2).

These great fundamental truths were sufficient to maintain the fervor of the early Christians and foster their unity. St. Paul rebuked the Ephesians for giving heed to fables and endless genealogies, and questions which had in them little of godly edification, for "the end of the commandment is charity, from a pure heart, and a good conscience and unfeigned faith" (2 Tim. 1:5).

## A Far Cry

It is a far cry from the peace and unity of the early Church and the wrangling and disputes of the subsequent centuries, with their harvest of heresies and hatreds. Indeed, all those centuries were cluttered with heresies which divided the Church, the Body of Christ, into so many warring factions.

No small portion of church history is that which deals with the following heresies, each of considerable importance: Montanism, Gnosticism, Docetism, Modalism, Subordinationism, Adoptionism, Arianism, Macedonianism, Nestorianism, Monophysitism, Monothetilism, Priscillianism, Donatism, Pelagianism, Semi-Pelagianism, Iconoclasm, Berengarianism, Waldensianism, Albigensianism and Catharism. If those of lesser importance were included, the number would easily be tripled. The list leads up to the Reformation, which brought hundreds of dissident denominations into existence and shook Christendom to its very foundations.

From this it is evident that the Church has been in strife from the days of the Apostles. Despite the efforts to implement the scriptural injunction to live in peace, understanding, unity and love, the Church has felt compelled to suppress heresy wherever and whenever it raised its head.

Clear and impressive are the words of the Apostle Paul to the Galatians: "But though we, or an angel from heaven, preach a gospel to you besides that which we have preached to you, let him be anathema. . . . . For I give you to understand, brethren, that the gospel which was preached by me is not according to man. For neither did I receive it of man, nor did I learn it; but by the revelation of Jesus Christ" (1:8-12).

With all due allowance for the Church's concern for unity and for safeguarding the deposit of divinely revealed truth, it is difficult to understand how the Church, in the name of the Prince of Peace, could have sanctioned the systematic cruelty, torture and burnings at the stake which the Inquisition inflicted upon its unfortunate victims. This is the question which comes inevitably to the minds of most educated people upon hearing the word *Inquisition*.

## *Why the Torture?*

Let us look at the circumstances which made such cruelty possible. The purpose is not to justify it but to understand the mentality which made it possible. We shall see persons starting from presuppositions utterly foreign to our own and fashioning their conduct accordingly. "We shall admit at every turn," acknowledges G. G. Coulton, "that we ourselves, believing as they did, should probably have acted as they did." [1]

The first observation that must be made is that there is a world of difference between the systems or codes of punishment existing in those days and in our own. Living in the United States in an era when capital punishment has not been meted out since June 29, 1972, to any criminal regardless of the atrocity of his crime or crimes, we are understandably shocked at the thought of burning a man alive for differing in religious belief or worship. Today we are light-years away from such a belief and such a commitment.

Furthermore, we differ radically from people of the Middle Ages in sensitivity to pain, and we take for granted daily comforts, of which our far-off ancestors scarcely dreamed. Moreover, we moderns can hardly realize the privations and sufferings which were the daily lot of people a thousand years ago. Thus in the seventy-two years from 987 to 1059, there were forty-eight years of famine or pestilence, two of which were marked by cannibalism.

## A Vivid Picture

In 1017 a chronicler, Ralph Glaber, a monk of Cluny, patronized by two of the greatest abbots of his time—William of Dijon and Odilo of Cluny—gave a vivid and candid picture of the customs and morals of an age when Christianity on the continent had reached an incredibly low ebb. Born in Burgundy before 1000, he died about 1050. A restless spirit himself, Glaber was one of the few Dark Age chroniclers who put real life into their story and make the reader feel like an eyewitness of stirring and even shocking events. Glaber wrote in Latin, and I present a free translation of some of the highlights of his revealing chronicle.

The corruptions which prevailed among men are dreadful to narrate. It grieves me to report an almost incredible thing: the pangs of starvation drove men to act like cannibals and devour human flesh. Unwary wayfarers were pounced upon by stronger men and, after being torn limb from limb, were cooked and devoured like animals. Fleeing from one town to another to escape the famine, persons were taken in at hostelries and killed during the night, to serve as food for those who entertained them. Even children were lured away with an apple or egg by persons who slew and devoured them.

In localities where a famine was raging, corpses were dug from their graves. Indeed, starvation created such a pitch of madness that beasts were safer from the ravisher than human beings. As an indication that the eating of human flesh had now become a well-established practice, an individual at Troyes brought it cooked for sale in the public market. When he was arrested, he made no attempt to deny the atrocious crime. Accordingly he was bound and burned at the stake. Another individual who dug up this man by night and devoured him was also burned in a similar manner. Some three miles from the city of Macon in the lonely forest is a church dedicated to St. John. There a murderous fiend had built a hut, and there he slaughtered a considerable number of travelers and made them his hideous food.

There a man and his wife took lodgings for the night. The husband happened to peer into the corners of the hut and to his horror he perceived the severed heads of men, women and children. His face grew pale as he realized that he was in a death-trap. Despite the desperate efforts of the murderous host to retain the couple, they escaped and hurried to the city, where the man reported his ghastly discovery to Count Eudes and the citizens. A band of men was at once despatched to investigate. To their horror they found the savage in his hut with no less than forty-eight heads of murdered wayfarers whose flesh he had devoured in such beastly and repulsive fashion. They brought the fiend to the city and tied him to a post in a barn, and, as I myself saw later on with my own eyes, they burned him at the stake.[2]

## Truce of God

To such savagery, induced by semistarvation, must be added the interminable strife between baron and baron, between baron and king, and invasions by Saracens. Instituted in Glaber's time, the Truce of God had only the limited success which attended, for instance, the League of Nations. Its chief support came from the Church, which threatened with anathema the ruler who violated the Truce. Glaber bewails the low morals of the clergy as a body and the greed of the prelates for money. He describes the Christian worshippers, when St. Peter's in Rome caught fire, threatening God with vengeance if he did not intervene.

The picture drawn by Glaber was corroborated by Ferdinand Lot:

The form of Christianity which triumphed in the West was of neither a high nor a pure quality. Even the best bishops were superstitious, believing in omens and haunted by fear of the devil. Their notion of the deity was too often that of a jealous vindictive God, who favored his devotees without troubling about their morality. What are we to say of the bulk of believers? Certain practices contributed to the degradation of Christian feeling, such as the use of "penitentials." Coming apparently from Ireland, these were tariffs of prices for the redemption of sins.

From this period the worship of God gave way to the worship of the Saints . . . Gradually differentiations between the Saints were set up which specialized the effects of their intervention, so that the healing Saints replaced the gods and heroes of antiquity . . . Left to itself, the human mind fell back wholly into paganism.[3]

Lea relates the case of a priest, charged with heresy, who was thrown into prison. The Inquisitors brought several theologians to refute him, but they found their match in him. Believing that torture would accomplish what disputation could not, the Inquisitors ordered him to be bound tightly to a pillar. Eating into the swelling flesh, the cords caused such exquisite torture that, when they visited him the next day, he begged piteously to be taken out and burned. Oddly refusing, they left him in his increasing agony for another twenty-four hours. By this time the intense pain and exhaustion had broken his spirit and he humbly recanted.

The incident illustrates the frequent use the Inquisitors made of prolonged torture to achieve their purpose. Guillem Carrec was confined in prison for nearly thirty years before he was willing to confess before the Inquisition at Carcassonne in 1321. The long confinement had weakened him physically and mentally and when he appeared before the Inquisition he was but a shadow of his former self.

In an auto-da-fé at Toulouse in 1299 Guillem Salvavert made a confession which was unsatisfactory to the Inquisitors. He was confined in prison until 1316—seventeen years—when he made another confession, which the Inquisitors again deemed unsatisfactory. Determined to crush him, they kept him in prison another three years. But he held unwaveringly to his previous confession. Finally the Inquisitor Bernard Gui, in consideration of his imprisonment for twenty years without a conviction, let him off with the penance of wearing crosses.

## Pope Orders Investigation

At the session of the Inquisition in 1319 were sentenced six unfortunate victims, who had recently died in prison after confinements ranging from one to eleven years. The long imprisonments in narrow dark cells, with many of the prisoners in chains, caused widespread hatred of the Inquisition among the rank and file. As some of the prisoners were among the most highly respected citizens of Albi, news of its cruelty reached Pope Clement V. His order, issued in 1310, for the immediate trial of all imprisoned suspects had been flagrantly disregarded by the Inquisition, which was a law unto itself.

Even though the pope reiterated his command, it was ignored by the Inquisition. Finally in 1319, Guillem Calverie and Isarn Colli were brought from their dungeon, in which they had been immured for almost twenty years. They promptly retracted the confessions that had been extorted from them by torture. This paved the way for what was probably the final scene in the horrible drama—death at the flaming stake.

When the Inquisitors wanted to get faster action, they made the imprisonment incredibly harsh. Chains and starvation in a stifling hole quickly brought confessions from reluctant lips. So widespread were the rumors of these and worse tortures that an official investigation of the prison at Carcassonne was conducted. It disclosed not only a woeful lack of beds and a deficiency of food but also the implements of the torture-chamber: the rack, burning coals and the *strappado*.

The rack was a triangular frame, on which the prisoner was stretched and bound so that he could not move. Attached to his arms and legs were cords connected with a windlass, which when turned dislocated the joints of the wrists and ankles.

In his *History of the Inquisition*, the French historian Jacques Marsollier describes the use of fire to extract confessions of guilt. After a good fire was started, he relates, the victim was stretched out on the ground, his feet manacled, and turned toward the flame. Fat, grease or some other combustible was rubbed upon them so that they would be severely burned. From time to time the torturer would place a screen between the victim's feet and the brazier, so that the Inquisitor might have the opportunity to resume his questioning. In a letter dated July 28, 1319, Pope John XXII refers to this type of torture that was inflicted upon a woman by the Inquisition at Toulouse. [4]

The *strappado* or vertical rack was equally painful. The hands of the prisoner were tied behind his back and he was raised by a rope attached to a pulley or windlass to the top of the gallows, or to the ceiling of the torture chamber. He was then let fall with a jerk to within a few inches of the floor. The torturers would repeat this several times. Sometimes they tied weights to the victim's feet to increase the shock of the fall and the piercing agony of the victim.

Still surviving in remarkable completeness is the prison in Carcassonne with its towers and narrow, dark cells wherein persons convicted of heresy by the Inquisition were confined. Thousands of people visit this museum each year to see the Torture Chamber with its instruments of torture. In the embrasure of a window in the upper story is the inscription made by a prisoner: "[Give me] food." The lower dungeon is reached by a trapdoor and is lighted by three deep loopholes. The stone pillar, rubbed and worn by prisoners' backs, still has the chains riveted to it.

It is a grim reminder of the cruelty and harshness meted out to all who incurred the enmity of the dreaded Inquisition. Uppermost in the minds of virtually all visitors is the unvoiced question: "How could an institution calling itself Christian inflict such cruel and inhuman punishment upon its members?"

## Violent Antagonism

The instruments of torture used by the Inquisitors, declares Lea, "were in such violent antagonism not only with the principles of Christianity but also with the practices of the Church that their use by the Inquisition, as a means of furthering the faith, is one of the saddest anomalies of that dismal period. . . . It is a noteworthy fact, however, that in the fragmentary documents of Inquisitorial proceedings which have reached us, the references to torture are singularly few." [5]

Except among the Visigoths, torture had been unknown among the barbarians who founded the nations of Europe, and their system of jurisprudence had grown up free from its contamination. What seem to be the earliest instances of the approved use of torture occur in Italy. When Pope Innocent IV in 1252 issued his bull *Ad extirpanda,* he authorized the use of torture for the discovery of heresy. Out of respect for the Church's age-old prohibition of torture, however, he forbade the Inquisitors and their assistants to administer it or to be present thereat.

That was to be turned over to the secular authorities. They were directed to force all captured heretics to confess and accuse their accomplices by torture which should not imperil life or injure limb, "just as thieves and robbers are forced to confess their crimes and accuse their accomplices."

In 1256, four years after the bull of Innocent IV, Pope Alexander IV authorized the Inquisitors and their associates to absolve each other and mutually grant dispensations for irregularities. This permission was repeatedly renewed and deemed to remove all impediments incurred by the use of torture under the direct supervision of the Inquisitor and his ministers. Unfortunately, the Inquisition speedily arrogated the administration of torture to its own officials.

In Naples in 1305 we find Frà Tomaso d'Aversa personally inflicting the most brutal tortures on the Spiritual Franciscans. When he discovered that the use of such measures did not compel them to convict themselves, he hit upon a new expedient: starving one of the younger brethren for a few days and then plying him with strong liquor. When the unfortunate victim was thoroughly fuddled, Frà Tomaso experienced no difficulty in getting him to admit that he and his forty comrades were all heretics. [6]

Toward the end of the thirteenth century Philip the Fair, king of France, in letters to the bishop, bailiff and Inquisitor of Toulouse, called attention to the cruelty of the Inquisitors. Similar complaints were carried by citizens and consuls to Pope Benedict XI. The Franciscan Bernard Delicieux was accused of plotting against Pope Benedict, Philip the Fair and the Inquisition. He was subjected to torture in 1319 by the Inquisition at Carcassonne. But he confessed to hostility only toward the Inquisition.

## Live Coals Hasten Confession

Jean Guiraud reports the case of a woman who was being tried at Poitiers for heresy by Jean de Belegnego, canon of Autun, in the bishop's name. She refused to convict herself until live coals were placed upon the soles of her feet. Under the stimulus of the terrible pain, the unfortunate victim screamed out her confession of error and mentioned the names of her alleged associates.

The canon explained that he used torture only because the jurymen, who assisted him, related that torture was used by the Inquisition at Toulouse. The woman died shortly afterward in prison. As her death might have been provoked or hastened by the torture, the canon asked for absolution for this from Pope John XXII. He was granted it in a bull of July 28, 1519. [7]

In the cases of Isarn Colli and Guillem Calverie, previously mentioned, the record states that they retracted their confessions made under torture. But in the confessions themselves there is nothing to indicate that it had been employed. In the 636 sentences, noted in the Register of Toulouse from 1309 to 1323, the only reference to torture is in the recital of the case of Calverie. There are, however, many instances in which the information wrung from the convicts, who had no hope to escape, could scarcely have been obtained in any other manner. During this period the Inquisition at Toulouse was conducted by Bernard Gui, and he expressed too emphatically his conviction of the utility of torture on both principals and witnesses to leave any doubt as to his use of it.

The investigation of the Inquisition's use of force and torture, instigated by Pope Clement V in 1306, led to an effort at reform which was agreed to by the Council of Vienne in 1311. The publication of that legislation was delayed, however, until October, 1317, when his successor, Pope John XXII, made it known to the world. The legislation sought to limit the use of torture, and to this end Pope John directed that it should not be administered without the concurrent action of bishop and Inquisitor, if this could be secured within eight days.

Remonstrating vigorously against this as crippling the efficiency of the Inquisition, Bernard Gui proposed to substitute for it the meaningless phrase that "torture should be employed only with mature and careful deliberation." His proposal went unheeded, and the regulation of Pope Clement V became the law of the Church. The Inquisitors were so long accustomed to having a free hand, however, that they honored the law more in the breach than in the observance.

## Psychological Pressure

The Inquisitors were adept in the use not only of physical torture but also of psychological torture. We have seen how they used prolonged imprisonment in a dark narrow cell to erode the resistance of the accused prisoner. They were experts in playing upon the emotions as well. One of their favorite tactics was to bring in the other members of the prisoner's family and urge them to beseech him to confess and thus be restored to his home and family.

Chroniclers depict many scenes of a wife and children visiting a prisoner and begging him, with tears, to take his place once more among his loved ones. One can well imagine the psychological pressure put upon the prisoner to yield to such tearful entreaties. This was one of the saddest and most revolting phases of the Inquisitors' willingness to use noble sentiments for ignoble ends.

The common procedure of the Inquisitors was to require that any confession made under torture be confirmed after removal from the torture-chamber. The custom was to continue the torture until the accused expressed his readiness to confess, whereupon he was unbound and carried into another room where his confession was made. In cases when the confession was extorted during the torture, it was read over afterward to the prisoner and he was asked if it were true. There was a rule that there should be an interval of twenty-four hours between the torture and the confession or its confirmation.

This was, however, generally ignored. Silence was construed to indicate assent, and the length of silence to be allowed was, as usual, left to the judge, with the admonition to consider the condition of the prisoner, whether male or female, simple or learned, young or old. If the prisoner retracted the confession, he could be taken back to the torture-chamber for a continuance of the torture, with little or no attention being paid to the pious proviso that the victim had not been "sufficiently" tortured already.

## Evidence of Good Faith

As evidence of good faith and sincerity, the tortured prisoner was expected to disclose the names of others, especially of his close friends and relatives, who might be suspected of heresy. In this way he would afford new customers for the Inquisition's torture-chambers.

If the suspected heretic did not confess freely and satisfy the Inquisitor, he would be tortured and brought back the next morning. The torture usually brought him back in a more compliant frame of mind. The record would invariably contain the notation that "this confession was made freely, without torture and away from the torture-chamber." To the sin of cruelty the Inquisitors did not hesitate to add that of mendacity.

Adept in twisting legislation to suit their purpose, cunning casuists suddenly discovered that the October, 1317, decree of Pope John XXII limiting the use of torture had spoken only of torture in general and had not specifically alluded to witnesses. Wherefore they concluded that the torture of witnesses was left to the sole judgment of the Inquisitor. This shocking abuse of the system then became the accepted practice.

It virtually enabled the Inquisitors to control the testimony of witnesses. What witness would want to testify contrary to the wishes of the Inquisitors and thereby incur tortures so cruel as to injure him perhaps for life? One may well wonder if a provision of this character could be found in any system of jurisprudence in the civilized world.

What makes this provision all the more heinous and incredible is that it was framed and put into operation in the name of the gentle and compassionate Christ and of the religion which he founded. What made this provision especially malignant was that it was calculated to so shape the testimony of the witness as to bring about a guilty verdict for even his dearest relatives and friends and thus have them burned to death at the stake. It is any wonder that despite the lapse of centuries, people still "see red" when they hear the name *Inquisition* mentioned or see it in print?

## Two Incriminating Witnesses

Eymeric, an experienced Inquisitor, states that when there are two incriminating witnesses, a person of good reputation may be tortured to ascertain the truth. If, however, he is of bad repute, he can be condemned without incriminating testimony or can be put to torture on the evidence of a single witness. On the other hand, the Inquisitor Zanghino states that the testimony of a single witness of good character is sufficient for the use of torture, without distinction of persons. The third Inquisitor, Bernardo di Como, maintained that ordinary or common reputation is enough to justify the application of torture.

In the course of time detailed directions were developed for the guidance of Inquisitors in this matter, but their uselessness was frankly acknowledged in the admission that, in the final analysis, the decision was to be left to the discretion of the judge. How little was required to warrant the exercise of this discretion becomes evident when jurists maintained it to be enough if the accused, on examination, was frightened and stammered or varied even slightly in his responses, without any objective evidence against him. [8]

It is worth noting that the rules adopted by the Inquisition in the administration of torture ultimately became those of the secular courts of Christendom. Eymeric, whose instructions on the subject are the most detailed, acknowledges the enormous difficulties which surrounded the subject and the notorious uncertainty of the result. If the torture should be moderate and the shedding of blood was to be scrupulously avoided, what then was moderation?

Some of the accused were so weak that, at the first turn of the pulleys, they would confess virtually anything requested of them. Others proved to be so stubborn that they would endure any torture rather than confess anything, even the truth. Prisoners who had already undergone torture might be either stronger or weaker for it; with some the arms were hardened, with others they were permanently weakened. In the last analysis, the application of torture and the amount of it depended entirely upon the judge.

## Applying the Torture

According to law, both the Inquisitor and the local bishop should be present. The various instruments of torture were shown to the prisoner, who was urged to confess his guilt. If he declined, he was stripped and bound by the executioners. He was again urged to confess and was assured of mercy in all cases in which mercy could be shown. Quite frequently this was sufficient to produce results, with the dread of the torments tipping the scales of decision.

If the prisoner proved obstinate, however, the torture was applied with gradually increased severity. If the obstinacy persisted, additional implements of torment were exhibited to the victim with the assurance that he would be subjected to each of them in turn. It would take a person of unusual courage and determination to resist, and probably most were ready to yield at this stage. If still undaunted, however, he was unbound and informed that the torment would be renewed on the next or the third day.

According to canon law, torture could be applied but once. Like virtually all other regulations for the protection of the accused, this one was easily circumvented. The Inquisitors did this by declaring that the next torment was not a repetition but a "continuance" of the torture. Regardless of the length of the interval, the casuists were able to continue it indefinitely. A further excuse was found in alleging that new evidence had been discovered, and hence renewed torture was necessary to purge it away.

Fresh solicitations were made during the interval to elicit confession. If these were ineffective, the accused was again subjected to the same tortures or to others even more painful and more likely to get the desired confession. If he still remained silent after torture deemed sufficient by his judges, some authorities maintained that he should be discharged and be given a declaration that nothing had been proved against him.

Others maintained that he should be remanded to prison and kept there. The trial of Bernard Delicieux in 1319 disclosed another tactic to elude the prohibition of repeated torture: the Inquisitors could at any moment demand further torment to satisfy their curiosity about a single point in the suspect's testimony. Thus they could continue the process indefinitely.

Inquisitors were greatly concerned with the retraction of confession, for it placed them in an embarrassing situation. In consequence of the methods used to procure the confession, retraction was likely to occur and stringent measures were adopted to prevent it. In theory, a distinction was made between confessions made "spontaneously" and those extracted by torture or its threat. In practice, however, the difference was ignored.

Nicolas Eymeric, a veteran Inquisitor, was alone in maintaining that, if the torture had been sufficient, the accused who persistently revoked his confession was entitled to a discharge. Some contended that the prisoner should be compelled to withdraw his revocation by repeating the torture. Others argued that such revocation impeded the progress of the Inquisition and this fact should be noted in the excommunications regularly published by parish priests and at the opening of every auto-da-fé. They maintained that the excommunication should also include the notaries who contumaciously assisted the accused in drawing up the revocations.

## General Assumption

The general assumption of Inquisitors was that the confession expressed the truth, while the retraction was perjury. Hence the prevalent view was that the retraction merely proved the accused to be an impenitent heretic, who had relapsed after confessing and humbly asking penance. What then was to be done with such an unruly recalcitrant? Nothing but to turn him over to the secular arm for punishment without a hearing.

It is true, however, that the case of Guillem Calverie was handled in a slightly different manner. Condemned in 1319 by Bernard Gui for retracting his confession, he was mercifully allowed fifteen days in which to withdraw his revocation. This was, however, a mere exception to the general rule. The latter is reflected in the emphatic statement of Zanghino that, if an accused had confessed and abjured and had been freed under penance, and if he later remarked in public that he had confessed under fear of expense or to escape more severe punishment, he was to be judged an impenitent heretic, liable to be burned at the stake.

A final complexity frequently confronted the Inquisitors: What was to be done when the retracted confession incriminated others besides the accused? The common answer was that, if such testimony was not to be used against them, the one who confessed was to be held liable for false witness. As virtually no confession which did not reveal the names of partners in guilt was deemed sufficient or adequate, the Inquisitors, who did not consider revocation as relapse, could at least imprison the accused for life as a false witness.

"The Inquisitorial process as thus perfected," observes Lea, "was sure of its victim. No one whom a judge wished to condemn could escape. The form in which it became naturalized in secular jurisprudence was less arbitrary and effective. Yet Sir John Fortescue, the chancellor of Henry VI, who in his exile had ample opportunity to observe its working, declared that it placed every man's life or limb at the mercy of any enemy who could suborn two unknown witnesses to swear against him." [9]

## Church Responsible

It is proved beyond question," points out the scholarly Abbé Vacandard, "that the Church, in the person of the Popes, used every means at her disposal, especially excommunication, to compel the state to enforce the infliction of the death penalty upon heretics. This excommunication, moreover, was all the more dreaded because, according to the canons, the one excommunicated, unless absolved from the censure, was regarded as a heretic himself within a year's time, and was therefore liable to the death penalty. The princes of the day, therefore, had no other way of escaping this penalty, except by faithfully carrying out the sentence of the Church. The Church is also responsible for having introduced torture into the proceedings of the Inquisition." [10]

"The data before us," continues Vacandard, "prove that the Church forgot her early traditions of toleration, and borrowed from the Roman jurisprudence, revived by legists [specialists in Roman law], laws and practices which remind one of the cruelty of ancient paganism." [11] Forgotten were the teachings of the gentle and compassionate Christ to love not only your neighbor but also your enemy. In their place were the teachings of the pagans, demanding an eye for an eye and a tooth for a tooth. Forgotten too was the spectacle of the dying Christ on the cross, praying for the forgiveness of his crucifiers: "Father, forgive them, for they know not what they do" (Luke 23:34).

The noted medievalist of Cambridge University, G. G. Coulton, characterizes the era in which the Church sanctioned the use of torture to extort confessions as the "blackest chapter" in her history, "for it shows the Church adding hypocrisy to exceptional cruelty." Similar is the judgment of the British Catholic scholar, Christopher Hollis. He points out that by sanctioning torture, the Church showed herself false to the early maxim enshrined in the first volume of the *Codex juris canonici*: "Confession should not be extorted, but rather should be brought forth of the man's own accord."

"It was not," Hollis continues, "that the thirteenth century had not yet risen to the standards of the twentieth; it was rather that she had fallen enormously below those of the eleventh." After mentioning all that can be said to render the Inquisitors' practice in this matter less odious than it might seem, he adds: "Yet, in face of the appalling truth that the popes sanctioned its employment at all, such petty details are of little importance." [12]

Hollis puts his finger on the crucial point, which can never be ignored in any honest appraisal of the Inquisition: repeated approval by popes of the use of torture to force confessions of alleged guilt. This violates the most basic teaching of Christ and constitutes the blackest and ugliest chapter in the long history of the Catholic Church.

Confession, the Church teaches, is good for the soul and this is a confession which must be made with honesty and candor. Any effort to twist that simple truth merely adds to the guilt. The world has moved a great distance—light years, in fact—from the papal reasoning of that day, and the Church has moved with it. The popes who established and supported the Inquisition were creatures of their day, but that day has long since passed, hopefully never to return.

## CHAPTER VI

# The Cathar Threat

You shall know the truth and the truth shall make you free.

JOHN 8:32

THE GREATEST THREAT not only to the unity of the Catholic Church but also to the very existence of Christian civilization since the Arians and Manichaeans in the early centuries, was that posed by the Cathars in the twelfth century. The word "Cathar" comes from the Greek word meaning "puritan." It was the name specifically applied to, or used by, several sects at various periods. In its more usual sense, Cathar is the general designation for the dualistic sects of the later Middle Ages, and it is in that sense that it is used here.

Despite the Gregorian reform movement and the new monastic trends in the eleventh century, religious life in western Europe had difficulty in maintaining its equilibrium. Some endeavored to appease their spiritual aspirations by a return to evangelical poverty and simplicity of life, from which it was not difficult to fall into heresy. This seems to be the origin of many sporadic movements superficially labeled Manichaean by contemporaries, but of which little is actually known.

Among historians there is a tendency to regard the Cathars as the lineal descendants of the Manichaeans. In many aspects the liturgy, organization and doctrine of the Cathars reproduce the liturgy, organization and doctrine of the early disciples of Manes.

The successive emergence of the Priscillianists, Paulicians and Bogomili, representatives to a considerable extent of similar principles, fairly establishes, according to N. A. Weber, "the historical continuity between the two extreme links of the chain—the Manichaeans of the third, and the Cathars of the twelfth century. In the present state of our knowledge, however, conclusive proofs in favor of the *genetical* dependence of the Cathars on the Manichaeans are lacking. Some differences between the two religious systems are too radical to find a sufficient explanation in the appeal to the evolution of human thought."[1]

## The Heresy of Dualism

The distinguishing characteristic of the Catharist creed was dualism: the belief in a good and an evil principle. The former created the invisible and spiritual, while the latter created the material world. Furthermore, there was a divergence of opinion as to the nature of these two principles. The absolute dualists admitted their perfect equality, while the mitigated dualists held that the beneficent principle alone was eternal and supreme, whereas the evil principle was a mere creature and consequently vastly inferior.

These two divergent interpretations of dualism coexisted in the East and West. In the East the Bogomili professed a modified form of dualism; in the West, the Albanenses in Italy and nearly all the non-Italian Cathars were rigid dualists. The dualist heresy, originating in the East, was not found in the West until the middle of the twelfth century, when its adherents were called Cathars, a traditional name for Manichaeans.

The heresy was carried from the Balkan Peninsula chiefly by knights returning from the Second Crusade. It spread rapidly in northern France, through the Rhine countries and down into southern France and into northern Italy. It secured an unusually large following in the episcopal city of Albi in France, whence the Cathars in that region came to be known as Albigensians. By the end of the twelfth century there were four Albigensian bishops, with sees at Carcassonne, Toulouse, Albi and Agen.

Excepting their agreement on the principle that the visible world was evil, there was no real unity of doctrine among the

Cathars. They discarded the sacraments of the Church, particullarly baptism of water and matrimony. The absolute dualists recognized parts of the Old Testament, but the vast majority accepted only the New Testament. The Cathars explained the creation of man by myths: Satan, the evil god, had imprisoned spirits in material bodies.

## One Salutary Way

To escape this evil world there was only one salutary way: that was to receive the *consolamentum*, an elaborate ceremony of initiation or spiritual baptism, administered by the imposition of hands. Considering as its only full-fledged members the *Perfect*, the Catharist church conferred upon them the *consolamentum*, which was their key to heaven. The *Perfect* were held to strict poverty and a rigorous asceticism, their diet being entirely vegetarian except for fish. They observed not merely one, but three lents each year.

For the most part the *Perfect* were poor peasants or craftsmen, and were accorded great honor and veneration by the ordinary Cathars, who were called Believers. In the hierarchy of the *Perfect*, deacons were above the ordinary *Perfect*, and at the top was the bishop who was assisted by a "major son" and a "minor son," with the former succeeding the bishop.

The Believers or ordinary Cathars lived according to their beliefs, with no fixed rules of morality. It was enough for them simply to believe that the *consolamentum*, if received shortly before their death, guaranteed their salvation. The Believers "worshiped" the *Perfect* during the ceremony of the *melioramentum*, designed to improve them spiritually, and listened dutifully to their preaching. Catharism was accepted by many of the lesser nobility, who for the most part were poor and turbulent, by peasants, craftsmen and especially by the burghers of the cities who profited from usury that the Cathars had legalized.

The Cathars rejected many teachings of the Catholic Church and assailed its hierarchical structure. Jesus was regarded merely as an angel who came to show the way to salvation, not to provide it. His human sufferings and death were but illusions. The Cathars denied the value of oaths and, at least in theory, the right to punish, thus undermining the basis of orderly government.

But by far the greatest danger, which the triumph of Catharism presented, was the extinction of the human race. This annihilation would be the direct result of the Catharist teaching that all sexual relations between the sexes should be avoided and that suicide was not only lawful but commendable. No salvation of the Cathars was possible without previous renunciation of marriage.

## Oppose Marriage

In the matter of sexual relations Cathars failed to make an essential distinction between marriage and debauchery, a distinction which Christians have always made. They viewed the former as merely a criminal and sacrilegious legalization of the latter. Their blind intransigence prevented them from seeing the radical difference between fornication and the marriage relationship, blessed by God at the dawn of human life and ordained by him as the sacred means for the propagation of the race.

It is a curious bit of irony that the most formidable enemy of the Catholic Church was a strange and weird creed that can scarcely be classified as Christian. Yet this hybrid doctrine spread so rapidly and resisted so stubbornly the desperate efforts at suppression that at one time, as Lea points out, "it may fairly be said to have threatened the permanent existence of Christianity itself." [2]

One suggested explanation of this is the curious fascination which the dualistic theory—the antagonism of co-equal good and evil principles—presents to those who consider the existence of evil as incompatible with the supremacy of an all-wise and beneficent God. When the doctrine of transmigration as a means of reward and retribution is added to dualism, the sufferings and frustrations of man seem to be fully accounted for. When one recalls how widespread and hopeless were those sufferings in the eleventh and twelfth centuries, one begins to realize how many might be inclined to accept so comforting an explanation.

Nevertheless this does not account for the fact that the dualism of the Cathars or Albigenses was not merely speculative dogma spun by philosophical theorists, but a faith which stirred such

fanaticism that its adherents shrank from no sacrifices in its propagation and placed themselves on the burning fagots with astounding joy. Perhaps the worldly and even scandalous lives of
so many nominal Catholics, clergy and even bishops, along with
the conviction of the speedy triumph of their own faith, may
partially account for the unselfish fervor which it aroused in the
poor and illiterate.

## Most Dangerous Rival

The Church early recognized Catharism as the most dangerous
of its rivals. As soon as it could mobilize the resources of the
State, it attacked the heresy with relentless fury and determination. In 1184 the Emperor Frederick I Barbarossa and Pope Lucius
III joined at Verona in issuing the decree *Ad abolendam*, which
formulated a procedure for ecclesiastical trial, after which an
obstinate heretic would be handed over to the secular arm for
punishment. This meant confiscation of property, exile or death,
frequently by burning, according to the custom of the time.

Against the Cathars the Inquisition launched its most vigorous
campaigns, seeking to achieve nothing less than their complete
eradication. This is illustrated in Bernard Gui's detailed accounts
of the trials of Cathars in his *Register*.

Scholars are unanimous in acknowledging the absolute sincerity
and honesty of Gui, a Dominican friar, bishop and Inquisitor.
His Inquisitor's manual, which he called *Practice of the Inquisition
into Heretical Perversity*, was written between 1320 and 1325.
It embodies some of the work of the Franciscan David of Augsburg, half a century earlier. He also wrote his *Register*, recording
the trials and condemnation of 930 alleged heretics between 1307
and 1323.

Writing in the *Register* under the year 1307, Gui gives a detailed
account of the trial of Stephana, daughter of Martin de Praud,
charged with being a Catharist heretic. We present some of its
highlights and quote some of Gui's revealing account, which
lists the heretical errors of the Cathars.

## *Stephana Denies Incarnation*

Stephana denies the Incarnation and the resurrection of the
flesh. The visible world is created not by God but by the devil;
the seven sacraments are naught; marriage is a carnal and profane
act. She believes in the heretics and in salvation through them.
The sign of the cross is devilish. She condemns "the whole Roman Church" as unholy, "saying that [its priests] cannot loose or
bind sinners, being rather sinners themselves." She "asserts [her
own heretical ministers] to be imitators of the Apostles, keeping
the same life and following as they did: with many other erroneous falsehoods." She has confessed before the Inquisitors
to having seen seven heretical *Perfect* at Toulouse, and to having
"adored" one of them. Gui continues:

Concerning which errors and heresies thou hast oftentimes been
admonished and exhorted with reasons and authorities from Holy
Scripture, and besought in the Lord's name, with soft words, both
by me as Inquisitor and my vicars, and by many religious of the Friars
Preachers and Minors and other Orders, with many other honorable
men, clergy and layfolk, of the city of Toulouse, and by your own
parents also, that ye should depart from these errors and return with
good and pure heart to your Holy Mother the Roman Church, outside of which there is no salvation, and shouldst leave that detestable
heretical sect which leadeth souls to damnation and eternal perdition;
yet thou wouldst not even so be persuaded, nor be converted to the
Catholic faith after long waiting, but rather thou persistest even to
this day, with hardened mind, in thine aforesaid obstinacy.

## *The Secular Arm*

She is therefore handed over to the secular arm.

Next day, Monday, she was better advised, seeing that the penalty
of fire was then prepared for her, and was imminent that very day.
She said that she said she would be converted to the Catholic faith
and return to the unity of the church. Whether she said this feignedly
or in truth of heart from fear of death * man's judgment cannot
define with certainty. It was first put before her and explained that

* *Sic*: such is the order in which the reporter writes all these words.

the time of grace was spent for her, and that she should think on the salvation of her soul and reveal fully whatsoever she knew of the fact of heresy, whether in herself or in others. She promised to do and say thus, and that she would fain die in the faith of the Holy Roman Church.

After long and solemn consultation with canonists and theologians, it was decided to stretch mercy so far as to give her a chance. She must abjure publicly, swear future fidelity and go straight to prison, in order that she might be prevented from infecting others, and that the judges might finally discover whether her penitence was feigned or sincere, "the sentence of her condemnation being in no other respect altered, unless it should appear clearly, by manifest evidense, that she was truly converted." [8]

## A Vivid Picture

We turn now from Gui's *Register* to the *Practica*, to his account entitled *Concerning the Manner and Way of Life of These Manichaeans*. We get a vivid picture of the manner in which the Inquisitors confronted the Cathars, who are here termed Manichaeans because they were adjudged to be repeating the errors of the latter. Because of its importance we quote it in full.

It is expedient that I should say a little on this subject, whereby they may be easier known and caught.

*First,* you must know that they swear in no case.

*Item,* they fast thrice a year; from Nov. 13 to Christmas; and from Quinquagesima to Easter, and from Whit-Sunday to the Feast of St. Peter and St. Paul (June 29). They call the first and last week of each of these Lents *a strict week;* for then they fast with bread and water, and the other weeks they confine themselves to bread and water for only three days a week. Throughout the rest of the year, they fast on bread and water thrice weekly, unless they be sick or on a journey.

*Item,* they never eat flesh, nor even touch it, nor cheese or eggs or aught that is born of the flesh by way of generation or coition.

*Item,* on no account would they kill any animal or fowl; for they say and believe that in beasts, and even in fowls, are those spirits which quit human bodies, when they have not been received into the Manichaean sect by laying on of hands according to their rite, and that they pass from body to body.

*Item*, they touch not any woman.

*Item*, at the beginning of their repast, when they are among believers or among themselves, they bless a loaf or a piece thereof, holding it in their hands, with a napkin or other white cloth hanging from their neck, repeating a Pater Noster and breaking the bread into small pieces. Such bread they call Bread of Holy Prayer, and Bread of Breaking; and their believers call it Blessed Bread, or Signed Bread; and, by way of Communion, they eat thereof at the beginning of the meal and distribute it among their believers.

*Item*, they teach their believers to show them reverence, which they call *melioramentum* but which we call *adoratio:* to wit, by bending the knees and inclining profoundly before them on some bench or even to the ground, with hands joined, inclining and rising thrice, and saying each time "Benedicite," and concluding at the end: "Good Christians, God's blessing and yours! Pray the Lord for us, that God may keep us from evil death and may bring us to a good end, or to the hands of faithful Christians."

And the heretic [leader] answers: "May you have that blessing from God and from us: may God bless you and snatch your soul from evil death and bring you to a good end." By *evil death*, the heretics signify death in the faith of the Roman Church; by *good end* and *the hands of faithful Christians* they signify that they should be received at their latter end into that sect and order of theirs, according to their own rite for that they call a good end. The aforesaid reverence, they say, is done not to themselves, but to the Holy Ghost, of whom they say that He is in them from the time when they were received into the sect and order which they profess to hold.

*Item*, they teach their believers to make with them the pact which they call The Covenant: to wit, that at their latter end they will be received into their sect and order; and from thenceforth the heretics may receive such an one in his sickness, even though he have lost the power of speech or of orderly memory.[4]

## How Cathars Preach

Gui then describes how the Cathars preach their doctrines. First, they boast themselves as good folk "who neither swear nor lie nor curse any man, nor slay man or beast," yet whom the Roman Church persecutes, even as the Pharisees did with Christ and His apostles. "*Item*, for the most part they speak to the layfolk of the evil lives of clergy and prelates of the Roman Church. And they enter into details, and dwell upon their pride and greed and avarice and unclean lives, and whatsoever other evils they know.

"And for this they quote authorities, according to their own exposition and understanding, from the Gospels and Epistles against the state of clergy and prelates and monks and friars and nuns, whom they call Pharisees and false prophets, such as say but do not. Then, little by little, they rend and vituperate all the Sacraments of the Church." The clergy (they say), in their greed, sell these empty things to the populace of dupes. "*Item*, they read from the Gospels and Epistles in the vulgar tongue, applying and expounding them in their own favour and against the state of the Roman Church, which it would be tedious to set forth here in full." [5]

Next to the oath, the easiest practical test for an Inquisitor was flesh-eating. Two Tuscans, charged with being Cathars, abjured before Pope Gregory IX. Two days later they demonstrated the sincerity of their conversion by eating flesh publicly, in the presence of several prelates, with a notary to prepare an official record of the fact.

Married defenders, charged with Catharism, generally drew attention to their marriage. The Inquisitor Guillaume Pelisso narrates an incident from his own experience somewhere about 1230. A certain John Weaver of Toulouse wanted to clear himself of the charge of Catharism. So he boasted in open court: "Lords, hear me. I am no heretic, for I have a wife and lie with her, and have children. And I eat flesh and lie and swear, and am a faithful Christian." [6]

What was said in private casual conversations would at times be cited in court against alleged heretics. Thus at Toulouse in 1247 it was reported against Pierre Garcias that he had said in a conversation with a Franciscan friar: "If I could hold that God who, among a thousand men He hath created, saved one and damned all the rest, I would rend him and tear him, tooth and nail, as a traitor; I defy Him as a false traitor and would spit in His face." He added the further heresy that, even among the angels fallen from heaven, "not one in a thousand shall be damned . . . and, if a man is to be saved, the spirit which could not do [sufficient] penance in one body passeth into another, to do penance there."

## A Revolting Practice

One of the most revolting practices of the Cathars was that of the so-called *Endura*, a voluntary fast unto death. Because Cathars had such a horror of the flesh, they often escaped from it by religious suicide, especially on their deathbed. In such a case the sick man was requested to choose between the death of a martyr or a confessor.

If he selected the former, a pillow or a wet cloth was placed over his face suffocating him, while a prayer was recited. If the latter, he starved to death.

If that proved too slow, a fellow Cathar would hasten the process by smothering him. The *Perfect* pressed suicide upon dying members, and in a few cases they had the cruelty to practice it even upon children. "One would think," observed a historian of the time, "that the world had gone back to those hateful days when unnatural mothers sacrificed their children to Moloch." [7]

Lea cites the case of a Cathar who vainly attempted to escape the stake by deliberately starving. A certain Pierre Raymond, who as a Cathar had been led to abjure and seek reconciliation at a session of the Inquisition in 1310, had been condemned to imprisonment, but later in his solitary cell repented of his weakness. The mental tortures became so acute that at last he defiantly proclaimed his relapse into heresy in which state he would live and die.

He only regretted that he could not have access to some minister of his faith in order to be "perfected" or raised to the state of the *Perfect*. He placed himself in *Endura* and, after six days of starvation, he was nearing the end he so desperately sought. He was hurriedly sentenced and a short session of the Inquisition was held so that, with a few other culprits, the stake might not be cheated of its prey. [8]

## Endura Ends in Murder

While the *Endura* was in theory a form of suicide, it often turned out to be murder. After administering the *consolamentum* to a sick person, one of the *Perfect*, fearful that the patient, if he recovered, would probably relapse from the rigid absolutism prescribed, often took matters into his own hands and, for the alleged good of his soul, starved him to death.

The *Perfect* would forbid the patient's family to feed him. When doubtful as to whether the family would obey the murderous prescription, the *Perfect* would either remain there or remove the sick person to the home of one of the *Perfect* to be sure he was starved to death.

One of the *Perfect*, named Raymond Belhot, administered the *consolamentum* to a sick girl, and ordered her mother not to give her anything to eat or drink.

"If she asks me for it," said the mother, "I will not have the heart to refuse."

"You must refuse her," replied Belhot, "or else cause great injury to her soul." [9]

To make sure that the sick girl got no nourishment, he returned frequently to the home and saw to it that she was starved to death. The magnitude and gravity of this menace may be judged from the fact that the *Endura*, according to the English historian A. L. Maycock, "put to death more victims in Languedoc than the stake of the Inquisition." [10]

Speaking out of long experience, Bernard Gui tells his fellow Inquisitors how difficult it is to bring heretics to justice. Conscience, he points out, bids us be careful not to punish the innocent. But, on the other hand, "our minds are even more distressed" by the fear of letting the guilty loose upon society. While excessive severity is regrettable, excessive laxity is even more lamentable.

## Faithful Scandalized

Furthermore, "faithful folk are scandalized when the business of the Inquisition, once set in motion against a man, is left in a sort of confusion. They are to some extent weakened in their faith, seeing that learned men are thus mocked by base and un-cultured persons; for they believe us to have at our fingers' end all the true reasons for faith, so clear and open that no man can stand up against us but that we know how to convict him forth-with, in such a fashion that layfolk themselves can clearly under-stand such reasons. Therefore, in such a case, it is not expedient to dispute concerning the faith against such astute heretics in the presence of layfolk."[11]

Cathars denied the Real Presence of Christ in the Holy Euchar-ist and considered transubstantiation as the worst of abomina-tions. This was in line with their basic religious principle that matter, in every form, was the work of the Evil Spirit. They in-terpreted the Gospel text, "This is my body," in a figurative sense, and thus anticipated the teaching of Carlstadt and Zwingli.

In line with their denial of the Real Presence, Cathars rejected the sacrifice of the Mass. They contended that God repudiated all sacrifices in accordance with the words of the prophet Hosea: "I will have mercy and not sacrifice" (6: 6). Cathars, said Bernard Gui, "declare that to know one's wife carnally is no less sin than incestuous intercourse with one's mother, daughter, or sister." [12] Cathars regarded the birth and conception of a child as essentially a devilish act since it brings into this world a creature who thereby becomes the property of the devil.

In the twelfth century the Cathars had acquired formidable followings in northern France, Germany and Italy, but more es-pecially in the country south of the Loire. After conducting missions among them in Aquitaine and Languedoc with but meager success, St. Bernard drew the following vivid picture of the flourishing character of the Cathars and of the sad condition of the Church.

What have we learned, and what do we learn each day? How much evil has the heretic Henry [of Lausanne] done, and is still doing, to the Church of God! The churches are without congregations, congregations without priests, priests without honor, and, to sum it all up in one word, there are now only Christians without Christ. The Churches are regarded like the synagogues, the sacraments are despised, festivals are no longer observed. Men die in their sins, souls appear before the terrible judgment seat without having been recon-ciled by penance or fortified by Holy Communion. Even the children of Christians are deprived of the Christian life by the refusal to give them the grace of baptism. How dreadful! Must such a man be listened to, and a whole people believe in him?[18]

Corroboration of this desolate picture was given by Count Raymond V of Toulouse. "Heresy," he declared, "has penetrated everywhere. It has introduced discord into all families, dividing husband and wife, son and father, daughter-in-law and mother-in-law. The priests themselves have been affected. The churches are deserted and are falling into ruin. I myself am doing all I can to stop this plague, but I feel that my powers are not equal to my task. The most important persons in my country have allowed themselves to be corrupted. The masses have followed their example, so that I neither dare nor am I able to repress the evil."[14]

## Center of Heresy

Lombardy was an active center of heresy in the eleventh century. Chronicles tell of a certain Girard who preached to the inhabitants of Monteforte, near Milan, doctrines closely resembling Catharism and Waldensianism by absolutely prohibiting marriage and the family life. Confronted with this challenge, the archbishop of Milan, Heribert, launched a campaign against the heretics at Monteforte, and took Girard and many of his followers prisoners.

He sought to save their lives by urging them to renounce their heresy. But the populace demanded vengeance. Accordingly a stake was erected opposite a cross, and the heretics were offered the choice between death by burning or abjuration before the cross. They stubbornly refused to abjure their heresy, however, and in spite of the protests of the archbishop were burned at the stake.

But, as in the early centuries of the Christian era, the Roman emperors discovered that the blood of martyrs was the seed of Christians, so ecclesiastical authorities discovered that fire does not extinguish heresy. Indeed it often stimulates its spread. The Catharist forces stirred civil, social and religious strife. In 1204 they aroused the inhabitants of Piacenza against the bishop who, with his priests, took refuge in Cremona.

The hatred and hostility of the heretics followed them there, and prompted the sectaries to expel the bishop of Cremona and many of his followers. It was not until 1207 that the Catholics of Piacenza were permitted to return to their city and resume their religious life and worship.

## Threat to Society

Conscious of the threat to social and political stability posed by the heretics, the emperors of the thirteenth century had enacted severe measures against them. The motivation was civil rather than religious or from any special attachment to the Holy See. This is illustrated particularly in the case of Emperor Frederick II. In the Bull of Egra, issued on July 12, 1213, he asserted his determination to eradicate heresy from all his territory.

On November 22, 1220, he published a Constitution, two articles of which were explicitly directed against the Cathars, Patarini, Speronists, Leonists, Arnaldists and circumcised heretics, and implicitly against all others. He considered all heretics as social revolutionaries, threatening the stability of his government.

Four years later he published an ordinance for the whole of Lombardy, decreeing the death penalty against heretics in the name of civil as well as of ecclesiastical law. He pointed out that, in bestowing upon him the imperial crown, the Lord had constituted him the guardian of the body of the Church, with the obligation of preserving it from the contamination of "scabby sheep."

In a letter addressed to Pope Gregory IX, the emperor developed his thesis with unmistakable clarity, saying:

The Church is internally torn asunder by false brethren, as by hidden vices, and externally by the attacks of political rebellions which make visible wounds. To these two evils Heavenly Providence has applied not two remedies but one only, under a double form: the anointing of the sacerdotal ministry, service for the spiritual cure of the internal vices of false brethren, vices which stain the noble essence of the soul; and the power of the imperial sword, which must pierce with its point the externally swollen wounds and, by conquering public foes, materially suppress by cutting away that which is rotten and dried up.

Such is in truth, Most Holy Father, the one though double remedy of our infirmity; and although these two things, the Priesthood and the Holy Empire, seem distinct in the terms which serve to designate them, they have in reality the same signification in virtue of their same origin, for both were from the beginning instituted by the Divine power . . . It is therefore to us two, who really are only one, and who assuredly believe the same, that it belongs to ensure in concert the salvation of the faith, to restore the rights of the Church as well as those of the Empire, by sharpening the swords entrusted to us against the destroyers of the faith and the rebels against the Empire.

## Two Hundred Heretics Burned

Thus does Frederick II make it clear that, in repressing heresy in the external form, the emperor acts not as the servant of the Church but as the direct representative of God, from whom he has received the plenitude of power. The pope's jurisdiction is thus confined to the internal forum. This enables one to understand why, even when in conflict with the Holy See and even when excommunicated, the emperor carried on against heresy a program of suppression which he regarded as inherent in the imperial dignity and office.

With such support from the secular power, the Inquisitors were enabled to carry on their difficult task. In 1273 the Inquisitors even attacked one of the citadels of the Waldenses, Cathars and the other neo-Manichaean sects at Sermione, near Verona. Here ruled a Catharist bishop, Laurence, surrounded by many refugees from Piedmont, France and Burgundy. The military expedition was led by Albert della Scala, head of the noted Veronese family of Scaliger, with the Inquisitor, Friar Tinnidio, and his assistant Frà Filippo Bonaccorsi actively participating.

The heretics were badly defeated and two hundred of them were burned at the stake on February 13, 1278, in the arena of Verona. "This," observes Jean Guiraud, "was one of the cruelest executions in the history of the Italian Inquisition."[15] One can well imagine what a horrible spectacle it was, with the tortured victims screaming in terror as the flames enveloped their bodies and gradually reduced them to bones and ashes. Yet the fact that the spectacle took place in a stadium would seem to indicate that it drew a large crowd to witness the cruel and monstrous scene.

That the burning did not eradicate heresy in Sermione, however, is apparent from the fact that on June 27, 1289—only eleven years later—Pope Nicholas IV is found congratulating Scaliger on the armed intervention which again was necessary to achieve the reconquest of Sermione. It shows the inherent futility of the Inquisition to eradicate a firmly held religious belief and to substitute for it a different one by brute force or the threat of it. Conscience is an impregnable fortress which, like the human soul, no material force can crush.

## Difficult to Understand

The Church recognizes this in the case of the early Christians who permitted themselves to be torn limb from limb by the savage beasts in the Roman arena or to be crucified therein rather than renounce their faith. The Church honors them as martyrs and points to them as saints who set an example for all Christians to follow. Hence it is difficult to understand the line of reasoning whereby the Church attempted to accomplish through the Inquisition what the Roman empire—the greatest in the ancient world—was unable to achieve, and was condemned for attempting.

While it is true that society must protect itself from heretics who, like the Cathars and Albigensians, attacked the very basis of human society by forbidding marriage and procreation, the means would seem to be restraining measures and education rather than burning the heretics to death. In short, the Church and its Inquisitorial Tribunal could condemn a heretic to death and ceremoniously turn him over to the secular arm to be burned to death, without killing the idea for which the heretic was willing to die. The only means by which the heretical idea can be extinguished or disproven is by demonstrating the truth of an opposing idea.

From the Pyrenees to Auvergne, from Marseilles to Bordeaux, the Cathars had apparently triumphed. Their churches were attended by the great bulk of the people, while Catholic churches were nearly deserted. At this critical juncture in 1209, Pope Innocent III sanctioned an armed crusade against the heretics, and a formidable army, led by a number of barons from northern

France, proceeded to ravage Toulouse and massacre the inhabitants, both Cathar and Catholic.

## Collapse of Cathars

This Albigensian Crusade, as it is commonly called, waged unrelenting war and devastated the country for many years. But it seems that the more orderly persecution sanctioned by King Louis IX, in conjunction with the Inquisition, had greater success in breaking the power of the Cathars. Great numbers of the heretics went underground and many of the French Cathars fled to Italy. Early in the thirteenth century the Dominican Order was established to provide learned preachers as apt and poor as the Cathars for the purpose (among others) of combating heresy. It was natural that they would be assigned by the papacy to inquiries into heresy. It was out of these inquiries, as we have previously noted, that the machinery of the Inquisition was gradually developed in the thirteenth century.

At about the same time the order of the Friars Minor, or Franciscans, was established and they proved almost equally effective against the Cathars. St. Francis directed his preaching to the poorer classes, to whom the Cathars had particularly appealed. Unlike their message, however, his was one of love and joy. With transparent earnestness and ardor, he brought home, as it had never been before, that the world was God's world and that it was good.

"It is likely," observes the *Encyclopaedia Britannica*, "that the collapse of the Cathars was as much due to the failure of their appeal as to the fires of the Inquisition, and it is noticeable that they disappeared both in France and in Italy at about the same time, although persecution was much more persistent north of the Alps. . . . . The Inquisition was their chief legacy to medieval Europe, for the future of the Church was to be directly influenced far more by the sects that preached a puritanism and a return to the primitive Church innocent of dualism." [16]

Moderns are generally familiar with the menace which the Moors presented to Christian Europe, for the Moors were of a different race, culture and religion. Few moderns are familiar, however, with the seriousness of the threat of the Cathars, for here the foe was of the European household, of the same race and culture, professing to practice primitive Christianity itself. Here the menace lay not in the military might of threatening invaders but in the realm of ideas—poisonous, revolutionary and explosive. Hence an institution, which would ferret out those ideas and thus enable both the Church and the State to contend against them intellectually, and to refute them, was obviously needed if the two institutions were to survive.

## CHAPTER VII

# The Confiscation Policy

Those who deny freedom to others deserve it not for themselves and, under a just God, cannot long retain it.

ABRAHAM LINCOLN

I F, BY THE MOVEMENT OF SOME MAGIC WAND, the reader could
be transported to Carcassonne, France, on a day in the thirteenth century, he would witness a most unusual parade: a motley group of people, preceded by a trumpeter, each carrying a part
of the partially decomposed body of one or more burned heretics.

Such parades were not uncommon because persons who had
died even several decades previously could be adjudged heretical
and all their property could be taken from their heirs, to be dis-
tributed among the heirs of the persons who had discovered only
recently evidence of that lapse from the faith years previously.
Among others who would share in the confiscated property
would be members of the Inquisition, church officials and the
public treasury.

Though not so severe or dramatic a penalty as death at the
stake or lifelong imprisonment, confiscation bore heavily upon
the victims of the Inquisition, their family and heirs. The crime of
heresy was equated with treason by public law and was punished
usually by death or imprisonment and always by confiscation.

The law decreed that all heretics forfeited their property on
the very day they wavered in faith. Confiscation did not apply,
however, to those penitents who deserved no severer punishment

than temporary imprisonment. The veteran Inquisitor Bernard Gui responded to those who objected to such exemption by demonstrating that there was no real pecuniary loss.

Secondary penances, he pointed out, are inflicted only upon those heretics who denounce their accomplices: but, by this denunciation, they ensure the discovery and arrest of the guilty ones who, without their aid, would have escaped punishment; the goods of those heretics are at once confiscated, which is certainly a positive gain. [1] Confiscation occurred in the case of all stubborn and relapsed heretics abandoned to the secular arm, of all penitents condemned to perpetual imprisonment and of all suspects who had managed to escape the Inquisition, either by flight or by death.

## Persecution of the Dead

The heretic who died peacefully in bed surrounded by the members of his family may have thought he was escaping the long arm of the Inquisitors. His happiness would have quickly turned to grief, however, if he knew that the Inquisitors, upon learning of his secret heresy, would regard him as contumacious, exhume his remains and confiscate his property. This last fact explains the incredible frequency of prosecutions against the dead and the appropriation of whatever they had left to their relatives and friends.

It is somewhat startling to learn that, of the 636 cases tried by Bernard Gui, no less than eighty-eight were posthumous. Confiscation occurred even when the legal heirs were model Catholics of unquestioned orthodoxy. They were the ones who were really being penalized and not the heretic who had passed beyond the Inquisitorial hands.

But mindful of the large revenue resulting from such confiscations, the Inquisitors brushed that argument aside, despite the fact that both logic and justice were on the other side. What helped to arouse great interest in the trials of the deceased by the Inquisition was the keen interest in learning what disposition was to be made of their property and personal possessions. Many were in hope that some of the confiscated material or property would go to them.

When the parade had passed through the city streets and wound up at the Inquisition center, the names of the deceased heretics were read aloud, and the living were threatened with a similar fate if they followed in the footsteps of the deceased. Ecclesiastical and lay princes shared with the Holy Office in Rome in these confiscations and thus won for the Inquisition the good will and support of these three influential forces. Lea aptly calls this sharing the "stimulant of pillage." Zeal for the work of the Inquisition, it was noted, languished when the number of confiscations dwindled.

"In our days," writes the Inquisitor Nicolas Eymeric rather gloomily, "there are no more rich heretics, so that princes, not seeing much money in prospect, will not put themselves to any expense; it is a pity that so salutary an institution as ours should be so uncertain of its future." [2]

## Merits Attention

As a general rule, historians have had little or nothing to say about the pecuniary aspect of the Inquisition. The first one to give it the attention it merited was Lea. "In addition," he observes, "to the misery inflicted by these wholesale confiscations on the thousands of innocent and helpless women and children thus stripped of everything, it would be almost impossible to exaggerate the evil they entailed upon all classes in the business of daily life." [3]

The contracts of a hidden heretic, as we have pointed out, were essentially null and void from the moment he wavered in faith and could actually be rescinded as soon as his guilt was discovered, either during his lifetime or after his death. With such a sword of Damocles over the head of every businessman, there was little or no security in commerce of any kind.

"While the horrors of the crowded dungeon can scarcely be exaggerated," remarks Lea, "yet more effective for evil and more widely exasperating was the sleepless watchfulness which was ever on the alert to plunder the rich and to wrench from the poor the hard-earned gains on which a family depended for support." [4]

Cruel as were the imperial edicts of pagan Rome against heresy,

they did not go to the extreme of indirectly punishing the innocent, as did the Inquisitorial legislation. Even when the Manichaeans were condemned to death by Roman law, their property
was confiscated only when their children were likewise heretics.
The Council of Tours, convoked by Pope Alexander III in 1163,
ordered all secular princes to imprison heretics and confiscate
their property.

In his Verona decretal of 1184, Pope Lucius endeavored to
secure for the Church the benefit of the confiscation which he
again declared to be incurred by heresy. One of the first acts of
Pope Innocent III in his double capacity of temporal prince and
head of Christendom, was to address a decretal to his subjects of
Viterbo, in which he declared:

In the lands subject to our temporal jurisdiction we order the
property of heretics to be confiscated; in other lands we command
this to be done by the temporal princes and powers, who, if they
show themselves negligent therein, shall be compelled to do it by ecclesiastical censures. Nor shall the property of heretics who withdraw
from heresy revert to them, unless some one pleases to take pity on
them. For as, according to the legal sanctions, in addition to capital
punishment, the property of those guilty of treason is confiscated,
and life simply is allowed to their children through mercy alone, so
much the more should those who wander from the faith and offend
the Son of God be cut off from Christ and be despoiled of their
temporal goods, since it is a far greater crime to assail spiritual than
temporal majesty.

## Responsibility of the Church

Hence the Church, as Lea points out, cannot escape the responsibility of weaving this penalty into European law as a punishment for spiritual aggressions. [5] The decretal of Innocent illustrates the fact that, at the beginning of the combat with heresy,
the greatest difficulty experienced by the Church in regard to
confiscation was to induce or coerce the temporal princes to do
what it held to be their duty in taking possession of heretical
property. This was probably the greatest of the offenses which
Raymond VI of Toulouse expiated so bitterly.

His son proclaimed Innocent's decretal regarding the confiscation of heretical property to reflect the law of the land and specified punishments for those who favored heretics in any way or who refused to aid their capture. After danger of armed resistance had disappeared, secular princes generally welcomed the opportunity of increasing their slender revenues, and the confiscation of the property of heretics and of promoters of heresy was widely recognized in European law.

In 1317 Gui learned through the confession of another heretic that the deceased Ricarda of Born had been led into heresy on her deathbed by notorious Cathars, and that Guillaume Ysarn, with others, received *consolamentum* from the same two missionaries at his death. Thereupon Gui issued the following sentence:

We condemn them as heretics, commanding that, in token of their perdition, the bones of both be disinterred, in so far as they may be distinguished from those of faithful folk, and burned outside the graveyard.

*Item*, that the houses wherein the said Ricarda and Guillaume were hereticated shall be torn down to the foundation, so that they be uninhabitable for evermore; and, as they have been dens of misbelievers, so let each become a place of filth, and take the place of a stinking dungheap.

In England the Assize of Clarendon in 1166 decreed that if any man received into his home any of the "exterminated" heretics of Oxford, "he shall be at the king's mercy and the house in which they were shall be carried out of the town and burned." Commenting on this decree, G. G. Coulton aptly remarks: "Those who were banished from Oxford in winter, with royal prohibition against their reception by any of the king's subjects, might just as well have been killed outright." [6]

## Financial Tie-up Harmful

The multiplication of trials for the sake of the spoils was occasionally denounced by popes. But since they took no effective measures to cut the evil tree at the root, it continued to flourish and grow. The worst greed was shown by the civil magistrates who either shared with the Inquisitors, or as in France, pocketed all the spoils on condition of bearing all the expenses. But in either case the financial tie-up was harmful to religion and undermined confidence in the Inquisition as a court of even-handed justice.

Further contributing to the lack of confidence in the Inquisition was the notorious venality of medieval courts. Virtually all were influenced by financial considerations, especially the ecclesiastical courts and particularly the center of all at Rome. Barons and abbots contended for the right of executing felons for the sake of their spoils. Undignified fights between ecclesiastics over the right to a putrefying corpse were all too frequent.

In 1270, relates G. G. Coulton, the lord of Mirepoix, who was the King's Marshal in Albigensian lands, demanded possession of the bones of certain heretics burned by the riverside at Carcassonne. He demanded this in virtue of his "peaceful possession of his right of burning heretics on his lands, when condemned to the fire by the Inquisitors of Carcassonne, and of taking their moveable goods if they were in the king's demesne." [7] The Inquisitors yielded to his demands but it is difficult to believe that they did so without regret.

Their arbitrary powers presented terrible temptations. "So assured were the officials," observes Lea, "that condemnation would follow trial, that they frequently did not await the result, but carried out the confiscation in advance. . . . The Inquisition so habituated men's minds to the belief that no one escaped, who had once fallen into its hands, that the officials considered themselves safe in acting upon the presumption." [8]

Confiscation was an ordinary resource of medieval law. In England, from the time of Alfred, property as well as life was forfeited for treason, a penalty which remained until 1870. In France murder, false witness, treason, homicide and rape were all punished with death and confiscation. By German feudal law the fief might be forfeited for a vast number of offenses. But the distinction was drawn that, if the offense was against the lord, the fief reverted to him; but if simply a crime, it descended to the heirs.

The records of the Inquisitorial prosecutions at Albi reveal that in 1300 a certain Jean Baudier was first examined on January 20, when he confessed nothing. At a second hearing on February 5, he confessed to acts of heresy and was condemned on March

7. Yet astonishingly enough his confiscated property was sold on January 29! This was prior not only to his sentence but also to his confession.

Similar is the case of Guillem Carrec. Accused of complicity in the plot to destroy the Inquisitorial records of Carcassonne in 1284, he was not sentenced until 1319. But again to the surprise of everyone interested in legal justice and fairness, we find the Count of Foix and the royal officials in 1301 quarreling over the ownership of his confiscated castle of Monteirat. [9]

## Incredible Rapacity

An even more striking illustration of the incredible rapacity with which the process of confiscation was conducted is cited by Lea. It is based on a report made by Jean d'Arsis, seneschal of Rouergue, to Alphonse of Poitiers in 1253. He made the report to show the care and zeal with which he was safeguarding the interests of his suzerain. The bishop of Rodez was conducting an episcopal Inquisition, and at Najac had turned over to the secular arm a certain Hugues Parair as a heretic. The seneschal burned him "incontinently" and collected more than 1,000 livres Tournois from his estate.

Sometime later he was surprised to learn that the bishop had cited before him at Rodez six other citizens of Najac. D'Arsis hurried there to make sure that no fraud was practiced on the count. The bishop explained to him that all these men were heretics and that he would see that the count got 100,000 sols from their confiscations. But he and his assessors entreated the seneschal to pass on a portion for the culprits and their children. This the loyal servitor bluntly refused.

Following evil counsel, and in fraud of the rights of the count, the bishop tried to elude the forfeiture by condemning the heretics to a much lighter penance. The seneschal understood his master's rights, however, and immediately seized the property, after which he allowed a pittance to the dispossessed and their children. He reported that, in addition to this, he was in possession of about 100,000 livres. He winds up by advising the count, if he did not wish to be defrauded, to appoint some one to watch and supervise the further Inquisitions of the bishop.

On the other hand, the bishops complained that Alphonse's agents allowed heretics, for a bribe, to withhold a portion or the whole of their confiscated property, or else they condemned to the flames those who did not deserve it in order to seize their estates. Despite all his greed, Alphonse was not unwilling to share the plunder with those who secured it for him, and some of his not entirely disinterested liberalities of this kind are on the record. Thus we have a 1268 letter of his assigning to the Inquisition a revenue of 100 livres annually on the confiscated estate of a heretic, and a 1270 letter, confirming the foundation of a chapel from a similar source.

## Additional Revenue

An additional source of Inquisitorial income was discovered in the system of fines for offenses and of payment for special mitigations. Efforts were made at first to keep it out of the Inquisition, as lending itself to suspicion of baser motives and as incompatible with the Inquisitorial profession of poverty, since nearly all were friars. In 1242 the Dominican General Chapter forbade it, and the Council of Narbonne in 1244 did likewise. But these prohibitions were generally ignored, and in 1251 Innocent IV explicitly authorized fines in cases where they appeared to be the only convenient penance.

A further source of Inquisitorial revenue was that of commuting for a fee the penance stipulated by the Inquisition tribunal. Long in vogue for the Crusades, this practice yielded immense sums all through the Middle Ages by redemption of Crusaders' vows. In theory such contributions were supposed to be applied to defray the working expenses of the Inquisition and for other pious purposes: in practice there was a great deal of graft and embezzlement.

In 1249 Pope Innocent IV rebuked Inquisitors for levying extortionate fines, to the disgrace of the Holy See and the scandal of the faithful. In 1302 Pope Boniface VIII publicly rebuked the Franciscan Inquisitors of Padua and Vicenza for extracting huge sums which they expended neither for the Church nor for their own Order. In 1311 at the Ecumenical Council of Vienne, Clement V based his reforming statutes partly upon his conviction that the Inquisitors often extorted money from the innocent and accepted bribes from the guilty.

In 1346 the Republic of Florence rose against their Inquisitor, and even refused a safe-conduct for his appearance before the investigators. One witness swore to sixty-six cases of extortion; in another case the sum amounted to 1,700 gold florins. Offering emphatic evidence of such extortion was a particularly well informed witness and a champion of orthodoxy, the Spaniard Alvarus Pelagius, a Franciscan friar.

## Pocketing the Spoils

Alvarus Pelagius testified that his fellow friars, when they were employed against heretics, regularly pocketed the spoils of their victims:

Wherein these Inquisitors commit two mortal sins; for whereas, by papal privilege, this money [earned by the Inquisitor] ought to be divided into three parts, one for the government of the land wherein the heretic dwells, another to the officials of the Holy Office, and the third for the diocesan bishop for necessary expenses for the Inquisition. Yet these Inquisitors, though no share has [thus] been assigned to any of them, usurp the whole for themselves, even though the Roman Church assigns to them no part for their expenses. Thus they are truly thieves and robbers of the Inquisition money, usurping it beside and contrary to the will of the Roman pontiffs and spending it abusively at their own pleasure upon their brethren and their kinsfolk.

Their second sin is that, whereas they ought to be Friars Minor and touch no money, yet they spend it as they please, and think themselves to be making a holy offering to God when they give alms of this money to their friaries or their brethren—alms, literally, of the mammon of unrighteousness—that is, of other men's money. And a third sin also, that they scarce punish any man accused of heresy except by condemning him to lose his money, in order that they may put it into their own purses. Therefore, I can scarce believe that any one of them escapeth that papal excommunication which is rehearsed in Canon Law.[10]

Such a system of confiscation, points out Abbé Vacandard, inflicted poverty upon thousands of innocent women and children, paralyzed ordinary social relations to a degree hard for us to understand, and broke down business guarantees, since no bargain made by a heretic was valid in law. The man might be denounced as a heretic and all his affairs cast into the melting-pot even before his death.

An illustration of the remorseless greed which seized every revenue connected with the confiscation of the holdings of a condemned heretic is found in the archives of the bishop of Albi. On the death of the Chevalier Guillem Prunelle and his wife Isabelle, the guardianship of their orphans would normally vest in the next of kin, the Chevalier Bernard de Montesquieu. But he had been burned for heresy some years previously and his estate, of course, was confiscated. The seneschal of Carcassonne insisted that the guardianship now formed part of the assets of the estate, and he accordingly assumed it.[11]

## Pitiless Methods

The harshness of the confiscation procedure was aggravated by the pitiless methods employed. As soon as a person was arrested for suspicion of heresy, his property was sequestrated and seized by the officials, to be restored to him in the rare cases in which his guilt might be declared not proven. Enforcing this rule in the most rigorous manner, officials inventoried every article of the person's furniture and provisions as well as his real estate.

Whether innocent or guilty, his family was turned outdoors to starve or depend upon the dubious charity of others. Whatever sympathy might ordinarily exist was likely to be chilled by the realization that any manifestation of it was dangerous. It would be impossible to estimate the amount of misery arising from this source alone. One may readily imagine that those who were active in the work of confiscation were not overly scrupulous in securing a share of the spoliations.

This is illustrated by a case which occurred in Carcassonne in 1304. Jacques de Polignac had been for twenty years keeper of the jail in that city. He and several of the officials employed on the confiscations were found to have appropriated a large amount of the confiscated material. Included was a considerable amount of valuable property, including a castle, several farms and other lands, vineyards, orchards and movables. It is pleasant to report that they were compelled to disgorge all of it and to suffer punishment at the king's pleasure. [12]

Another interesting case occurred in Flanders at a time when in that region the Inquisition had become so nearly dormant that the usages of confiscation were almost forgotten. The bishop of Tournay and the vicar of the Inquisition condemned at Lille a number of heretics, who were duly burned. They confiscated the property, claiming the movables for the Church and the Inquisitor, and the real estate for the state treasury.

This aroused the magistrates of Lille who boldly intervened. They declared that among the liberties of their town was the privilege that no citizen could forfeit both body and goods. Acting in behalf of the children of one of the victims, they appealed to the pope.

The counselor of the suzerain, Philip the Good of Burgundy, with a clearer perception of the law, declared that the whole confiscations inured to him. But the ecclesiastics declared the rule to be invariable that the real estate goes to the municipal treasury and the other possessions go to the Church.

Both sides agreed to leave the decision to the duke himself. With wisdom he settled the matter in 1430, with general consent, by deciding that the sentence of confiscation should be treated as not rendered, and the property left to the heirs, expressly declaring, however, that the rights of the Church, Inquisition, city and state were reserved without prejudice in the unlikely event that such a case would again occur.

## The Prescription of Time

The prescription of time against the Church, Lea notes, had to be forty years and against the Vatican one hundred years. The prescription ran, not from the commission of crime, but from its detection. Although some canonists maintained that the proceedings against the deceased heretic had to be started within five years after death, others asserted that there was no limit. The practice of the Inquisition shows that the latter opinion was followed.

A further provision, lessening the likelihood of good Catholics coming into the possession, was that they must at no time have had a knowledge that the former owner was a heretic. Indeed he must have died with an unsullied reputation for orthodoxy. Both requirements must have placed a grave doubt on titles.[13]

From what we have said thus far, it is clear that the prosecution of the dead was a mockery in which defense was virtually impossible and confiscation inevitable. How unexpectedly the dreaded blow might fall is shown in the case of Gherardo of Florence. A consul of the city in 1218, he was rich and powerful, and a member of one of the oldest and noblest houses in Italy.

He was denounced as a heretic on his deathbed (between 1246 and 1250). But the matter remained a secret until 1313—at least sixty-three years after his death—when Frà Grimaldo, the Inquisitor of Florence, brought a successful prosecution against his memory. Included in the condemnation were his children, Nerlo, Cante, Bertuccio and Ugolino, and his grandchildren, Goccia, Frà Giovanni, Coppo, Gherardo, prior of St. Quirico, Marco, Goccino and Baldino. This did not imply that they were heretics. But it did mean that they were disinherited and subjected to the disabilities of descendants of heretics. While such proceedings were acclaimed as exhibitions of holy zeal, no man could feel secure in his possessions, whether derived from descent or purchase.[14]

Somewhat different in character but equally illustrative is the case of Geraud de Puy-Germer. His father had been condemned for heresy in the time of Raymond VII of Toulouse, who was bighearted enough to restore the confiscated estates. Yet, twenty years after the demise of the count in 1268, the zealous agents of Alphonse of Poitiers seized them as still liable to confiscation. Thereupon Geraud appealed to Alphonse who ordered an investigation, with what result is not known.

## Cloud of Uncertainty

Not only were all alienations made by heretics set aside and the property wrested from the purchasers, observes Lea, but all debts contracted by them, and all hypothecations and liens given to secure loans, were null and void. Thus uncertainty clouded every obligation into which a person could enter. Although St. Louis mitigated the rigors of confiscations in Languedoc, the utmost concession he made was that creditors should be paid for debts contracted by culprits before they became heretics, while all claims arising subsequent to an act of heresy were rejected.

Since no one can be certain of the orthodoxy of another, it is easy to imagine the amount of distrust that must have enveloped every bargain and every sale in the most ordinary transactions of daily life. The blighting influence of such widespread doubt can be readily perceived, since it came at a time when the industrial and commercial development of Europe was beginning to usher in the dawn of modern culture.

Hence it was that the Inquisition not only repressed the spiritual striving of the thirteenth century but also retarded the progress of commercial enterprise. As the Inquisition was comparatively unknown in England and the Netherlands, they gained the predominance in commerce and industry, which brought freedom, wealth, power and progress in its wake.

The commonwealths of Italy recognized the disabilities inflicted upon their real estate merchants through the confiscation by the Inquisition. In Florence a remedy was sought by requiring the seller of property to provide security against possible future sentences of confiscation—the security being that of a third party. This was only replacing one evil by another of scarcely less magnitude. Accordingly, the republic explained to Pope Martin IV the intolerable inconvenience and the scandals which had occurred and the yet greater ones threatened as a result of the confiscation of the real estate of heretics in the hands of *bona fide* purchasers. In a special bull of November 22, 1283, the pontiff forbade the Florentine Inquisitors in the future to seize such property. [15]

## "Constipated Purses"

Theoretically the bishops were liable for the expenses of the Inquisitors, and at first those of Languedoc sought to obtain funds from them. They suggested that at least the pecuniary penances inflicted for pious uses should be devoted to paying their notaries and clerks. But the bishops turned deaf ears to their pleas. This prompted Guy Foucoix—the future Pope Clement

IV—to remark that "their hands were tenacious and their purses constipated." He recommended that the pecuniary penances be used to defray the expenses of the Inquisitors, provided it be done decently and without scandalizing the people.

Throughout central and northern Italy the fines and confiscations fully supported the Inquisition. In Venice the state took all the profits and defrayed all the expenses. The same policy was at first pursued in Naples by the Angevine monarchs. At the Council of Béziers in 1246, the Cardinal Legate of Albano reminded the bishops that it was their duty to defray the expenses of the Inquisition in accordance with the instructions of the Council of Montpellier.

As would be expected, St. Louis of France set an edifying example in this matter. In 1248 we find him defraying the expenses of all the Inquisitions in all the domains of the crown. In addition, he assumed the cost of the prisons and prisoners sentenced by the Inquisition.

Both princes and religious superiors complained about the luxury and extravagance of not a few Inquisitors. The Dominican provincial chapters of Montpellier and Avignon rebuked some of their Inquisitors for departing from the simplicity and poverty of the religious life and taking on many of the airs of the nobility. In a confidential letter of 1268, Alphonse of Poitiers complains of the vast expenditures of Pons de Poyet and Etienne de Gatine, Inquisitors of Toulouse, and instructs his agent to try to persuade them to remove to Lavaur, where less extravagance can be hoped for.

## Avarice and Fanaticism

With the appearance of great generosity, Alphonse offered to put at their disposal the castle of Lavaur or any other that might be fit to serve as a prison. At the same time he craftily wrote to them, explaining that, in order to enable them to extend their operations, he would place an enormous castle in their hands.[16]

An army, it is said, travels on its stomach. Without food, it would do little traveling and less fighting. Prosecution, as a steady and continuous program, rested essentially upon persecution. "It was this," says Lea, "which supplied the fuel to keep up the fires of zeal, and when it was lacking the business of defending the faith languished lamentably. . . . There is an intimate connection between the activity of persecuting zeal and the material results to be derived from it." [17] When that close connection is weakened and ultimately destroyed, persecution comes to a dead stop like a motorcar which has run out of gas.

Of course, it would be both inaccurate and unfair to say that greed and avarice were the impelling motives of the Inquisition. But it is fair to say that the thought of financial support was never far from the minds of the Inquisitors and their backers. Without that financial support their work would have been much less effective and it would have sunk into comparative insignificance as soon as the first frenzied zeal of bigotry had burned itself out.

"This zeal," observes Lea, "might have lasted for a generation, to be followed by a period of comparative inaction, until a fresh onslaught would have been excited by the recrudescence of heresy. Under a succession of such spasmodic attacks Catharism might perhaps have never been completely rooted out. By confiscation the heretics were forced to furnish the means for their own destruction. Avarice joined hands with fanaticism, and between them they supplied motive power for a hundred years of fierce, unremitting, unrelenting persecution, which in the end accomplished its main purpose." [18]

# CHAPTER VIII

# The Spanish Inquisition

Wide differences of opinion in matters of religious, political and social belief must exist if conscience and intellect alike are not to be stunted.

THEODORE ROOSEVELT

THROUGHOUT THE MIDDLE AGES the heterogeneous culture of Spain with its many Saracen and Jewish elements was but slightly disturbed. Merely local and spasmodic efforts were taken to rid the peninsula of heretics, chiefly immigrants from Languedoc. In 1317 the archbishop of Compostella wrote to the Inquisitor Bernard Gui asking what should be done with the Languedocian heretics who had recently settled in his diocese: "For, up to the present, the proper manner of dealing with them is unknown in these parts." [1]

Though the famous Inquisitor Nicolas Eymeric had set up his tribunal there, he frequently bewailed its poverty and the lack of effective support from the secular authorities. "The fact that so little came into its exchequer from confiscation," observes A. S. Turberville, "and that so ardent and active an Inquisitor should apparently have accomplished so little seems mainly to prove that heresy was not a serious menace in Aragon at that time." [2]

The Spanish Inquisition, however, properly begins with the reign of Ferdinand and Isabella. During the struggle of 780 years with the Moors, the Spaniards had succeeded in preserving their Catholic faith and their nationality; and these two had become so fused as to be regarded by them as one. Originally the conquered Saracens were allowed the free exercise of their religion. But repeated revolts along with attempts to procure another Mohammedan invasion from Africa caused the Spanish sovereigns in 1501 to issue a decree ordering all Moors to leave Castile and Granada, except those who would embrace Christianity.

Though most of the Moors received baptism, many secretly apostatized, and others adulterated their Christian rites with Moslem practices. After having resisted popular demands for the banishment of the Jews, the Spanish government decided to acquiesce on the grounds that the foes of Christianity had formed a league, threatening the freedom and the sovereignty of Spain. The Spanish people had long yearned for some means of cementing the religious and political unity of the nation. The throne saw in the Inquisition an agency calculated to achieve this unity.

Accordingly Ferdinand and Isabella established the Inquisition in 1480 along nationalist and royalist lines, whereas Sixtus IV had wished it to be set up after the form and spirit of the Middle Ages. So displeased was the pontiff at the action of the Spanish sovereigns that he placed the Spanish ambassador under arrest. Ferdinand retaliated by arresting the papal envoy and recalling all his subjects from the Roman states. Ultimately Rome yielded and permitted the Inquisition to be introduced into Aragon and Castile.

Disturbed by complaints concerning the rigor and rapacity of the tribunal, the pontiff ordered the Inquisitors to proceed only in accord with the bishops and not to extend their inquiries into other provinces. He also instituted a papal judge to hear all appeals from the Spanish tribunal and he quashed many of its indictments. So dissatisfied was the pope with the highhanded, cruel and despotic actions of the Inquisitors that in a Brief of January 29, 1482, he threatened them with deposition—a step he would have taken but for the intervention of the Spanish throne.

According to the directions of Rome, the judges were to be at least forty years old, of unblemished reputation, noted for virtue and wisdom, masters of theology, or doctors or licentiates of canon law, and they were to follow the usual ecclesiastical rules and regulations. At the request of the Spanish monarch, Sixtus IV bestowed on the Dominican Tomas Torquemada, the office of Grand Inquisitor, the institution of which rendered possible the high degree of centralized authority which characterized the Spanish Inquisition. Torquemado became the true organizer of the Inquisition in the Iberian peninsula; it speedily ramified from Seville to Cordova, Jaen, Villareal and Toledo. By 1538 there were nineteen courts, to which three were later added in Spanish America: Mexico, Lima and Cartagena.

Failure marked the attempts to introduce it into Italy, while the efforts to establish it in the Netherlands entailed disastrous consequences for Spain. In the Iberian peninsula, however, it remained operative into the nineteenth century. While originally called into being against secret Judaism and secret Mohammedanism, it served to repel Protestantism in the sixteenth century but was ineffective against French Rationalism and immorality in the eighteenth. It was abrogated by King Joseph Bonaparte in 1808, restored in modified form by Ferdinand VII in 1814, only to be abolished by the Revolution in 1820. It was not, however, until May 8, 1869, that the principle of religious liberty was proclaimed in the peninsula, and even since then it has been limited by the Constitution of 1876, which prohibited the *public* celebration of dissident religions until comparatively recent years.

## Organization of Inquisition

A glance at the organization of the Spanish Inquisition will show its peculiarly monarchical and centralized character. At the head of the Inquisition was the Grand Inquisitor, nominated by the crown and confirmed by the pope. By virtue of his papal credentials, he enjoyed authority to delegate his powers to other suitable persons and to receive appeals from all Spanish courts. He was assisted by a High Council consisting of five members—the so-called Apostolic Inquisitors.

The officials of the supreme tribunal were appointed by the Grand Inquisitor after consultation with the king. The former held office for life and had the authority to appoint, transfer, remove from office, visit, inspect and call to account all Inquisitors and officials of the lower courts. All power was concentrated in the supreme tribunal. It decided disputed questions and heard appeals; without its permission no priest, knight or nobleman could be incarcerated and no auto-da-fé held. Everyone was subject to it, not excepting priests and bishops.

It claimed almost complete autonomy and did not hesitate, despite protests from Rome, to initiate proceedings against bishops and archbishops. Closely allied with the crown, the Inquisition frequently asserted its independence of Rome; it declared the decisions of the Roman Congregation of the Index to be valid for Spain only if countersigned by its Holy Office in Madrid. It acted in frequent opposition to Rome and joined with the crown in resisting appeals to the pope.

It had the temerity to attack the orthodoxy of Carranza, archbishop of Toledo and a distinguished Dominican theologian. Despite the approval of Carranza's book *Comments on the Christian Catechism* by the Council of Trent, the Spanish Inquisition placed it on the Index. Displeased with such action, Pius IV protested against it and called the case to Rome, but King Philip declared that the first prelate of Spain should be tried only in Spain. The pontiff compromised by sending a legate and two other judges to conduct the examination, but the Inquisitors managed to prolong the investigation until the new pope, Pius V, ascended the chair of Peter.

This pontiff repeatedly protested to Philip that he was not kept informed of the progress of the case, and it was only by threatening the monarch with excommunication that he succeeded in having Carranza sent to Rome. This was in May, 1567, after nearly eight years' imprisonment under the Spanish Inquisitors.

## Political Character

So independent of Rome did the Inquisitors feel at times that they twice imprisoned St. Ignatius Loyola, the founder of the Jesuits, in the beginning of his career. Even St. Theresa did not escape their suspicious zeal: she was accused of misconduct and several times denounced. One of her works, *Conceptos del Amor Divino*, was placed on the Index and she herself was saved only by the personal influence of Philip II.

The Spanish Inquisition thus became virtually an *imperium in imperio*, a state within a state. At the peak of their power, the Inquisitors paid no taxes and gave no account of their confiscations. They claimed for themselves and their agents the right of bearing arms, and they did not scruple to prosecute their critics and adversaries under the charge of heresy.

It is distinguished from its medieval counterpart by its monarchical constitution, its greater consequent centralization of authority, and by the constant and legally provided-for influence of the crown on all official appointments and the progress of its trials. In short, it was to a considerable extent a *political* institution. The monarch appointed the Grand Inquisitor; he confirmed the nomination of the assessors. He kept the tribunal dependent upon him and was capable at almost any time of thwarting, frustrating and terminating it. He used it repeatedly against his enemies and even made it serve as his ally in his differences with Rome. "If there was any place in the world," observes Abbé Vacandard, "where the State interfered unjustly in the trials of the Inquisition, it was in the kingdom of Philip II." [3]

When Cardinal Ximenes protested against Ferdinand's appointment of a layman to the council of the Inquisition, the monarch asked indignantly: "Do you not know that if the tribunal possesses jurisdiction, it derives it from the king?" Thus clearly did he show that he regarded himself as the real power behind the Inquisition, which he could withdraw at will.

## Ranke Testifies

The Protestant historian Ranke regarded the Spanish Inquisition as a political institution for two reasons: the Inquisitors were royal officers receiving their appointment from the king who could dismiss them at will; the institution served continuously to enrich the royal treasury. Developing this last point, Ranke says:

It was even believed and asserted from the beginning that the kings had been moved to establish this tribunal more by a hankering after the wealth it confiscated than by motives of piety . . . Segni says that the Inquisition was invented to rob the wealthy of their property and the powerful of their influence. As Charles V knew no other means of bringing certain punishment on the bishops who had taken part in the insurrection of the Communidades, he chose to have them judged by the Inquisition . . . Under Philip it interfered in matters of trade and of arts, of customs and marine. How much further could it go, when it pronounced it heresy to sell horses or munitions to France? . . . In spirit, and above all in tendency, it was a political institution. The Pope had an interest in thwarting it, and he did so as often as he could.

In 1812 the Spanish Cortes, or parliament, having convened to draft a new constitution for the kingdom, appointed a committee to report on the Inquisition. Their report declares that the Inquisition "was an institution demanded and established by the Spanish monarchs in difficult circumstances," and "that it could decree nothing without the consent of the king." Then the committee frankly declares: "The Inquisition is a royal authority, the Inquisitor is a royal agent, and all his ordinances are null and void unless they have the royal sanction. The king's power suspends and revokes at will every member of the tribunal, and the very moment royal authority would disappear, the tribunal would accompany it."

## Ecclesiastical Complexion

The testimony of these various authorities indicates that the Spanish Inquisition had a political complexion and that the monarch exercised enormous control, even at times opposing and thwarting the wishes of the Holy See. From the facts already mentioned, some writers have concluded that it was essentially and predominantly a political institution. But this is going too far. Despite all the influence of the king, it was predominantly an ecclesiastical tribunal: the Holy See sanctioned the institution and accorded to the Grand Inquisitor canonical installation and therewith judicial authority concerning matters of faith. From him jurisdiction passed down to the subsidiary tribunals under his control.

How else can it be explained that the popes always admitted appeals from the Inquisition to the Holy See, called to themselves entire trials, at any stage of the proceedings intervened in the legislation, exempted whole classes of believers from its jurisdiction and even deposed Grand Inquisitors? No, the theory of its being essentially a political institution won't jell: it was predominantly ecclesiastical. This is candidly acknowledged by the

*Catholic Encyclopedia:* "The predominant ecclesiastical nature of the institution can hardly be doubted."

The Church must, therefore, bear her share of responsibility for the proceedings of this tribunal, so many of whose actions were marked by cruelty and savagery. They have left black stains on the pages of history and their somber shadow falls upon both crown and papacy and shows that their occupants were the children of their day.

## The Background

Now let us sketch the background of the establishment of the Inquisition in Spain and show how it operated. Up until 1480 Spain had been one of the least Inquisition-ridden countries in Europe. Even though there were few remnants of Latin culture, the stimulating influence of the Moors and the Jews had helped to keep Spain both active and creative. In this peninsula jutting out into the Mediterranean there was a mixture of races and of creeds, duplicated in no other land. It demonstrated that in such situations there occurs a natural process of adaptation so long as no aggressive proselytism interferes with the ordinary man's willingness to live and let live.

In the beginning the Spanish problem involved only the relation between Christian and Jew. The Council of Toledo in 633 passed a decree, later incorporated into canon law, which disturbed this happy and peaceful situation. It declared that a Jew, forcibly baptized in infancy or forced to accept conversion under fear of death, was thenceforth a Christian subject, so that a relapse might bring him to the stake.

Under such aggressive pressure the country soon became filled with *conversos* (Jewish converts), Christians in name but frequently still Jews at heart. Instead of solving the problem of enormous diversity and increasing toleration, the decree aggravated it immensely. Then in 711 came the Saracen invasion, making the problem a three-cornered affair involving Christian, Jew and Moslem.

In 1096 when El Cid conquered Valencia, the surrender was signed by leading Christian and Moslem citizens. As Christians gradually reconquered Spain, they became increasingly concerned with the preservation of their religion and its advancement. Canon law decreed that the Christian who aided the Saracens was an abettor of heresy and thus a subject for burning. In 1215 the Lateran Council decreed that all Jews should wear a badge of infamy, and in 1371 Henry II of Castile prescribed it also for the Moors: a red circle on the left shoulder.

## Ferdinand and Isabella

At the Council of Vienne in 1311, Pope Clement V directed all princes to prohibit the Moors from permitting the muezzin to make his public call of prayer from his minaret. This was generally disregarded, so the decree was repeated at the Council of Tarragona in 1329. Again ignored, it was repeated by the Council of Torlosa in 1429, but it was not until the reign of Ferdinand and Isabella that the decree of Vienne was at last enforced.

Its prescriptions were more readily enforced, with cupidity probably being the chief motive. At the Council of Zamora in 1313, the bishops of Spain invoked the curse of God and St. Peter upon the long-standing privilege whereby Jewish witnesses were needed to testify against Jewish defendants. In addition they issued decrees calculated to cut off all intercourse between the two communities. No longer should churches be profaned by attendance of Moors and Jews at Mass.

The expertise of Jews as physicians and surgeons led to their widespread patronage by Christians. Rumors were circulated, however, that Jews took advantage of their privileged position to bring about the deaths of some of their Christian clients. Hence a law was passed forbidding the employment of Jewish physicians under the threat of excommunication. This was re-enacted in 1335 and 1412.

Yet in 1462 a Franciscan preacher complained that many nobles and even bishops had Jews as their physicians. He claimed that these doctors boasted among themselves as to who had caused the most Christian deaths. Nevertheless in 1469, when the king of Aragon suffered from a double cataract, he was careful to have a Jewish oculist remove them. Similarly in 1480 the Dominicans obtained permission to be treated by Jewish physicians on the grounds that there were so few non-Jewish physicians in Spain.

## Isolating Jews and Moors

In 1412 it was decreed that Jews and Moors should be isolated in their own ghettos, behind an impenetrable wall with only one gate. Furthermore, they were forbidden to attend Christian funerals or weddings.

The repetition of these laws discloses the difficulty of enforcing them. But, as Lea observes, "they answered the purpose of inflicting an ineffaceable stigma upon their victims and of keeping up a wholesale feeling of antagonism on the part of the population at large." [4]

As a result of these oppressive measures the Jews in Spain experienced more distressing alternations than elsewhere between comparative prosperity on the one hand, and robbery and massacre on the other. The Hebrews were too numerous an ethnic group to be liquidated wholesale until Spain became a totalitarian state under Ferdinand and Isabella. The Church did all it could, however, to keep them in the position assigned to them by canon law: that of slaves to Christians.

In 1348 when the Black Death was ravaging Spain, the rumor was widespread that it was traceable to poisoned wells. Some accused the lepers of the crime; but a greater number fastened it on the Jews. To the enduring credit of Pope Clement VI, he pointed out the absurdity of the charge. He showed how the plague raged in districts where there were no Jews. He followed this up by directing all prelates to proclaim to their flocks that Jews were not to be beaten, wounded or slain on this charge, and he ordered that all offenders should be excommunicated.

In 1391 a terrible "Holy War against the Jews" was launched by the archdeacon of Seville, Martinez. Under his leadership a mob tore down synagogues and stormed the ghettos. The survivors escaped only by accepting baptism. The conflagration spread to Valencia, where several hundred were slain. It moved on to Barcelona, Toledo, Palma, Saragossa and other cities, where the choice was always between baptism or the sword.

The *conversos* gradually became so numerous as to constitute a definite class in Spain. As early as 1449 some of the noblest houses had Jewish blood in them and their members were persons of more than ordinary ability. King Ferdinand himself was of such a family; so too was the Inquisitor Torquemado and his next successor in the Inquisitorship General. So likewise was a contemporary, the archbishop of Granada.

We find evidence of great differences in the zeal with which the Inquisitors did their work and in the support which they received. Thus in 1244 the Bishop of Elne and a Dominican friar, acting as Inquisitors, had condemned Ramon Malleolis and Helena, his wife, as heretics. But they succeeded in appealing to Pope Gregory IX, who referred the case to the archdeacon of Besalu and the sacristan of Girona. These acquitted the accused couple and had their possessions restored to them. The Inquisition, however, carried the case back to Rome, and Innocent finally confirmed the conviction.

Four years later Innocent IV wrote to the bishop of Lerida, instructing him how to treat heretics who voluntarily return to the Church. The clear implication here is that the Inquisitors were both ill-informed and inactive. Dissatisfied with the results, King Jayme in 1254 wrote to Innocent requesting more vigor and zeal in ridding the country of heretics. As a result, the pope confided the choice of Inquisitors to the Dominican priors of Barcelona, Lerida, Perpignan and Elne, each one to act within his own diocese.

## Exhuming Bones

Meanwhile the Inquisitors had not been inactive elsewhere. Inquisitor Fray Pedro de Cadreyta of Urgel, with his colleague Fray Pedro de Tonenes and Arnaldo, bishop of Barcelona, had rendered final judgment on January 11, 1257, against the memory of Ramon, Count of Urgel, as a relapsed heretic whose bones were to be exhumed. But with unusual clemency the Inquisitors admitted the widow and the son to reconciliation and did not deprive them of their estates.

Twelve years later we find Cadreyta, together with another colleague, Fray Guillen de Colonico and Abril, bishop of Urgel, condemning the memory of Arnaldo, Visconde of Castelbo and of his daughter Ermessende. Though both had been dead for more than thirty years, the Inquisition ordered their bones to be exhumed and their property confiscated.

Although there must have been many condemnations of living persons during this period, the only record that has come down to us is that of Berenguer de Amoros who was burned at the stake in 1263. That the living had indeed been objects of fierce persecution seems to be indicated by the stoning to death of the hated Cadreyta by the outraged people of Urgel.

With the opening of the fourteenth century, the Inquisition proceeded with increased vigor. This is evidenced by the greatly increased number of heretics turned over to the secular arm. In 1314 Inquisitor Fray Bernardo Puigercos discovered a batch of alleged heretics, some of whom he burned and others he exiled. That the Aragonese did not relish the methods of the Inquisitors was shown in 1325 by the action of the Cortes in prohibiting, with the assent of King Jayme II, the Inquisitorial process and the use of torture.

## *The Model Inquisitor*

The most noteworthy Inquisitor of whom the Aragonese Inquisition can boast is Nicolas Eymeric. Trained in various branches of learning, he was the author of numerous published works, including his *Directorium Inquisitorium*. In it for the first time, he systematized the procedure of the Inquisition and outlined the principles and details which should guide the Inquisitor in all his acts. His model Inquisitor should be thoroughly familiar with all the intricacies of doctrine and with all the aberrations of heresy, both past and current.

"At a time when the Inquisition was declining and falling into contempt," observes Lea, "he boldly insisted on its most extreme prerogatives as an imprescriptible privilege. If he assumed that the heretic had but one right—that of choosing between submission and the stake—he was in this but the conscientious exponent of his age, and his writings are instinct with the conviction that the work of the Inquisitor is the salvation of souls." [5]

Around the middle of the fifteenth century various members of the nobility and persons of influence in Spain were able to do what few individuals had done previously: disregard the decision of the Inquisition, which normally was able to terrify the accused into the immediate acceptance of its decisions. Thus in 1423 Fray

Pedro Salazo, Inquisitor of Roselton and Cerdana, condemned as a heretic a hermit, Pedro Fraserii who was widely reverenced for his holiness.

## A Rare Acquittal

He accused the witnesses as being his personal enemies and offered to clear himself before a proper judge. His friends lodged an appeal with Pope Martin V, who referred the case, with power to decide, to Bernardo, abbot of the Benedictine Abbey of Arles in the diocese of Elne. The latter acquitted the hermit without further ado. It is pleasant to discover occasional cases of this character, which show that now and then popes did overrule the normally absolute and despotic power of the dreaded Inquisition.

Against the poor and friendless, however, the Inquisition retained its absolute and despotic power. The Waldenses had continued to spread and about 1,440 were discovered. While some were reconciled, the majority were burned to death as alleged obstinate heretics by Miguel Ferriz, Inquisitor of Aragon, and Martin Trilles of Valencia. Among the number was an unfortunate woman, Leonor, wife of Doctor Jayme de Leminanna. She steadfastly refused to perform the penance assigned to her by the Inquisition of Cartagena, and was abandoned to the secular arm to be burned alive at the stake.

# CHAPTER IX

## Expulsions from Spain

Toleration is good for all, or it is good for none.

EDMUND BURKE

ONE OF THE DARKEST CHAPTERS in the history of the Inquisition in Spain is that which records its refined cruelty and torture of alleged heretics, probably unparalleled in any other country. We say this even though it would seem difficult to surpass the agony of being burned alive, which was the penalty commonly inflicted upon defendants turned over to the secular arm.

The *Directorium Inquisitorum* by Eymeric, Inquisitor of Aragon, printed in Barcelona and passed through many editions, gives a full account of the various methods of torture. A book by Simancas, a Spanish bishop, covering similar ground, was published in 1569. In it the bishop denounces the protests made in 1522 by the philosopher Luis Vives against the use of torture. In 1585 Suarez de Paz published in Salamanca his book, *Ecclesiastical and Secular Practice*, in which he upholds, on the analogy of the usage adopted in trials for treason, the legality of torturing anyone over fourteen years of age who was suspected of heresy, and of scourging those under fourteen.[1]

These and later books show that virtually the whole surface of the body was liable to pain. Regardless of their sex, the victims were commonly stripped naked, and then usually given a small covering round the loins. Neither age nor youth afforded any protection. A girl of thirteen, who survived the torture, was then subjected to a hundred lashes. Incredible as it seems, a feeble old man of seventy-six, and old women of seventy-eight, eighty, ninety and even ninety-six are recorded to have been tortured and/or burned alive.

Even pregnancy offered no immunity, except that a woman with child was tortured in a sitting position, instead of being strapped down on planks. The customary accompaniments of the use of torture included the cutting through of the skin and muscle to the bone by tight cords, the tearing away of the skin and flesh, the cutting off of fingers and toes, the dislocation and fracture of arms and crippling for life.[2]

During the entire time of the torture, the secretary of the Inquisition stood by, recording every act of torture and every shriek of agony uttered by the victim, every question addressed to him and every word he spoke. By way of a typical example, Lea prints extensive portions of the original record of how the Inquisition of Toledo in 1568 tortured a woman who, because she declined to eat pork, was suspected of being secretly inclined to Judaism. The sickening account of the proceedings fills two and a half pages of fine print.

Despite her frantic cries for mercy, her declaration of innocence, her screams of pain and her pleas for death, the Inquisitor simply repeated the demand, "Tell the truth."[3] One can well imagine the screams of pain and the pitiful cries for death which filled the average torture chamber, making it a terrible nightmare.

## A Relic Speaks

The visitor to the Horniman Museum in southeast London finds his attention drawn to an unusual exhibit: a steel torture-chair that comes from Cuenca, a city about midway between Valencia and Madrid. It includes a movable seat, with pinion and rack, manacles for feet and hands and, most unusual of all, a skeleton-helmet with screws to put pressure on the top of the head, to pierce the ears and to torture the nose and the chin.

In addition, there is a gag for the mouth with rack-action for forcing the mouth open and dragging forward the tongue, screw-forceps for extracting toenails, single and double thumbscrews, and various other padlocks, buckles, chains, keys and turnscrews. Excavated with the chair was a steel whip, having eight thongs, each of which ends in a blade. Engraved on the mouth-gag are the words "Santo Oficio Caballero"—the noble Holy Office, namely the Inquisition, and the date 1676. What a monument to the Roman Congregation in charge of the Inquisition.

Standing before that barbarous instrument, which sought to torture virtually every nerve in the victim's body, the spectator is afforded a glimpse into the incredible savagery with which the Spanish Inquisition sought to eradicate all so-called heretics and impose the Catholic faith upon Moors and Jews.

## Motivation of Inquisitors

That steel chair with all its myriad adjuncts for torture reveals more vividly than words the cruel and revolting measures devised by the Inquisition to achieve its end. The exhibit seems to proclaim to all the visitors the message it thundered especially to the Jews and Moors of Spain: "We shall get you into the Catholic religion even if we have to drag you through the torments of hell. You probably won't believe that we are your friends and benefactors.

"But in reality we are, for these pains, culminating with burning you alive at the stake, will only last for a few minutes. We are saving you, however, from the pains of hell which will torture every nerve cell in your body for a thousand million billion years with demons stoking the fires with ever hotter coals."

That steel chair speaks to the visitor with myriad tongues. It lays bare before him the motivation not only of the Inquisitors who condemned the victims to the tortures and lit the flames at the stakes, but also of the theologians, popes and secular princes and kings who backed these tribunals.

They sought to regulate and control not only the actions of men but also the thoughts that stirred in the silent kingdom of their souls. It is any wonder that Catholics and non-Catholics alike shudder with horror at the mention of the word "Inquisition"? The Inquisition was probably the chief source of pain and torture for centuries in the countries of Europe.

In 1522 the Emperor Charles V introduced the Inquisition,

with all its horrible cruelties, into the Netherlands. Historian Cecil J. Cadoux reports that a man sentenced to be burned alive would frequently be prevented from speaking by having his tongue screwed tight between two irons. The tip of the tongue would be burned with a red-hot iron causing it to swell up so that it could not be drawn back.

"The practice of burying women heretics alive," Cadoux reports, "is another indication of the degree of cruelty which marked the Spanish kings' attempts to suppress religious freedom among their subjects in the Low Countries. The law of 1535 imposing this dreadful penalty had fallen into desuetude, when in 1597 it was called again into operation at the demand of the Jesuits.

"An unoffending woman-servant of forty, Anna van den Hove, who read her Bible and held Protestant views, was in that year brought to Brussels, and called upon by the authorities to renounce her errors. On steadfastly refusing she was led out of the city and solemnly buried alive."[4]

Referring to this horrible deed, the historian J. L. Motley says: "Of all the religious murders done in that hideous 16th century in the Netherlands, the burial of the Antwerp servant-maid was the last and the worst. The worst, because it was a cynical and deliberate attempt to revive the demon, whose thirst for blood had been at last allayed, and who had sunk into repose."[5]

## Variety of Tortures

Lecky, the historian, who has made extensive study of the tortures inflicted by the medieval Inquisition, points out that what strikes one most is not their diabolical barbarity but their extraordinary variety, which indicates how long their contrivers had worked on the problem and the consummate skill which they brought to their task. Nothing was left undone to squeeze out the last bit of pain from the writhing victim. To this end the victim was not infrequently roasted over a slow fire so that he would suffer the maximum agony.[6]

What was the total number of persons burned at the stake during the entire period of the Inquisition in Spain? This is impossible to answer with accuracy because of the lack of precise statistics. Juan Antonio Florente states that between 1480 and 1808 nearly 32,000 persons were burned by the Inquisition in Spain. But his veracity has been questioned by virtually all scholars.

When Napoleon invaded Spain and placed his brother Joseph on the throne Florente played the role of a Quisling and became an enthusiastic *Afrancesado*, as all patriotic Spaniards styled partisans of the new regime. It has long been a favorite technique of usurpers to ransack the archives of dispossessed princes and to publish whatever might be turned or twisted to their discredit.

Accordingly, in 1800 Joseph Bonaparte commissioned Florente, an ex-secretary of the Inquisition who had been dismissed for sundry irregularities, to "smear" the Inquisition so that the natives might be prompted to accept the "tyranny-crushing" rule of a foreign usurper. When the venal agent's work appeared, it was found teeming with insults to Rome, the Spanish Church and his country. His partisanship led him to many inaccuracies and even outright falsehoods.

## Number of Burnings

A far more reliable scholar, Henry Charles Lea, went back to the actual records for seven or eight chief towns (or provinces) in Spain for various specified periods, commencing with 1480 or soon thereafter. The total of such annual averages amounted to approximately 130 burnings per year, while the estimate for the whole of Spain was 150. Although these averages are generally considered to reflect the realities in the first few decades, those of later years would doubtless be considerably higher, as Cadoux points out.

The French historian Langlois reports that twelve hundred *conversos*, penitents, obdurate and relapsed heretics were present at the Inquisition session in Toledo in 1487, and according to the most conservative estimate, Torquemado sentenced to the stake about two thousand heretics in twelve years.[7] Two contemporary historians, Pulgar and Marineo Siculo, agree with this estimate. "During this same period," says Pulgar, "15,000 heretics did penance and were reconciled to the Church."[8]

In 1478 the two sovereigns, Ferdinand and Isabella, procured a bull from Pope Sixtus IV, establishing the Inquisition in Spain. They insisted upon earmarking all confiscated property for the crown, whereas in Italy it had gone to the popes and Inquisitors, and elsewhere had been split in varying proportions.

Moreover, in contrast with all other countries, the Spanish Inquisitors were to be appointed not by the pope but by the crown. This was a concession which Sixtus subsequently regretted, for it offered a strong temptation to the Inquisitors and their officials to enrich themselves by stretching every point for the condemnation of wealthy suspects or by accepting bribes for their release. Furthermore, the vast extension of the Inquisitorial machinery over so large a country made even the lowest officials untouchable not only by secular magistrates but also by exalted prelates. This made them virtually irresponsible in an age of comparatively lax commercial and judicial morality.

The result was that no one was safe from his neighbors, servants or even his children. All might fall under threats of torture from Inquisitors and thus give false incriminating testimony. This is illustrated in the case of Archbishop Hernando de Talavera of Granada, whose property the Inquisitor decided to confiscate for himself. Like many other high officials, Talavera had a strain of Jewish blood. The accusation against him rested upon the testimony of a woman who had been tortured as being a Jewish prophetess.

She was threatened with further torture unless she agreed to testify to have witnessed in Talavera's palace things the Inquisitor dictated to her. The Inquisitor Lucero was a criminal, thief and scoundrel of the blackest dye. He invented the myth of a vast conspiracy, alleged to have ramifications throughout Spain for replacing Christianity with Judaism. He pictured these conspirators as riding by night on demon goats. He instructed his prisoners to bear false witness against a prominent preacher, and on the strength of such stories he was convicted by the Inquisition.

Whereupon Lucero burned, in a single batch, 107 unfortunate victims, charged with attending Talavera's sermons. This kind of skullduggery continued from 1501 to 1507, when a noble of Cordova complained to the royal secretary that Lucero and his fellow Inquisitors "were able to defame the whole kingdom, to destroy without God or justice, a great part of it, slaying, robbing and violating maids and wives, to the great dishonor of the Christian religion." [9]

So great was the scandal that the Supreme Committee, greatly influenced by Cardinal Ximenes, tried Lucero publicly. He and his co-conspirators were convicted and sent in chains to Burgos. Incredible as it seems, Ferdinand still defended Lucero, who retired to a rich canonry which was one of his Inquisitorial confiscations. The only reason offered by historians for Ferdinand's action was that he himself had shared in Lucero's plunder.

## Extraordinary Document

In 1482 Pope Sixtus IV issued what Lea rightly characterizes as "the most extraordinary bull in the history of the Inquisition: extraordinary because, for the first time, heresy was declared to be like any other crime, entitled to a fair trial and simple justice." The pontiff complained that the Inquisitors of Aragon had been motivated for some time past not by zeal for the faith but by cupidity; and he proceeded to decree amendments of procedure which were to override all conflicting papal decrees and must be followed henceforth under pain of excommunication, or even, if need be, by appeal to the secular arm. These new provisions set aside some of the most important and characteristic points of Inquisitorial procedure.

The bull declared that slaves and unfit witnesses were no longer to be heard against the accused; evidence for the defense must be freely admitted; counsel must be allowed for defense; and any heretic freely acknowledging past guilt under seal to Inquisitor or bishop should be penanced only secretly and given a certificate to free him from further harassment for the past. This bull, if carried out, would have revolutionized Inquisitorial procedure, and put an end to bribery and flagrant deprivation of human rights.

But Ferdinand ignored the bull and acted as though no such document were issued. By so doing he virtually defied the excommunication which would have fallen upon a Christian of less power and standing than the king. After five months' delay, Sixtus tamely and shamefully conceded all the disputed points, and came to an arrangement which permitted Ferdinand to extend his Castilian Inquisition to Aragon and all his other dominions.

This failure to stand up for elementary human rights of the poor and underprivileged made a mockery of all the noble promises contained in the bull. It was a tragic surrender to a king who used papal authority only to advance his own selfish interests. Moreover, it paved the way, as we shall see, for one of the most heartrending tragedies in human history: an attempt virtually to destroy a race.

The conquest of Granada in 1492 brought all Spain under the power of Ferdinand and Isabella. With holdings greater than that of the average Spaniard, the Jews had contributed more than their share to that victory. Now their help was less needed. Always unpopular, they were the special objects of discrimination and injustice. In operation now for nearly twelve years, the Inquisition had not only increased animosity to the Jews but also stiffened the resistance of those Jews to whom their religion was dearer than life itself.

Their leaders sensed the coming of the hurricane of destruction against them and offered large sums as a ransom. There is general agreement that Ferdinand inclined toward acceptance, while Isabella was adamant against it.

## Decree Expulsion

Accordingly, the government passed a decree, signed on March 30, 1492, for the complete expulsion of the Jews, though it was not published in Barcelona until May 1. The decree gave the entire Jewish population only until July 31 to leave Spain under penalty of death for delay or for subsequent return.

As one can readily see, this meant that their possessions must be sold at greatly reduced prices and that in many cases they were unable to collect their debts. Moreover, for those who overstayed their time, total confiscation was rigorously enforced. Carrying what possessions they could, the Jews reached the seaport only to be confronted with an export duty per head, the equivalent of the daily wage of more than 120 laborers.

"In those circumstances," says G. G. Coulton, "these decrees were responsible for one of the most pitiful stories recorded in

history. It brought out the mutual helpfulness which even the
most orthodox writers of the Middle Ages noted in these Jews:
but the roads to the seaports were crowded with processions of
indescribable misery." [10]

Similar is the observation of Lea: "There was no Christian who
did not pity them; everywhere they were invited to conversion
and some were baptized; but very few, for the rabbis encouraged
them and made the women and children play on the timbrel. . . .
most of them had evil fate, robbery and murder by sea and in the
lands of their refuge." [11]

The historian Henry Kamen estimates that of the refugees
who fled from Spain before and during the great exodus of 1492,
a great number went to Portugal, perhaps as many as 120,000 in
all, swelling the Jewish community in Portugal to about a fifth
of the country's total population. The permission to reside in Portugal, at the price of nearly a ducat per person, was limited to
six months, after which they faced the virtually unvarying condition of conversion or expulsion. The wealthier Jews purchased
further toleration, while the poorer went into exile again, over the
sea and across to Africa.[12]

## Barbarous Treatment

No less pitiful than the story of the wholesale expulsion of the
Jews from Spain is that of the Moriscos, or Moors, who had
accepted the Spanish rule after their conquest by Ferdinand and
Isabella. Cardinal Richelieu characterized it as one of the "most
barbarous" in human annals.[13] Under unrelenting pressure by
the Church, most accepted baptism, but remained Moslems at
heart. The merely nominal Catholicity of most of the Moriscos
was largely due to the lack of sufficient clergy to instruct them
thoroughly. As a consequence of the activities of the Inquisition,
the Moriscos were reduced to external conformity in many sec-
tions of Spain, especially in Castile, where many of them abandoned their native dress and language.

From time to time rumors were circulated that the Moslems in
great numbers, with the aid of the Moriscos, would invade Spain
and re-establish Mohammedan rule. Accordingly, Philip II decided on a policy of repression: their ancestral language, amuse-

ments, dress and even their baths, public or private, were forbidden. Although Charles V in 1518 had solemnly sworn to them that he would neither expel these new subjects nor make forced conversions, Pope Clement VII issued a brief in 1524 absolving Charles from his oath. Still in force was the Inquisitorial law of talebearing, even within the same household, pitting children against their parents and wives against their husbands.

Under such unnatural conditions the mania for purity of blood became a sort of idolatry in Spanish society. Caught between the two millstones of religious and political oppression, the Moriscos were ground into abject slavery and irreligion. Determined to rid Spain of their presence, Philip II considered two measures proposed by two bishops. One was to appoint special Inquisitors who would so thin them out that the miserable remnant would constitute no threat nor give any further trouble. The other prelate suggested "deportation to Newfoundland, where they would speedily perish, especially if the precaution were taken of castrating all the males, old and young." [14]

## Expulsion of Moors

Finally, in 1609, wholesale expulsion was agreed upon. Under penalty of death, all Moriscos were to start within three days of the proclamation in their town or village and head for the ports assigned to them. In some localities they were even forbidden to sell their goods. Even when permitted, their treasured possessions went as cheap as the spoils of a plundered city.

On shipboard many of the refugees were plundered again and many of the women and children were taken as slaves. For violating the prohibition to carry money or jewels with them, more than thirty refugees were hanged in Burgos, while those who managed to reach Africa had to contend with the hostility and thievery of the Arabs. How many managed to survive? A contemporary chronicler estimated that only about one-third of the refugees survived the horrible nightmare.

Vacandard places the number of persons banished from Spain at 500,000—about one-sixteenth of the total population. [15] "Behold," wrote Brother Bleda, "the most glorious event in Spain since the times of the Apostles; religious unity is now secured; an era of prosperity is certainly about to dawn." [16] The era of prosperity so confidently predicted by the Dominican zealot never arrived.

The cruel and inhuman measure, which delighted him so much, in reality greatly weakened Spain by depriving her of hundreds of thousands of her citizens, many of whom were among her most skillful, industrious and best-disciplined workers. The eviction thus proved to be a great economic disaster, which took centuries to mitigate, if not to overcome.

## Disturbing Questions

As one reads the story of these two mammoth expulsions, certain thoughts and questions inevitably arise. First in regard to that of the Jews: Why, one wonders, did not the highest Vatican officials, including the sovereign pontiff, the college of cardinals, bishops, priests and religious, raise their voices in protest against such cruel and brutal treatment of a people from whose loins came the Incarnate Christ?

True, news spread slowly in those days. But two months elapsed from the time of the announcement of the forthcoming expulsion of the Jews and its beginning. Even more disturbing is the question: Why were condemnations not issued before, during, or after this un-Christian, unjust and inhuman action? Why did not Catholic sovereigns of other countries condemn it and do something to prevent it?

The same questions might be asked in regard to the Moriscos. Here the announcement of the forthcoming eviction was made only a few days before it began. But still the expulsion required considerable time to complete, thus enabling condemnations to be issued by the officials and dignitaries mentioned. Doubtless in asking these questions the reader has in the back of his mind the memory of the worldwide condemnation of the Nazi attempt virtually to annihilate the Jewish population of Germany in the incineration centers which have made Dachau, Auschwitz and Buchenwald the horrible symbols of genocide.

Strong protests were made not only by the officials of all Churches but also by the heads of all governments. Indeed, it was the horrible treatment of the Jews that led many nations to enter the war. The answer to the questions we have raised is doubtless to be found in the enormous progress in ethical and religious thought since the Inquisition. The world does move and its inhabitants move with it. The people living at the time of the Inquisition were the children of their day just as we are the creatures of our era. This twofold truth we have previously mentioned, but its importance and relevance warrant its repetition.

## Undermine Justice

To illustrate this truth, we cite the curious and intriguing case of Juan de Ribera, who became archbishop of Valencia in 1568. He is the man characterized by Coulton as the "main author and executioner" of the plans for the expulsion of the Jews and Moors from Spain. Yet he was formally beatified—one degree below canonization or sainthood, but to whom one may pray with the Church's approval. Beatification is thus designed to reflect the Church's belief that the person so honored is of unusual holiness and may serve as a model for all Christians. Thus do different eras reflect different concepts of holiness.

The expulsion of more than half a million Moors and Jews from Spain is styled by Coulton as the "crowning victory of a despotic State in partnership with a despotic Church. . . . In this matter of persecution, king and pope had one mind and one aim; and they did the uncivilized job with civilized thoroughness. Kings and clergy grew more and more despotic at the expense of national prosperity." [17]

In 1586 the population of Spain was estimated to be eight million but by 1700 it had dwindled to five million. In that interval the Inquisition courts had increased to twenty-two, with an army of 20,000 salaried and privileged satellites, and played a significant part in the decline of the population. It was strong and bold enough to defy the crown more successfully than any pope. In the words of Professor Diercks, it had "utterly ruined and undermined the sense of justice among the population." [18] With that conclusion virtually all scholars will find themselves in hearty agreement.

## CHAPTER X

# The Witch-Hunt Mania

There is the foul fiend Flippertigibbet. He begins at cur-
few, and waits till the first cock. He . . . squints the eye
and makes the hairlip.

WILLIAM SHAKESPEARE

I N THE BRITISH MUSEUM IN LONDON is a picture, "The Tortures
of the Inquisition" by Picart, which daily attracts many visitors. In one corner of the dungeon there sits on the floor a hand-
cuffed prisoner near a blazing fire. A torturer is holding a burning fagot close to his bare feet, causing him to shriek with pain.
Another prisoner lies stretched out on a cot, while his torturers
are pouring a stream of water into his opened mouth. A third
victim is suspended high in the air, and is about to be dropped
within inches of the floor. The sudden jolt will almost pull his
arms, tied together at his back, from their sockets.

The idea was to torture the prisoners to such an extent that the
excruciating pain would compel the unfortunates to confess that
they held some heretical doctrine. It might be, however, that they
themselves were not charged with heresy, but were merely witnesses who were being tortured in the belief that they were more
likely to testify against suspected heretics if they were put to
torture.

Horrible and revolting scenes such as this were enacted by the
Inquisition in various countries of Europe, and even in some of
their colonies, from the thirteenth to the eighteenth centuries.
Incredible as it seems to us today, the charge that brought most

of these victims to the dungeons and to a still worse fate—being burned alive at the stake—was participation in some form of witch-craft. While precise statistics are lacking, many scholars estimate, as we shall show in greater detail later on, that the total number of victims of the witchcraft mania ran into the hundreds of thousands and perhaps passed the million mark. This is probably the high-water mark for death meted out for any religious belief.

There arise at once in the reader's mind the questions: Of what concern to the Inquisition was the belief or nonbelief of a person in witches? Isn't this the business solely of the individual? To answer these questions we must explain what is meant by witch-craft and what has been its history.

## What Witchcraft Is

As commonly understood, witchcraft embodies the idea of a diabolical pact or at least an appeal to the intervention of evil spirits. This supernatural aid was usually invoked to bring about the death of some obnoxious person, or to arouse the passion of love in those who are objects of desire, or to call up the dead, or to bring disaster or impotence upon rivals, enemies and oppressors, fancied or real.

Hence witchcraft, broadly speaking, may be defined as the practice of black magic, sorcery or any form of intercourse with demons or evil spirits in order, through supernatural aid, to accomplish evil of various kinds. Its essential theological heresy consists in attributing to creatures the power that belongs to God alone. To the theologian there is no substantial difference between witchcraft, soothsaying, necromancy, wizardry, magic and sorcery. As a consequence Inquisitors felt convinced that, as guardians of the integrity of the Christian faith, they were obliged to deal with the heresy of witchcraft in all its forms.

Witchcraft is found in nearly all periods of human history. The earliest evidence of this traffic with the spirit world in Europe survives from the prehistoric past. A horned creature, doubtless connected with witchery, is found carved on rocks or painted on the walls of caves, at archeological sites dating back to 30,000 B.C. and spanning the territory from the Soviet Union to Spain with its famous Altamira Cave.

According to the Egyptologist Margaret Murray, witchery as practiced in Western Christendom was a carryover from pagan worship. Most scholars are of the opinion that the supposed activities of witches with evil spirits were in fact hallucinations. In ancient Babylonia and Egypt witchery played a marked role in the life of the people, as existing records clearly show. It will be sufficient to cite a short section from the recovered Code of Hammurabi of approximately 2000 B.C.

"If a man," it is there prescribed, "has had a charge of witchcraft upon a man and has not justified it, he upon whom the witchcraft is laid shall go to the holy river and if the holy river overcome him, he who accused him shall take to himself his house."[1]

## *Witchery and the Bible*

In the Bible, references to witchery are frequent and the condemnations of such practices are strong. "There must never be anyone among you," says Deuteronomy, "who makes his son or daughter pass through fire, who practices divination, who is a soothsayer, augur or sorcerer, who uses charms, consults ghosts or spirits, or calls up the dead. For the man who does these things is detestable to Yahweh your God; it is because of these detestable practices that Yahweh your God is driving these nations before you" (18:10-12).

In similar vein Exodus declares: "You shall not permit a witch to live" (22:18). Leviticus likewise decrees capital punishment for witchcraft: "Any man or woman who is a necromancer or magician must be put to death by stoning; their blood shall be on their own heads" (20:27).

The New Testament continues the refrain of the Old. Thus the Apostle Paul, in writing to the Galatians, links soothsayers with idolators and other wicked persons: "When self-indulgence is at work the results are obvious: fornication, gross indecency and sexual irresponsibility; idolatry and sorcery; feuds and wrangling, jealousy, bad temper and quarrels; disagreements, factions, envy; drunkenness, orgies and similar things" (5:19-20).

The early Church set her face sternly against any commerce with evil spirits. Thus the Council of Elvira in 306 refused the

Holy Viaticum to those who had killed a man by their witchcraft and adds the reason that such a crime could not be effected "without idolatry," devil worship and idolatry then being convertible terms.

Eight years later the Council of Ancyra (Ankara) imposed five years of penance upon those who consulted magicians, and here again the offense is treated as being a practical participation in paganism. This legislation reflected the mind of the Church for many centuries. Thus the Council of Paderborn in 785 decreed that sorcerers are to be reduced to serfdom and made over to the service of the Church.

Furthermore the Council declared: "Whosoever, blinded by the devil and infected with pagan errors, holds another person for a witch that eats human flesh, and therefore burns her, eats her flesh, or gives it to others to eat, shall be punished with death." During the first thirteen centuries, the Christian Church made unmistakably clear her opposition to witchcraft and sought to discourage any participation in it.

## A Famous Text

The classic compilation of canon law is known as Gratian's *Decretum*. The witchcraft canon, which was incorporated into the *Decretum* and is known as *Canon episcopi* from its opening word, *episcopi*, first appears in the little chapters of Charles the Bald for the year 872. It has been widely quoted as reflecting the mind of the Church on the subject of witchcraft and sorcery, and has become a famous text. It follows:

Bishops and their officials must labor with all their strength to uproot thoroughly from their parishes the pernicious art of sorcery and malefice invented by the Devil, and if they find a man or woman follower of this wickedness to eject them foully disgraced from their parishes. For the Apostle says, "A man that is a heretic after the first and second admonition avoid." Those are held captive by the Devil who, leaving their Creator, seek the aid of the Devil. And so Holy Church must be cleansed of this pest.

It is also not to be omitted that some wicked women, perverted by the Devil, seduced by illusions and phantasms of demons, believe and profess themselves, in the hours of night, to ride upon certain beasts with Diana, the goddess of pagans, and an innumerable multitude of women, and in the silence of the dead of night to traverse great spaces of earth, and to obey her commands as of their mistress, and to be summoned to her service on certain nights. But I wish it were they alone who perished in their faithlessness and did not draw many with them into the destruction of infidelity. For an innumerable multitude, deceived by this false opinion, believe this to be true, and so believing wander from the right faith and are involved in the error of the pagans when they think that there is anything of divinity or power except the one God. Wherefore the priests throughout their churches should preach with all insistence to the people that they may know this to be in every way false and that such phantasms are imposed on the minds of infidels and not by the divine but by the malignant spirit.

Thus Satan himself, who transfigures himself into an angel of light, when he has captured the mind of a miserable woman and has subjugated her to himself by infidelity and incredulity, immediately transforms himself into the species and similitudes of different personages and deluding the mind which he holds captive and exhibiting things, joyful or mournful, and persons, known and unknown, leads it through devious ways, and while the spirit alone endures this, the faithless mind thinks these things happen not in the spirit but in the body. Who is there that is not led out of himself in dreams and nocturnal visions, and sees much when sleeping which he had never seen waking?

Who is so stupid and foolish as to think that all these things which are only done in spirit happen in the body, when the Prophet Ezekiel saw visions of the Lord in spirit and not in the body, and the Apostle John saw and heard the mysteries of the Apocalypse in the spirit and not in the body, as he himself says "I was in the spirit"? And Paul does not dare to say that he was rapt in the body. It is therefore to be proclaimed publicly to all that whoever believes such things or similar to these loses the faith, and he who has not the right faith in God is not of God but of whom he believes, that is, of the Devil. For of our Lord it is written "All things were made by Him." Whoever therefore believes that anything can be made, or that any creature can be changed to better or worse or be transformed into another species or similitude, except by the Creator himself who made everything and through whom all things were made, is beyond doubt an infidel.[2]

## Use of Torture

During the first thirteen centuries of the Christian era individual prosecutions of suspected witches occasionally took place and in some of these torture, permitted by the Roman civil law, was apparently employed. In 860 Pope Nicholas I forbade the use of torture, and a similar decree may be found in the Pseudo-Isadorian Decretals. In 1080 Pope Gregory wrote to King Harald of Denmark forbidding witches to be executed upon the presumption of their having caused storms or failure of crops or pestilence.

Despite these efforts and perhaps encouraged by the very sermons preached against it, belief in witchcraft continued to make headway. The rise of the dualist heresy, which attributed real power to Satan as the equal opponent of God, made many people more conscious of demonic agents and their alleged power to affect their lives.

Once witchery was thought to involve demonic possession, heresy and the rejection of God, it came within the scope of the Inquisition. This papal institution formulated the basic legal principles that were to be followed in the markedly increasing number of witch trials in the thirteenth and fourteenth centuries. For the first time witchery was prosecuted under German imperial law with the encouragement of King Henry VII in 1224, and all involved in demonology were threatened with burning at the stake.

The obsession with witchcraft spread like a plague through all levels of society, prompting the Inquisitors to redouble their efforts to stem the tide. Pope Alexander IV ruled in 1258 that the Inquisitors should confine their intervention to those cases in which there was some clear presumption of heretical belief. But they found this easy to do because of the confessions of persons charged with heretical dealings with demons of various sorts.

## Women Confess

Thus the records of the Inquisition at Toulouse show that women confessed to the following: attending witches' sabbat on Friday nights; having intercourse with the devil in the form of a goat; casting spells and committing sacrilege at Holy Communion on the devil's instruction; making a brew of poisonous herbs together with parts of human and animal corpses and pieces of clothing from the hanged; believing that the devil was God's equal and ruled over the earth; making a pact with the devil; eating the corpses of stolen newborn children; causing neighbors' wheat to rot, sheep to sicken and vineyards to be smitten with frost; and causing persons to die by melting wax images dressed in part of their clothing. One accused woman first claimed innocence, but after torture she confessed to being a witch.

The important thing to note here is that all these activities, unmistakably evil in themselves, in their consequences and in their example, were firmly believed to have actually occurred, and the punishment for persisting in them was death in accordance with the biblical command: "You shall not permit a witch to live" (Exod. 22:18).

It is interesting to note also that the first case thus far discovered of a witch burned to death, after judicial sentence of an Inquisitor, occurred at Toulouse in 1275. The Inquisitor was Hugues de Baniol.[3] The woman, most likely half demented, "confessed" to having given birth to a monster after intercourse with an evil spirit and to have nourished it with babies' flesh which she obtained in her nightly expeditions.

Unfortunately, the possibility of such carnal intercourse between human beings and demons was accepted by some of the greatest Christian philosophers and theologians, including even St. Thomas Aquinas and St. Bonaventure.

## An Unfortunate Papal Bull

Even more unfortunate was the bull of Pope Innocent VIII, *Summis desiderantes affectibus* (Desiring with Supreme Ardor), so called from its opening Latin words, issued on December 5, 1484. The pope was prompted to issue the bull by the complaints of two Dominican Inquisitors, Henry Institoris and James Sprenger, that local ecclesiastical authorities were failing to assist them in their search for heretical witches. The bull has generally been considered the beginning of the persecution of witches and is, therefore, one of the most basic documents in the study of medieval witchcraft.

In it the pope declares:

Desiring with supreme ardor, as pastoral solicitude requires, that the Catholic faith in our days everywhere grow and flourish as much as possible, and that all heretical pravity be put far from the territories of the faithful, we freely declare and anew decree this by which our pious desire may be fulfilled, and, all errors being rooted out by our toil as with the hoe of a wise laborer, zeal and devotion to this faith may take deeper hold on the hearts of the faithful themselves.

It has recently come to our ears, not without great pain to us, that in some parts of upper Germany, as well as in the provinces, cities, territories, regions, and dioceses of Mainz, Köln, Trier, Salzburg, and Bremen, many persons of both sexes, heedless of their own salvation and forsaking the Catholic faith, give themselves over to devils male and female, and by their incantations, charms, and conjurings, and by abominable superstitions and sortileges, offences, crimes, and misdeeds, ruin and cause to perish the offspring of women, the foal of animals, the products of the earth, the grapes of vines, and the fruits of trees, as well as men and women, cattle and flocks and herds and animals of every kind, vineyards also and orchards, meadows, pastures harvests, grains and other fruits of the earth; that they afflict and torture with dire pains and anguish, both internal and external, these men, women, cattle, flocks, herds, and animals, and hinder men from begetting and women from conceiving, and prevent all consummation of marriage.

## Enemy of Mankind

The pope then continues:

Moreover, they deny with sacrilegious lips the faith they received in holy baptism; and that, at the instigation of the enemy of mankind they do not fear to commit and perpetrate many abominable offences and crimes, at the risk of their own souls, to the insult of the divine majesty and to the pernicious example and scandal of multitudes.

Although our beloved sons Henricus Institoris and Jacobus Sprenger, of the order of Friars Preachers, professors of theology, have been and still are deputed by our apostolic letters as inquisitors of heretical pravity, the former in the aforesaid parts of upper Germany, including the provinces, cities, territories, dioceses, and other places as above, and the latter throughout certain parts of the course of the Rhine; nevertheless certain of the clergy and of the laity of those parts, seeking to be wise above what is fitting, because in the said letter of deputation the aforesaid provinces, cities, dioceses, territories, and other places, and the persons and offences in question were not individually and specifically named, do not blush obstinately to assert that these are not at all included in the said parts and that therefore it is illicit for the aforesaid inquisitors to exercise their office of inquisition in the provinces, cities, dioceses, territories, and other places aforesaid, and that they ought not to be permitted to proceed to the punishment, imprisonment, and correction of the aforesaid persons for the offences and crimes above named. Wherefore in the provinces, cities, dioceses, territories, and places aforesaid such offences and crimes, not without evident damage to their souls and risk of eternal salvation, go unpunished.

We therefore, desiring, as is our duty, to remove all impediments by which in any way the said inquisitors are hindered in the exercise of their office, and to prevent the taint of heretical pravity and of other like evils from spreading their infection to the ruin of others who are innocent, the zeal of religion especially impelling us, in order that the provinces, cities, dioceses, territories, and places aforesaid in the parts of upper Germany may not be deprived of the office of inquisition which is their due, do hereby decree, by virtue of our apostolic authority, that it shall be permitted to the said inquisitors in these regions to exercise their office of inquisition and to proceed to the correction, imprisonment, and punishment of the aforesaid persons for their said offences and crimes, in all respects and altogether precisely as if the provinces, cities, territories, places, persons, and offences aforesaid were expressly named in the said letter . . . .

Let no man, therefore, dare to infringe this page of our declaration, extension, grant, and mandate, or with rash hardihood to contradict it. If any presume to attempt this, let him know that he incurs the wrath of almighty God and of the blessed apostles Peter and Paul.[4]

## Astonishment of People

People were understandably astonished at the pope's admission that men and women can have sexual relations with demons and that witches by their magical incantations can injure harvests, vineyards, orchards and fields. It is true, of course, that the immediate and direct object of the bull was simply to ratify the powers, already conferred upon the Inquisitors Henry Institoris and James Sprenger, to deal with persons of every class and with every form of crime—for example, with witchcraft as well as heresy—and it requested the bishop of Strasburg to lend the Inquisitors all possible assistance.

Indirectly, however, by specifying the evil practices charged against the witches—for example, their intercourse with incubi and succubi (male and female spirits), their interference with the parturition of women and animals, the damage they did to cattle and the fruits of the earth, their power and malice in the infliction of pain and disease, the hindrance caused to men in their conjugal relations, and the witches' repudiation of the faith of their baptism—the pope, as the *Catholic Encyclopedia* points out, "must no doubt be considered to affirm the reality of these alleged phenomena." ⁵

In discussing this point, Ludwig Pastor, author of the famous *History of the Popes*, remarks: "The question whether the pope believed in them [the activities of the evil spirits] has nothing to do with the subject. His judgment on this point has no greater importance than attaches to a papal decree in any other nondogmatic question, e.g. in a dispute about a benefice." But "The learned historian is wrong," Vacandard points out, "for the pope's views made a great difference in this particular case. Many canonists cited it as proof, and the Inquisitors acted on it in their tribunals." ⁶

## Hammer of Witches

Scarcely less disastrous than the bull of Innocent VIII was the publication in 1486 of the book *Malleus maleficarum* (*The Hammer of Witches*) by the Inquisitors Institoris and Sprenger. The work is divided into three parts. The first and second deal with the reality of witchcraft as depicted in the Bible as well as its nature, horrors and the manner of eradicating it. The third part formulates the practical rules for procedure, whether the trial be conducted in ecclesiastical or secular court.

The volume maintained that the origin of witchery was "carnal lust," said to be insatiable in certain women. It said that those suspected of sorcery should be investigated, if necessary, with torture and that convicted witches, if penitent, should be condemned to life imprisonment and, if unrepentant, should be handed over to the law for execution.

The book included as a preface Pope Innocent VIII's bull *Summis desiderantes affectibus* and contained as an appendix an alleged decision in its favor by the Faculty of Theology at the University of Cologne. With such impressive claims to speak with the highest authority, the volume seemed to present Christian Europe with a complete, authoritative and effective method of dealing with the witches in its midst.

Add to this the fact that it was reproduced by the printing press, and we can safely say that no other book exercised such wide influence in shaping public opinion on witchcraft as *Malleus maleficarum*. Neither did any other work reflect so authentically the spirit and ethos of the Inquisition.

In 1572 Augustus of Saxony imposed the penalty of burning for participation in witchcraft of all kinds, including fortune-telling. Martin Luther, John Calvin and other Protestant reformers joined in the hue and cry, calling for the extermination of witches of all sorts.

## Luther Speaks Out

"I should have no compassion on these witches," Luther once wrote. "I would burn all of them." [7] He shared and reinforced the witchcraft beliefs of the people of his day. In his Commentary on St. Paul's Epistle to the Galatians, he described the awesome power and skill of sorcerers, enchanters and witches as agents of the devil:

*Who hath bewitched you, that you should not believe the truth?* Here have ye another commendation of this goodly righteousness of the law, and of your own righteousness, namely, that it maketh us to contemn the truth: It bewitcheth us in such sort, that we do not believe nor obey the truth, but rebel against it.

Paul calleth the Galatians foolish and bewitched, comparing them to children to whom witchcraft doth much harm. As though he should say: It happeneth to you as it doth to children, whom witches, sorcerers, and enchanters are wont to charm by their enchantments, and by the illusions of the devil.

Afterwards, in the fifth chapter, he rehearseth sorcery among the works of the flesh, which is a kind of witchcraft, whereby he plainly testifieth, that indeed such witchcraft and sorcery there is, and that it may be done. Moreover, it cannot be denied but that the devil liveth, yea, and reigneth throughout the whole world. Witchcraft and sorcery therefore are the works of the devil; whereby he doth not hurt only men, but also, by the permission of God, he sometimes destroyeth them. Furthermore, we are all subject to the devil, both in body and goods; and we be strangers in this world, whereof he is the prince and god. Therefore the bread which we eat, the drink which we drink, the garments which we wear, yea, the air, and whatsoever we live by in the flesh, is under his dominion.. . .

Of witchcraft I have spoken before, in the third chapter. This vice was very common in these our days, before the light and truth of the gospel was revealed. When I was a child, there were many witches and sorcerers, which bewitched both cattle and men, but specially children, and did great harm also otherwise; but now, in the light of the gospel, these things be not so commonly heard of, for the gospel thrusteth the devil out of his seat, with all his illusions. But now he bewitcheth men and much more horribly, namely, with spiritual sorcery and witchcraft.[8]

## Calvin and Demons

The man who probably ranks second only to Luther in the leadership of the Reformation was John Calvin, author of the *Institutes of the Christian Religion*. A favorite theme of his was that of the role and power of Satan and the pact between him and the witch. In his *Institutes* he elaborates what he judges to be the biblical bases of demonological belief, as shown in the following excerpt.

*The devils in the purposes of God: Scripture forearms us against the adversary.* All that Scripture teaches concerning devils aims at arousing us to take precaution against their stratagems and contrivances, and also to make us equip ourselves with those weapons which are strong and powerful enough to vanquish these most powerful foes. For when Satan is called the god (2 Cor. 4:4) and prince (John 12:31) of this world, when he is spoken of as a strong armed man (Luke 11:21; cf. Matt. 12:29), the spirit who holds power over the air (Eph. 2:2), a roaring lion (1 Peter 5:8), these descriptions serve only to make us more cautious and watchful, and thus more prepared to take up the struggle. This also sometimes is noted explicitly: for Peter, after he has said that devil "prowls around like a roaring lion seeking someone to devour" (1 Peter 5:8), immediately subjoins the exhortation that with faith we steadfastly resist him (1 Peter 5:9). And Paul, after he has warned us that our struggle is not with flesh and blood, but with princes of the air, with the powers of darkness, and spiritual wickedness (Eph. 6:12), forthwith bids us put on that armor capable of sustaining so great and dangerous a contest (Eph. 6:13 ff.).

We have been forewarned that an enemy relentlessly threatens us, an enemy who is the very embodiment of rash boldness, of military prowess, of crafty wiles, of untiring zeal and haste, of every conceivable weapon and of skill in the science of warfare. We must, then, bend our every effort to this goal: that we should not let ourselves be overwhelmed by carelessness or faintheartedness, but on the contrary, with courage rekindled stand our ground in combat. Since this military service ends only in death, let us urge ourselves to perseverance. Indeed, conscious of our weakness and ignorance, let us especially call upon God's help, relying upon him alone in whatever we attempt, since it is he alone who can supply us with counsel and strength, courage and armor.

Calvin then continued:

Moreover, in order that we may be aroused and exhorted all the more to carry this out, Scripture makes known that there are not one, not two, nor a few foes, but great armies, which wage war against us. For Mary Magdalene is said to have been freed from seven demons by which she was possessed (Mark 16:9; Luke 8:2), and Christ bears witness that usually after a demon has once been cast out, if you make room for him again, he will take with him seven spirits more wicked than he and return to his empty possession (Matt. 12:43-45). Indeed, a whole legion is said to have assailed one man (Luke 8:30). We are therefore taught by these examples that we have to wage war against an infinite number of enemies, lest, despising their fewness, we should be too remiss to give battle, or, thinking that we are sometimes afforded some respite, we should yield to idleness.

But the frequent mention of Satan or the devil in the singular denotes the empire of wickedness opposed to the Kingdom of Righteousness. For as the church and fellowship of the saints has Christ as Head, so the faction of the impious and impiety itself are depicted for us together with their prince who holds supreme sway over them. For this reason, it was said: "Depart, . . . you cursed, into the eternal fire, prepared for the devil and his angels" (Matt. 25:41).[9]

## Baleful Influence

Owing in part to the influence of the *Hammer of Witches*, denunciation, ordeals and torture were used in the prosecution of suspected witches. During the entire fifteenth century France was beset with the witchcraft mania, and the French victims of the sixteenth century frequently confessed that they were guilty of lycanthropy: assuming the form and characteristics of a wolf. The Parlement of Paris in 1641 abolished ordeal by water, but even in 1670 there were severe witch persecutions in Normandy and Rouen.

Spain was free of the burning of sorcerers prior to the sixteenth century, but in the seventeenth century the Inquisition of Toledo alone handled 151 witch cases. Sentences to the galleys or life imprisonment were frequently handed out. In Italy in the fifteenth and sixteenth centuries, witchcraft trials frequently ended with the death of the accused.

Owing largely to the influence of John Calvin the persecution of witches spread first through the Romansch cantons of Switzerland. In Russia capital punishment for witchery was virtually unknown in the eleventh century, but belief in it developed rapidly there. Even as late as the nineteenth century peasants murdered alleged witches.

In Denmark numerous sentences were meted out in witchcraft trials between 1572 and 1652, while in 1776 the Polish Parliament prohibited such trials. In 1670 in the Danish area of Mora alone, twenty-two women were executed, while in Iceland a man was burned at the stake for magic in 1685.

## Witchcraft in England

The trials for witchcraft in England were most numerous in the seventeenth century, but the absence of judicial torture doubtless made the trials proportionately less numerous than they were on the continent.

The methods employed by Matthew Hopkins, one of the most noted witch hunters, however, were not far removed from actual torture. His practice was to prick any bodily excrescence on the accused, which was believed to be an extra pap for suckling imps. Such parts, if insensible, were thought to prove the accused was a witch. Another technique was to compel the suspect to roam about all night, since only when at rest could a witch summon her familiars who would frighten her accusers away.

The last trial for witchery in England took place in 1712, when Jane Wenham was convicted but not executed. In Scotland witch trials were held only after the Reformation, and the last official burning took place there in 1727. One of the last cases in Germany was that of Johannes Junius, the burgomaster of Bamberg in Bavaria. He was pricked with a knife, possibly one with a retractable point, and did not feel it. This was presumptive evidence of guilt. Under the unbearable pain of torture, he confessed to devilish acts, called out the names of neighbors seen at witches' sabbat, and was burned alive in 1628.

English settlers in colonial America carried with them the belief in witchery. After a lengthy witch trial at Salem, Massachusetts, in 1692, as a consequence of charges by a group of teen-age girls, more than thirty persons were convicted of witchcraft, some after torture. One of the executed men received the unusual punishment of being crushed to death between heavily weighted planks.

## A Vast Holocaust

The number of persons executed, usually by being burned alive at the stake, on the charge of witchcraft, can only be estimated. Kors and Peters, editors of *Witchcraft in Europe*, say: "It is impossible to calculate accurately the total number of convicted witches who were burned at the stake or hanged between the fourteenth and seventeenth centuries, but few students begin guessing below the range of fifty to one hundred thousand, and some would double or triple that figure. However great the actual count of victims, witnesses all convey the impression that the witches existed in great numbers and that convictions and executions consumed them in great numbers." [10]

Writing in the symposium, *Witchcraft: Confessions and Accusations*, Norman Cohn describes the multitude put to death during the war on witchcraft in the sixteenth and seventeenth centuries as a "vast holocaust" and adds, "Nobody knows how many people perished at the stake during those two centuries, but responsible estimates vary from 200,000 to a million." [11] The *Encyclopaedia Britannica* reports: "The victims of the witchcraft trials have been variously estimated to number from the hundreds of thousands to the millions."

Describing the frequency with which witches were burned alive in the sixteenth century, Lea observes: "Protestant and Catholic rivalled each other in the madness of the hour. Witches were burned no longer in ones or twos, but in scores and hundreds. A bishop of Geneva is said to have burned five hundred within three months, a bishop of Bamburg six hundred, a bishop of Würzburg nine hundred. Eight hundred were condemned, apparently in one body, by the Senate of Savoy. . . . . Parame [in his *History of the Inquisition*] boasts that in a century and a half from the commencement of the sect in 1404, the Holy Office had burned at least thirty thousand witches who, if they had been left unpunished, would easily have brought the whole world to destruction." [12]

Resistance to the witchcraft mania, in both beliefs and practices, was present from the start especially among clergy and physicians. In Italy the philosopher Giordano Bruno, 1548–1600, was burned at the stake as a heretic because he declared publicly that many so-called witches were simply psychologically disturbed old women. St. Vincent de Paul (1581-1660) added his voice to others opposing the witch mania.

The first evidence of decline in the intensity of the witch hunts came in Spain (1610), where the Inquisitor Alonso Salazar y Frias investigated the witch burnings at Logrono, Navarre. He found that most of the accusations had been false and that no single act of witchcraft had occurred in all the burnings.

He ordered that the Spanish Inquisition was not to accept accusations without independent evidence and that torture was not to be used. But most significant seems to have been his order that the accused's property was not to be confiscated as a result of the conviction. At any rate, the number of accusations of witchery dropped markedly.

## *The Curtain Falls*

In Germany in 1623 Pope Gregory XV issued his constitution *Omnipotentis* in which he commanded that persons who had entered into a pact with the devil or who had practiced black magic or had caused the death of another, should be turned over to the secular arm for execution. If the action of the malefactor did not, however, bring about the death of another, he should atone alone for his crime by life imprisonment. In Germany at this time there was much suffering from witchcraft persecutions, especially during the Thirty Years' War.

Probably the stoutest opposition to the witchcraft persecutions in Germany came from the Jesuit Friederich von Spee. In 1631 he published his *Cautio criminalis* in which he fought on the side of humanity and enlightenment against the witch craze. His well-reasoned protests helped to speed its abolition in a number of places, especially at Mainz, and led to its gradual suppression. Joining him in his campaign of enlightenment were the Protestants Lambert Daneau and Christian Thomasius.

The last witch trials were held at Würzburg in 1749, at Endlingen in 1751 and at Kempten in 1775. The curtain was rung down gradually on these trials in France after the edict of Louis XIV in 1682.

The witch hunt had spent its fury, its work was done, and it slowly moved off the stage, leaving behind it an ocean of blood, a sea of corpses and the memory of deliberate torture, pain and agony with few, if any, parallels in the religious history of the race.

## CHAPTER XI

# The Sabbat: Heart of Witchcraft

They are neither men nor women,
They are neither brute nor human,
They are Ghouls!

EDGAR ALLAN POE

IN LOOKING BACK AT THE WITCHCRAFT MANIA which held so many millions of Europeans in its weird hysterical grasp, there is one feature that deserves special attention, for it was the craft's most distinctive and striking characteristic: the sabbat. This was a midnight assembly (Thursday night was favored) of the witches and sorcerers held in medieval and Renaissance times to renew allegiance to the devil and to celebrate rites and orgies. Its distinguishing feature was the worship of Satan.

To it men and women were transported through the air, either spontaneously or astride a broomstick or stool, or mounted on a demon in the form of a goat, a dog or some other animal. Stripped of the devil-worship, now first introduced, such assemblies are found in the beliefs of many races.

In the medieval period the first reference to such an assemblage occurs in a fragment, not later than the ninth century, in which it is treated as a diabolical illusion. This fragment came to be known as the *Canon episcopi*, which we have presented in the previous chapter. As shown in that document, the Church in its efforts to suppress these relics of paganism denounced as heretical the belief in the reality of such delusions.

As part of canon law this remained immutable. But alongside of it there grew up with the heresy reports of secret meetings in which the members adored the devil in the form of a cat or other animal and engaged in obscene rites, including kissing Lucifer, in the form of a cat, under its tail. In the middle of the thirteenth century Thomas of Cantimpre, a Dominican, describes how demons transport men from one region to another and delude them into worshiping mortals as gods. Others, he declares, carry away women, replacing them with insensible images.

## Abandonment to Satan

When peasant witches were examined by Inquisitors as to their dealings with Satan, they could scarcely keep, under unbearable torture, from satisfying the curiosity of their examiners with stories of their nocturnal flights and the orgiastic rites at the sabbats. Finally the time came when the confession of a witch was regarded as incomplete without an account of her attendance at a sabbat, which was the unmistakable evidence of her abandonment to Satan. So widespread and detailed were these stories that they could not be ignored without discrediting the whole structure of witchcraft.

Inquisitors and demonologists were at a loss to square the reported facts with the denunciations by the Church of such beliefs as heresy. In 1458 the Inquisitor Nicholas Jaquerius sought to solve the difficulty by declaring that the existing sect of witches was radically different from the heretics mentioned in the *Canon episcopi*. He presented, in evidence of their bodily presence at the sabbat, many cases which had come before him in his official capacity as Inquisitor.

Among the cases cited was one of a man who, as a child fifty-five years before, had been brought to a sabbat with his infant brother, and presented to Satan in the form of a goat, who with his hoofs had imprinted on them an indelible mark—the stigma of the devil. Jaquerius added, reasonably enough, that even if the affair is an illusion, it is nonetheless heretical. Thirty years later the Inquisitor James Sprenger, who did much to formulate belief and organize persecution, endeavored to solve the difficulty by arguing that, while the devil undoubtedly possessed the power of transportation, the presence of the witch was only mental.

## Mere Delusions?

Along about 1500 the scholarly jurist Gianfrancesco Ponzinibio wrote a tract on witchcraft, in which he upheld the reasoning in *Canon episcopi* and applied it to all magic and sorcery, which he treated as mere delusions. He exposed the fallacy of the argument that existing witches belonged to a different sect and contended that their confessions are not to be received, since what they confess is illusory and impossible. He further argued that their evidence as to their associates is to be rejected, since they are deluded and can only delude others.

His line of reasoning, so clear and convincing to contemporary man, aroused the ire of Silvestro Mozzolino of Prierio, Master of the Sacred Palace and later Dominican General. To deny the corporal presence of witches at the sabbat, he declared, is to discredit the enormous number of cases tried by the Inquisition and consequently to discredit both the Inquisitors and the laws themselves.

His successor to the mastership of the Sacred Palace, Bartolomeo de Spina, displayed still greater wrath against Ponzinibio and his arguments. "O wonderful presumption!" he thundered, "O detestable insanity! Only heretics abjure, only heresies are abjured before Inquisitors.

"Is then that belief a heresy which Inquisitors defend, and according to which they judge the enemies of the faith to be worthy of extreme damnation? . . . Must then all the theologians and judges, the Inquisitors themselves of all Italy, France, Germany and Spain, holding this opinion abjure before the Inquisition?" He concludes by calling upon the Inquisition to take prompt and vigorous action against Ponzinibio as vehemently suspect of heresy, as a defender of heretics and an impeder of the Holy Office.[1]

## Dangerous to Dispute

"This sufficiently shows," observes Lea, "that the new beliefs completely conquered the old. The question had passed beyond the range of reason and argument, and everywhere throughout Europe the witches' sabbat was accepted as an established fact, which it was dangerous to dispute. Jurists and canonists might amuse themselves by debating it theoretically; practically it had become the veriest commonplace of the courts, both secular and ecclesiastical."[2]

There were but a few variations in the detailed reports of the sabbats, due most likely to the fact that the same leading questions were customarily put by the Inquisitorial judges to those charged with witchery. One of the first acts of the witch was to obtain a consecrated wafer by pretending to receive Holy Communion and then bringing the wafer home. This was fed to a toad which was then burned. The ashes were mixed with the blood of an infant, preferably unbaptized.

To this were added the powdered bone of a man and certain herbs. With this curious mixture the witch anointed the palms of her hands and a stick or stool which she placed between her legs and she was at once flown to the place of the meeting. On some occasions, however, the ride was made on a demon in the form of a dog, a goat or a horse.

The sabbats were held in a great variety of places: a wood, a valley, a field near a village, a cemetery, a ruined building, a semideserted church and sometimes a house belonging to one of the initiates. On one exceptional occasion a sabbat was held in the very heart of the city of Bordeaux. The assemblage generally lasted till dawn, before which those in attendance were not permitted to depart.

In his work on witchery Bartolomeo de Spina, O.P., relates that a peasant who lived in the district of Mirandola had occasion to rise early one morning and drive to a neighboring village. He found himself crossing a waste tract of considerable extent which lay between him and his destination. Off in the distance, he suddenly caught sight of what seemed to be numerous fires flitting to and fro.

## Glimpse at a Sabbat

As he drew closer, he perceived that these were none other than lanterns held by a large group of persons, some of whom were performing a fantastic dance. Others were seated, partaking of food and drinking wine. Others, unabashed, were engaged in the most unrestrained debauchery, publicly performing the sexual act with every kind of indecency.

The horrified peasant realized that he was witnessing the revels of the sabbat. Crossing himself fervently and uttering a prayer, he drove as speedily as possible from the accursed spot. It was not, however, before he recognized some of the company as notorious evildoers and persons who were already under suspicion of witchcraft. Although the witches must have noticed his presence, they made no attempt to catch him.[3]

Another instance is related by a Dominican, Fra Paolo de Caspan. Antonio de Palavisini, the parish priest of Caspan in the Valtelina, an area infested by witches, most solemnly affirmed that, when going before daybreak to celebrate an early Mass at a shrine near the village, he saw through the clearings in the wood a gathering of men and women with lanterns. They were seated in a circle and their actions showed that they were witches engaged in lascivious rites and orgies.[4]

A refreshing difference of opinion concerning the reality of the activities at the sabbat was expressed by a Benedictine priest, Dom Augustin Calmet: "To attempt to give a description of the sabbat is to attempt a description of what does not exist, and what has never existed save in the fantastic and disordered imagination of warlocks (sorcerers) and witches. The pictures which have been drawn of these assemblies are merely the phantasy of those who dreamed that they had actually been borne, body and soul, through the air to the sabbat."

After quoting these words, Montague Summers in a book, *The History of Witchcraft and Demonology*, published in 1926, comments: "Happy Sceptic! But unfortunately the sabbat did—and does—take place; formerly in deserted wastes, on the hillside, in secluded spots, now, as often as not, in the privacy of vaults and cellars, and in those lone empty houses, innocently placarded 'To Be Sold.' "[5]

When the presiding officer at the sabbat was a human being, a man, he would sometimes appear in a grotesque and hideous disguise, sometimes with no attempt at concealment. More frequently, however, the masquerade took the form of an animal, whence it passed to the sorcerer and the witch.

As early as the *Liber poenitentialis* of St. Theodore, archbishop of Canterbury (668-690), we have a strong prohibition of this foul mummery. "If anyone at the kalends of January," reads the prohibition, "goes about as a stag or a bull, that is making himself into a wild animal and dressing in the skin of a herd animal, and putting on the head of beasts, those who in such wise transform themselves into the appearance of a wild animal, penance for three years because this is devilish."[6]

Satan, or the master of the sabbat who presided in place of Satan, was adored by the witches by genuflections, gestures, obeisances and prostrations. Their principal act of homage, however, was the *osculum infame*. Curiously this impious and lewd ritual is discerned in the religious rites of virtually all tribes and races.

## Bull of Boniface

In a bull of Pope Boniface VIII, issued on June 8, 1303, reference is made to the case of Walter Langton, bishop of Lichfield and Coventry (1296-1322) and treasurer of Edward I, when this prelate was accused of sorcery and homage to Satan: "For some time past it has come to our ears that our Venerable Brother Walter, Bishop of Coventry and Lichfield has been commonly defamed and accused both in the realm of England and elsewhere, of paying homage to the Devil by kissing his posterior, and that he hath had frequent colloquies with evil spirits." The bishop cleared himself of these charges with the compurgators. The bull, it is worth noting, shows clearly the belief of the pope in the type of devil who presides at the sabbats and has commerce of various hideous kinds with the witches who fly on broomsticks through the air.

After worshiping the devil at the sabbat, those in attendance engaged in dancing, singing and playing music. Music customarily accompanied the dancers and there is abundant evidence that various instruments were used: violins, flutes, tambourines, citterns, hautboys and, in Scotland, the pipes. The service ended in the most hideous discords and bestial clamor.

Philip Ludwig Elich thus describes the confused scene: "The whole foul mob and stinkard rabble sing the most abominable songs in honor of the devil. One witch yells, Haar, haar; a second hag, Devil, Devil; jump hither, jump thither; another, Sabaoth, Sabaoth, etc.; and so the whole wild orgy waxes frantic . . . with screeching, hissing, howling, caterwauling, and whooping lewd wassail."[7] The climax of all the horrors of the sabbat was that appalling blasphemy by which the Mass was mocked and burlesqued in hideous fashion in what is called a Black Mass.

Describing how the liturgy is burlesqued in every detail at the sabbat, Paul Grilland says: "Those witches who have solemnly devoted themselves to the devil's service, worship him in particular manner with ceremonial sacrifices, which they offer to the devil, imitating in all respects the worship of Almighty God, with vestments, lights and every other ritual observance. They have a set liturgy in which they are instructed, so that they worship and praise him externally, just as we worship the true God."[8]

## Cotton Mather

Surprising in this connection is the statement of Cotton Mather that the New England witches "met in Hellish *Rendezvous,* wherein the Confessors [i.e., the accused who confessed] do say, they have had their Diabolical Sacraments imitating the *Baptism* and the *Supper* of our Lord."[9] Eight of the confessing witches at the Salem, Massachusetts, trial in 1692 pointed to a minister, the Rev. George Burroughs, as the Chief of the Salem witches, who presided at their sabbats and administered the witch sacraments.

In 1597 the Parlement of Paris found Jean Belon, curé of S. Pierre-des-Lampes in the Bourges diocese, guilty of desecrating the sacrament and of repeated celebration of diabolical ceremonies at the sabbats. A year later the Parlement of Bordeaux sentenced to death at the stake Pierre Aupetic, curé of Pageas, near Chalus Limousin. He confessed that for more than twenty years he had attended sabbats, especially those at Mathegoutte and Puy-de-Dome, where he worshiped the devil and performed diabolical masses in his honor.[10]

In 1609 the Parlement of Bordeaux, disturbed by the growing number of sorcerers who infested that region and drew people to sabbats where Satan's masses were celebrated, decided to do something about it. They sent in a number of agents who arrested seven priests on the charge of officiating at such masses at the sabbats. Two, Migalena, an old man of seventy and Pierre Bocal, aged twenty-seven, were burned at the stake. Others wisely quit that territory.

## A Well-Known Case

A well-known case of witchery occured in 1450, when the Inquisitor of Como, Bartolomeo de Homate, the magistrate Lorenzo du Concorezzo and the notary Giovanni da Fossato went to a sabbat at Mendrisio and witnessed the "goings on" from a hiding place. They went either out of curiosity or because they doubted the witches whom they were trying.

The presiding demon pretended not to be aware of their presence. In due course he dismissed the assembly. Then suddenly he recalled his followers and set them on the officials, who were so severely beaten that they died within fifteen days.[11]

Ordericus Vitalis relates that in January, 1091, in Bonneville, Gualchelm, the priest connected with the Church of St. Albin of Angers, was returning at night after administering the sacrament of extreme unction to a dying man in a distant part of his parish. Suddenly he was met on the road by a huge crowd on foot and on horseback, men and women, knights and priests, abbots and bishops.

Withdrawing to one side, he watched them pass and recognized quite a few, some of whom had recently died. Suddenly realizing that they were spirits, he said to himself, "This is doubtless the troop of Herlechim, of which I have often heard, but never believed." The priest was ill for a week after this unexpected adventure, but lived in good health for fifteen years.[12]

Martin le Franc (ca. 1440), secretary to the Anti-Pope Felix V, in his "Champion des Dames" dedicated to Philip the Good of Burgundy, makes his "Adversaire" describe the sabbat in nearly its perfected form, as he heard it from the confession of an old woman who reported that she had frequented it since she was sixteen. At the sabbat in Valpute, about ten thousand women came riding on sticks. The demon presided, in the form of a cat, whom they all adored.

He taught them all kinds of crime and gave them an ointment with which they killed more than one hundred men and infants;

also a powder with which to raise tempests. After feasting on many sorts of delicious food, they copulated, with demons serving the women who had no men. Finally they flew away on sticks. More than six hundred had confessed, without torture, that they had made destructive hailstorms.[13]

## A Shocking Case

A shocking case is reported in the narrative of Madeleine Bavent, a Franciscan nun of the Third Order, attached to the convent of SS. Louis and Elizabeth at Louviers. Her confessions, written at length under the direction of her confessor, des Marets, an Oratorian, meticulously describe scenes of the most hideous blasphemy, in which were involved three chaplains: David; Maturin Picard, the curé of Mesnil-Jourdain; and Thomas Boullé, his sometime assistant. Among other monstrous things, they had revived the heresy of the Adamites, an early Gnostic sect, and celebrated Mass in a state of stark nudity amid circumstances of the grossest indecency.

Upon one Good Friday Picard and Boullé had forced the nun to defile the crucifix and to break a consecrated host, throw the fragments upon the ground and trample upon them. At the time of her writing, David and Picard were dead, but Boullé was burned alive at the stake in Rouen on August 21, 1647.[14]

The witch had but one serious occupation: works of evil. Abandoned, soul and body, to Satan, she was the instrument which he used to effect his malignant purposes. Demonologists contend that the witch was as necessary to the demon as the demon to the witch, and that neither can operate effectively without the other. Unlike magicians and sorcerers who earned their livelihood by selling their services, sometimes for good purposes and sometimes for bad, the witch was wholly evil, delighting in the exercise of her powers for the destruction of her neighbors.

By simply laying a hand upon a woman, a witch can cause abortion or dry up her milk if she is nursing. She can bring plagues of locusts and caterpillars, which devour the harvests. She can render men impotent and women barren and cause horses to become suddenly mad under their riders. Witches can bring death to infants by thrusting needles under the nails of an infant and then sucking the blood. They can transform themselves into cats and other animals. "Ludicrous as all this may seem," observes Lea, "every one of these details has served as the basis of charges under which countless human beings have perished in flames."[15]

When the blasphemous liturgy of the sabbat was completed, all present engaged in the most promiscuous debauchery, only pausing in their activities to spur themselves to new enormities by spiced foods and copious drafts of wine. "You may well suppose," writes Henri Boguet, "that every kind of obscenity is practiced here, yea, even those abominations, for which Heaven poured down fire and brimstone on Sodom and Gomorrah, are quite common in these assemblies."[16]

The scholarly Dominican Sebastian Michaelis, who on January 10, 1611, examined Madeleine de la Palud in regard to her participation in sabbats, writes that she disclosed the most unhallowed orgies. Inquisitor Jean Bodin reports that a large number of witches whom he tried acknowledged their frequenting the sabbat.

In 1459 a considerable number of men and women were burned at Arras, many of whom had accused one another. Many confessed that at night they had been transported through the air to the "hellish dances" at the sabbat. In 1485 Inquisitor Sprenger executed a large number of sorcerers in the Constance district, and "almost all without exception confessed that the devil had connection with them, after he had compelled them to renounce God and their holy faith."[17] Many converted witches also confessed to engaging in these abominations.

## Sacrifice of Children

Now and then we find evidence that animals were sacrificed at the sabbat to the demon. The second charge against Dame Alice Kyteler, prosecuted in 1324 for sorcery by Richard de Ledrede, Bishop of Ossory, was "that she was wont to offer sacrifices to devils of live animals." These she and her company tore limb from limb and made oblation, by scattering them at crossways, to a certain demon who was called Robin, son of Artes (Robin Artisson), one of hell's lesser princes.[18]

There is abundant evidence that children, usually tender babes as yet unbaptized, were sacrificed at the sabbat. Not infrequently these were the witches' own offspring. As a witch was often the midwife of a village, she had unusual opportunities of stifling a child at birth as a nonsabbatical victim to Satan. "There are no persons who can do more cunning harm to the Catholic faith than midwives," says the *Malleus maleficarum*.[19]

An excellent example of child-sacrifice on a large scale is that of Gilles de Rois (1440). In the Inquisitorial process against him 140 children are explicitly named. Some authorities place the total at eight hundred victims. Their blood, brains and bones were used to concoct magic philters.

Not less shocking was the traffic in child victims by Abbé Guibourg and his associates in 1680. The sacrifice of an infant at the blasphemous mass was so common, reports Montague Summers, that Guibourg paid not more than a crown-piece for his victim. These sacrilegious ceremonies were frequently performed at the insistence of Madame de Montespan in order that Louis XIV should remain faithful to her, reject all other mistresses, repudiate his queen and raise her to the throne.[20]

The customary procedure was to cut the child's throat and have his blood drain into the chalice. It was then permitted to fall upon the naked flesh of the inquirer, who lay stretched along the altar. La Voisin estimated that a total of fifteen hundred infants had been thus murdered. This is not unlikely, as an enormous number of persons, including a multitude of ecclesiastics, were implicated. Many of the most prominent in France had assisted at these blasphemous orgies.

No less than 246 men and women in all ranks and grades of society were brought to trial. Some thirty-six persons of humbler station went to the scaffold, while 147 were imprisoned for longer or shorter terms. Not a few found it convenient to leave the country or at least to obscure themselves in distant chateaux.

## Responsibility for Witchcraft

In an article in *The Encyclopedia of Witchcraft and Demonology*, Russel Hope Robbins says, "Were it not for the Inquisition, the Catholic tribunal charged with exposing and punishing unorthodoxy, not one person would have died for witchcraft."[21] This is an exaggeration with which few scholars will agree. Like the governments of the European nations which enacted criminal laws based upon the assumption that witches were real persons capable of harming individuals and destroying crops, the Church too must bear its share of responsibility for supporting such laws with religious sanctions. But many other factors were involved in spreading belief in witchcraft.

A more balanced judgment, as Henry A. Kelly points out, is expressed by Lynn Thorndike:

> It is possible to overemphasize the somewhat tenuous connection between magic and heresy. The witch was probably to some extent a scapegoat for the ills which then oppressed society. When we reflect that by the fifteenth century medieval culture was declining; that economic prosperity, political freedom and self-government, chivalry, and public charity were waning; that the fourteenth century had been marked by the terrible Black Death which demoralized society and never ceased its visitations thenceforth during the entire time of the witchcraft delusion, and by the perhaps worse pest of mercenary soldiers who, aided by artillery and firearms, made all wars from the Hundred Years' to the Thirty Years' so cruel, devastating, and financially exhausing—when we consider this, we may incline to regard the witchcraft delusion as in congenial company, and to view it as a sociological rather than theological or intellectual phenomenon, produced largely by popular fear and superstition, and by an undiscriminating wave of "law-enforcement" which swept over the secular more than the ecclesiastical courts, and raged in lands where the Inquisition had hardly functioned.
>
> . . . During the years from 1230 to 1430 the number of trials for magic before secular judges was large and ever growing. . . . We may agree, however, . . . that in so far as the witchcraft delusion was led up to by previous writings, it received countenance from works of theologians, canonists, and inquisitors rather than from medieval writers on nature and medicine, who were far more inclined to account for the supposed magical activities of demons by natural causes or human imagination.[22]

## Concluding Observations

Montague Summers concludes his lengthy discussion of the sabbat by saying: "A candid consideration will show that for every detail of the sabbat, however fanatically presented and exaggerated in the witch-trials of so many centuries, there is ample warrant and unimpeachable evidence. There is some hallucination, no doubt; there is lurid imagination, and vanity which paints the colors thick; but there is a solid stratum of fact, and very terrible fact throughout."[23]

After a similarly lengthy discussion of witchcraft in general and the sabbat in particular, Lea says: "No one can read the evidence adduced at a witch-trial or the confessions of the accused, without seeing how every accident and every misfortune and every case of sickness or death which had occurred in the vicinity for years was thus explained, and how the circle of suspicion widened so that every conviction brought new victims; burnings multiplied, and the terrified community was ready to believe that a half or more of its members were slaves of Satan, and that it would never be free from their malignant vengeance until they should all be exterminated. For more than two centuries this craze [witchcraft] was perpetually breaking out in one part of Europe after another, carefully nursed and stimulated by popes and inquisitors like Innocent VIII and Leo X, Sprenger and Inquisitor Bernard of Como and Bishop Binsfield, and the amount of human misery thence arising is simply incomputable."[24]

In the closing paragraph of its scholarly article on witchcraft the *Catholic Encyclopedia* says: "The question of the reality of witchcraft is one upon which it is not easy to pass a confident judgment. In the face of Holy Scripture and the teaching of the Fathers and theologians, the abstract possibility of a pact with the Devil and of diabolical interference in human affairs can hardly be denied, but no one can read the literature of the subject without realizing the awful cruelties to which this belief led and without being convinced that in 99 cases out of 100 the allegations rest upon nothing better than pure delusion."[25]

In a chapter, "The Myth of Satan and His Human Servants" in the symposium *Witchcraft: Confessions and Accusations*, Norman Cohn points out that the Inquisitors built up a fantasy of a mysterious sect, endowed with supernatural powers, flying on broomsticks or on animals to nocturnal assemblies. At Satan's bidding they waged incessant war on Christians and on Christendom. Were these witches real beings or imaginary creatures?

"This sect," he answers, "was wholly imaginary. Whereas heretical sects did at least exist, there was no sect of witches. That is not to deny that some individuals attempted various forms of sorcery—they certainly did; but they were not an organized body, they did not fly through the air, and they did not worship Satan. The sect of witches was a fantasy. To make it seem a reality, the Inquisitors tortured people until they not only confessed that they themselves attended the sabbat but denounced others for attending it. In this way they created the preconditions for the great witch-hunt which was to sweep large areas of Continental Europe long after the Inquisition had ceased to function there."[26]

We think that today virtually all scholars will agree with Professor Cohn's conclusion that the sect of witches against which the Inquisitors battled for several centuries was a fantasy, pure and simple. It was a fantasy, however, not peculiar to the Inquisitors but shared generally by the people of that day.

## CHAPTER XII

# Joan of Arc

They lived unknown
Till persecution dragged them into fame
and chased them up to heaven.
                                    WILLIAM COWPER

IN THE PREVIOUS CHAPTERS we have shown the procedure of the Inquisition in condemning thousands of persons to life imprisonment and other thousands to the stake to be burned alive for some alleged deviation in doctrine or for some alleged involvement in witchery. If the Christian countries of Europe were to be freed from the myriad heretics and witches infesting their landscape, there was a need for methods which would deal with them wholesale. Thus in 1487 the University of Cologne thundered a warning to the public that to contend against the reality of witchcraft was to incur the guilt of impeding the Inquisition: a guilt which was characterized as "constructive heresy."

Witches were no longer led to the stake in ones or twos, but in fifties and hundreds. A bishop of Geneva is reported to have burned five hundred within three months, a bishop of Würzburg nine hundred, and a bishop of Bamburg six hundred. The Senate of Savoy is said to have condemned some eight hundred, apparently in one body.[1]

Important and necessary as it is to show how numerous were the victims of the persecuting mania of the Inquisitors, it is not less important to disclose in greater detail and depth the suffering and agony of the victims. This can best be done, we think, by focusing our attention upon a few well-known individual victims. This will enable us the better to perceive the anguish and torment which each of the individual victims of the Inquisition experienced. This is the study in depth to which we now turn.

Probably the most famous victim of the Inquisition was Joan of Arc, the Maid of Orléans. The greatest national heroine of the people of France, she played a decisive role in the revival of France at a critical juncture in the Hundred Years' War. Born at Domrémy in Champagne, probably on January 6, 1412, Joan had three brothers and one sister, Catherine, who died young. Her father, Jacques, was a peasant farmer. She learned her religion and her prayers from her mother, Isabelle, who also taught her to sew. Like many other children of her state in life, Joan never learned to read or write.

## Her Voices

At the age of thirteen and a half, in the summer of 1425, Joan first became conscious of what she afterward came to call her "voices" or her "counsel." At first it was simply a voice, as if someone had spoken quite close to her.

Accompanying the voice was a blaze of light, and later on in some way she discerned the appearance of those who spoke to her, identifying them individually as St. Michael, St. Margaret, St. Catherine and others. Joan was always reluctant to speak of these voices, which were to guide her throughout her short life and to disclose her chief mission: the deliverance of the French kingdom from English control.

The treaty of Troyes (May 20, 1420) had made the English king, Henry V, king of France, pushing aside the legitimate heir, the future Charles VII. This was made possible because of the madness of Charles VI, French military reverses, and the alliance between England and Burgundy. After the successive deaths of Charles VI and Henry V, the duke of Bedford, regent of France for his ten-year-old nephew, Henry VI, undertook to complete the conquest of the kingdom by tracking down the dauphin (Charles VII), who had taken refuge beyond the Loire, and by putting Orléans under siege.

Although five years had passed since his father had died, the dauphin had still not been consecrated at Reims, the traditional place for the crowning of French kings. This was because Reims was well within the territory held by his enemies. As long as he remained unconsecrated, the legitimacy of his claim to be king of France was open to grave question in the minds of the people.

At the insistence of her voices, Joan left Domrémy and went to her "uncle" Durand Laxart (actually the husband of her mother's cousin), whom she persuaded to escort her in May, 1428, to Robert de Baudricourt, captain of Vaucouleurs, the nearest stronghold still loyal to the dauphin. But Baudricourt, a rude and dissolute soldier, paid scant attention to Joan on her mission. He advised the cousin who accompanied her: "Take her home to her father and give her a good spanking."

Meanwhile the military situation of King Charles and his supporters was growing more desperate. Orléans was surrounded on October 12, 1428, and by the end of the year complete defeat seemed imminent. Joan's voices became more insistent. In vain she resisted, saying to them: "I am a poor girl. I do not know how to ride or fight." But the voices only grew more urgent.

## Joan Leaves Domrémy

Yielding at last, Joan left Domrémy in January, 1429, and again visited Vaucouleurs. Although Baudricourt was still skeptical, Joan stayed on in the town, and her persistence gradually made an impression on him. On February 17 she announced that a great defeat had befallen French arms outside Orléans. As this was officially confirmed a few days later, her cause gained strength and she was permitted to seek an audience with the king.

With an escort of six men-at-arms, Joan set out. At her own request, she was attired in male costume as a protection for her modesty in the rough life of the camp. Those who knew her intimately declared that there was something about her which repressed any unseemly thought in her regard. On March 8 she was admitted into the presence of Charles VII.

To test her the king had disguised himself and hidden among his courtiers. But Joan went straight to him. She informed him that she wished to go and make war against the English and that she would have him crowned at Reims. On the dauphin's orders she was at once interrogated by ecclesiastical authorities in the presence of Jean, duc d'Alençon. A further examination was held at Poitiers, where for three weeks Joan was questioned by eminent theologians and canonists.

She told them that it was not at Poitiers but at Orléans that she would give proof of her mission. In their report on the examination the ecclesiastics suggested that in view of the desperate situation of Orléans, the dauphin would be well advised to make use of her. Accordingly he provided her with a military household, which included an Augustinian monk, Jean Pasquerel, who was her chaplain and confessor. Here she was joined by her two brothers, Jean and Pierre.

Instead of the sword offered by the king, she begged that a search be made for an ancient sword buried, as she disclosed, behind the altar of the church of St. Catherine-de-Fierbois. It was found on the exact spot indicated by her voices. There was made for her at the same time a standard bearing the words *Jesus*, *Maria*, with a picture of God the Father, and kneeling angels presenting a fleur-de-lis.

Joan predicted that "she would save Orléans and would compel the English to raise the siege, that she herself in a battle before Orléans would be wounded by an arrow but would not die of it and that the king, in the course of the coming summer, would be crowned at Reims, together with other things which the king keeps secret."[2] Before launching her campaign, Joan called upon the king of England to withdraw his forces from French soil.

Upon receiving no reply, Joan, by a rapid movement, entered Orléans on April 30, 1429; her presence had a magical effect upon the soldiers. By May 8 the English forts which encircled the city had all been captured, and the siege raised, though on May 7 Joan was wounded in the breast by an arrow. The Maid strongly urged that they follow up this great victory with all possible speed and drive the English out of France.

## A Year to Live

It is probable that she did this partly out of a sound military instinct and partly because her voices had already told her that she had but a year to live. But the apathetic king and his advisers, particularly La Trémoille and the archbishop of Reims, were intolerably slow to capitalize upon their great victory at Orléans. At Joan's urging, however, a short campaign was begun upon the Loire, which, after a series of successes, ended on June 18 with a brilliant victory at Patay. Here the English reinforcements dispatched from Paris under Sir John Fastolf were completely routed.

This opened the way to Reims, but the Maid had great difficulty in persuading the commanders not to retire before Troyes, which was at first closed against them. Yielding to the Maid's urging, they captured the town and then still reluctantly followed her to Reims. Here in the great cathedral on Sunday, July 17, 1429, Charles VII was solemnly crowned, with the Maid and her standard close to the altar.

"As it had shared in the toil," she explained, "it was just that it should share in the victory." It was a dramatic spectacle, dear to the people of France, and it has been reproduced many times in their history books and works of art. It was probably the happiest and proudest moment in the life of the Maid of Orléans. Perhaps she could draw upon the cherished memory of that scene for courage and strength to endure the agony of her confinement in irons in the bleak prison where she was waiting for the curtain to fall upon one of the most agonizing scenes in French history.

After the coronation ceremony, Joan knelt before Charles, calling him her king for the first time. That very day she wrote to the duke of Burgundy, calling upon him to make peace with his king and withdraw his garrisons from the royal fortresses. The principal goal of Joan's mission had now been accomplished, and some authorities maintain that it was her wish to return home, but she was detained with the army against her will. The evidence is somewhat conflicting, and it is probable that she was distressed by the apathy of the king and his chief advisers, who seem to have had precious little ability to work out military plans and strategies, and were content to put off till tomorrow many things which demanded action today.

An abortive attempt on Paris was launched at the end of August. St. Denis was taken with little opposition, but the assault on Paris was not seriously supported. While heroically cheering on her men to fill the moat, she was shot through the thigh with a bolt from a crossbow. With great reluctance Joan followed the duc d'Alençon's order to withdraw. The reverse undoubtedly impaired her prestige and shortly afterward, when a truce was signed with the duke of Burgundy, the Maid laid down her arms upon the altar of St. Denis.

## Idol of the French

The inactivity of the following winter, spent for the most part amid the worldliness and jealousy of the court, must have been a trying experience for the Maid. It may well have been with the idea of consoling her that the king on December 29, 1429, ennobled Joan and her family. It was April before Joan was able to take the sword again at the conclusion of the truce.

Moreover her voices told her that she would be taken prisoner before Midsummer Day (June 25). The fulfillment of that prophecy was not long delayed. Everywhere acclaimed, the Maid of Orléans was now, according to the chronicler Georges Chastellain, the "idol of the French."[3] She confided to Renaud de Chartres, archbishop of Reims, that she would like now to go back to tending her parents' flocks.

At sunrise on May 24 she was joined with others in defense of Compiègne against the attack of Burgundians. In the evening she attempted a sortie, but her small troop of five hundred encountered a much larger force. Her troops were driven back and retired, fighting desperately. By some mistake or panic of Guillaum de Flavy, who was in command, the drawbridge was raised while many of those who made the sortie still remained outside, Joan among the number.

Pulled down from her horse, she became the prisoner of a follower of John of Luxemburg. Some have accused de Flavy of deliberate treachery, but no adequate reason or evidence has been presented to support such a charge. In fact, he continued to hold Campiègne for his king. Joan's incessant thought during the early months of her captivity was to free herself and come to assist him in defending the town.

Here the spotlight is focused upon the incredible apathy and ingratitude of Charles and his advisers in leaving the Maid to her fate. If they could not rescue her by military force, they had other prisoners such as the earl of Warwick, for whom she could have been exchanged. She was sold by John of Luxemburg to the English for a sum which would be the equivalent of about $110,000 in modern currency.

## Pierre Cauchon

Partly because they feared the prisoner with a superstitious terror and partly because they were ashamed of the dread which she inspired, the British were determined at all costs to take Joan's life. Although they could not put her to death for having beaten them, they could get her condemned as a witch and a heretic. Moreover they had already in their hands an apt tool in Pierre Cauchon, the bishop of Beauvais, an ambitious and unscrupulous man who was the creature of the Burgundian party.

They used as a pretext for invoking his authority the fact that Campiègne, where Joan was captured, was in the diocese of Beauvais. But as Beauvais was still in the hands of the French, the trial took place at Rouen, which see was then vacant. This raised not a few points of technical legality, which were summarily settled by the parties concerned. The English paid the expenses of the bishop and of the Inquisitor. At that time Jean Graveran was Inquisitor for France and he appointed Frère Jean le Maître as his vicar or deputy for Rouen, and the latter reluctantly agreed to attend and thus give special authority to the whole proceedings. Actually he came only to the later sessions.

During the entire trial Cauchon's assessors were almost entirely Frenchmen, for the most part theologians and doctors of the University of Paris. Preliminary sessions of the court took place in January, but it was only on February 21, 1431, that Jean appeared for the first time before her judges. This nineteen-year-old girl, apparently with no formal schooling, was allowed no advocate in a trial which pitted her against learned theologians and doctors of the University of Paris.

Yet she managed not only to hold her own but frequently to make them appear unreasonable and irrelevant in their finicky questioning and juridical maneuvering. Though accused in an ecclesiastical court, she was illegally confined in the Castle of

Rouen, a secular prison, where she was guarded by dissolute English soldiers. Of this Joan frequently complained, asking to be in a church prison, where she would have had female attendants. It was for the better protection of her modesty that she persisted in retaining her male attire. This latter seemed to the Inquisitorial judges to be a heinous and even capital offense, to which they persisted in returning times without number.

## Attempts to Escape

Frustrated at every turn, Joan sought to escape by jumping from the window of the tower of Beaurevoir. She landed in the moat, where she was found unconcious. Not seriously injured, she was taken to Arras, a town belonging to the duke of Burgundy, when she had recovered. Her leap was termed an "act of presumption" for which she was repeatedly browbeaten by her judges.

It also served as a pretext for the harshness shown during her confinement at Rouen, where she was at first kept in an iron cage, chained by the neck, hands and feet. Moreover she was allowed no spiritual privileges, such as attendance at Mass or reception of Holy Communion, because of alleged heresy and the "monstrous" male garb she was wearing.

Although her offenses against the English were well known, Joan was brought to trial before a court concerned exclusively with matters of faith and morals. Her judges were to be the bishop of Beauvais and the Vice-Inquisitor of France, thus making the trial an ecclesiastical proceeding. Between February 21 and March 24, Joan was interrogated about a dozen times. The trial proper commenced a day or two later and it required two days for the Maid to answer the seventy charges drawn up against her.

These were grounded chiefly on the claim that her whole attitude and behavior displayed blasphemous presumption: in particular, that she claimed for her pronouncements the authority of divine revelation; endorsed her letters with the names of Jesus and Mary; prophesied the future; immodestly wore men's clothing; dared to claim that her saints spoke in French and not in English.

## *The Church Militant*

Probably the most serious charge was that of preferring what she assumed to be the direct commands of God to those of the "Church Militant." Here she was at a disadvantage because of her lack of education. She did not understand the phrase, and though eager and anxious to appeal to the pope, hesitated to pledge herself to accept in advance the judgment of the court which was trying her, as this would inevitably be made the test of her submission.

Like the brave warrior that she was, she struggled valiantly to avoid the trap, saying that she was aware that the Church Militant could not err; but it was to God that she held herself answerable for her words and actions. "God," observes Coulton, "for all practical circumstances at Rouen, was the Church Militant and the Church Militant was the Inquisition."[3a]

When Joan was brought before her judges, the president requested her to speak the whole truth without evasion. Her answer was remarkable and explains certain obscurities in her language used later on in the trial.

"I do not know," she said, "upon what you wish to question me. It may be that you will ask me something that I cannot tell you. About my father and my mother, and about everything that I have done since my arrival in France, I swear to answer freely. But about the revelations I have from God, I have never said or revealed anything except to King Charles only, and I will reveal nothing, though it cost me my head."

She explained that she had been forbidden by her "counsel" to discuss these matters. She added that in the course of eight days she would be quite certain as to what she should be silent about and what she should disclose; her voices would have instructed her. Kneeling, her two hands on the Gospels, she swore to do this. She then gave an account of her early years. When Cauchon warned her not to try to escape, she replied:

## *"If I Escape"*

"I do not accept that warning. If I escape, let no one accuse me of having broken my word, for I have given it to no one." When she complained of being in chains and having irons on her feet, Cauchon pointed out that she had tried before to escape.

"It is true," she replied, "I have tried to escape and I would try again." Even at that first examination Joan displayed a courageous determination not to accuse anyone or throw upon anyone else the responsibility for things which might justly or unjustly be imputed to her. She kept till the day of her death her resolution never to utter a single word of recrimination against the traitors and ingrates who, by abandoning or deliberately opposing her, had brought her to her present straits. She never even mentioned La Trémoille and mentioned, only to bless, the king who had deserted her.

The judges were eager to learn what she had told the king and what secret she had revealed to gain his confidence. But any matter which even touched upon her relations with Charles VII remained shrouded in mystery in the answers she made to their repeated questioning.

"When the voice pointed out your king to you," asked Cauchon, "was there any light in the room?"

"Pass on to something else," she replied.

"Did you see an angel hovering over your king?"

"Spare me. Pass on to something else."

Two days later (February 24) there was a third hearing at which sixty judges were present. When the Maid was requested for the third time to swear that she would speak the whole truth without reservation, she replied:

## A Heavy Responsibility

"Grant me permission to speak. By my faith, you might ask me such questions that I should not be able to speak the truth, for instance, concerning the revelations; for perchance you might force me to tell what I have sworn not to tell, and thus I should be perjured, which you ought not to desire. I tell you weigh well your words when you say that you are my judge. You are taking upon yourself a heavy responsibility and you overwhelm me. I have twice taken my oath, that is sufficient."

They finally extracted from her this oath: "I swear to speak the truth about those things which I know and which touch the case."

When Joan thought that Cauchon was pressing her for irrelevant details she did not hesitate to call him to account. Thus, when he wanted to know if Joan gave thanks on bended knee to the voice, Joan broke off and turning to the judge said: "You call yourself my judge. Beware of what you do, for truly I am sent by God, and you are putting yourself in great danger!"

"Joan," asked Cauchon, "are you in a state of grace?"

Here was a trap laid for her. If she answered "Yes," she would have been accused of pride and presumption. If she said "No," it would have been the equivalent of admitting the crimes charged against her. The question was so palpably unfair that one of the judges spoke out: "She is not bound to answer."

"If I am not, may God put me in one. If I am, may God keep me there. I should be the most unhappy woman in the world if I knew myself not to be in a state of grace. But if I were in mortal sin, the voice would not come to me."[4]

Joan was at her best in handling the questions which were designed to show that the so-called saints, in her frequent visions, were in fact demonical illusions. Asked what part of them she saw, she answered: "The face." Asked how they spoke if they had no other members, she answered: "I leave that to God." Asked if St. Margaret spoke in English when she appeared to the Maid, Joan answered: "Why should she speak in English, when she is not on the English side?"[5]

After Joan had mentioned that St. Michael was one of the saints who appeared to her, the judges asked what garments he wore. Joan replied, "I do not know." Asked if he was naked, Joan replied: "Think you that God has not the wherewithal to clothe him?"

## "One at a Time"

The judges sought to confuse and bewilder her by the number, irrelevance and incoherence of their queries. To add to the confusion they not infrequently questioned her together, intermingling their questions without waiting for an answer. At times she felt obliged to say to them: "Good, my lords, speak one at a time."

At the sixth hearing, on March 3, they increased their interrogations, repeating some that had been answered a dozen times. They adjured her to put aside her masculine attire.

"The time has not yet come," she said.

"Have you not said that escutcheons made in your likeness are lucky?"

"No, I said to our men: 'Force your way fearlessly among the English.' And I went myself."

The judges inquired about Friar Richard, the Franciscan preacher, who had followed her since the entrance into Troyes. Laughingly she recalled the incident "when the people of Troyes, doubting whether I came from God, sent the Friar out to meet me. He approached, making the sign of the cross and sprinkling holy water. 'Approach fearlessly,' I said to him, 'I shall not fly away.' "

Here was an instance of the good humor and utter simplicity, which she displayed throughout her life and even during the strain and miseries of the trial. "That this uneducated and ignorant peasant girl of nineteen," remarks L. Petit de Julleville, "depressed by her chains and her forsaken condition, should have been able to retain this alertness of mind, standing alone before fifty solemn, scowling, hostile doctors, seems scarcely less astounding than her victories. During the trial she astonished everyone and frequently embarrassed her enemies by the aptness, decision and clearness of her answers."[6]

## The Only Fault

The judges recurred to what was probably the only fault she had ever committed, namely, the leap at Beaurevoir, for which there were extenuating circumstances.

"I had been in that prison for four months," she explained. "I was told that the English were approaching. My voices forbade me to leap, but I was afraid of the English. Commending myself to God and to our Lady, I took the leap. I was wounded, but St. Catherine comforted me and told me I should recover."

"Did you not," they asked, "upon seeing yourself recaptured, give way to rage? Did you not blaspheme?"

"Never! And it is not my habit to swear."

On March 17 the examinations terminated. No less than seventy propositions were then drawn up, forming a disorderly, confused and unfair presentation of Joan's "crimes." But after she had heard and had replied to them, another set of twelve were drafted, better organized and less extravagantly worded. A large majority of the twenty-two judges who participated in the hearing declared Joan's visions and voices to be "false and diabolical."

Furthermore, they decided that, if she refused to retract, she would be handed over to the secular arm, which was merely a polite way of saying that she would be burned alive at the stake. Then on April 18 and May 2 certain formal admonitions, the first private, and then public, were administered to the pitiful victim. She refused, however, to make any submission which the judges would have regarded as satisfactory. Accordingly on May 9 she was threatened with torture, but refused to budge.

Meanwhile the twelve propositions were submitted to the University of Paris, which being extremely English in sympathy, denounced the Maid in violent terms. Fortified by this approval, the judges, forty-seven in number, held a final deliberation and forty-two reaffirmed that Joan should be declared heretical and handed over to the civil power if she still refused to retract.

## A Final Warning

Another warning was given in the prison on May 22, but Joan remained unshaken. The next day a stake was erected in the cemetery of St. Ouen, and in the presence of a large crowd she received the solemn admonition for the last time. Joan made a courageous protest against the preacher's insulting references to her king, Charles VII. By this time she was completely exhausted in body and mind.

For the first time her courage failed her. She agreed to sign some sort of retraction, but what its precise terms were will never be known. In the official record of the process there is inserted a form of retraction which is most humiliating. It is a long document which would have required a half hour to read.

What was read aloud to Joan and was signed by her must have been something quite different, for five witnesses at the rehabilitation, including the official who read it aloud, testified that it was only a matter of a few lines. Even so, Joan did not sign unconditionally, but plainly declared that she only retracted so far as it was God's will. In virtue of this concession, however, Joan was not then burned, but conducted back to prison.

The Burgundians and the English were enraged at the possibility of her escaping, but Cauchon is said to have placated them by saying "We shall have her yet." Unquestionably Joan's position would, in case of a relapse, be worse than before, since no second retraction could save her from the flames. Furthermore, as one of the points upon which she had been condemned was the wearing of male attire, a resumption of that apparel would itself constitute a relapse into heresy.

This is precisely what happened a few days later. This may have been traceable to any one of several possible causes. It may have been owing, as was afterward alleged, to a trap laid by her jailers in connivance with Cauchon.

It may have been due to a desire to defend her modesty from outrage. It may have been because her women's garments were taken from her. It may have been simply because she felt convinced that her enemies were determined to have her blood upon one pretext or another.

## A Unanimous Decision

On May 29, a court of thirty-seven Inquisitorial judges decided unanimously that Joan must be considered a lapsed heretic. The next morning, May 30, 1431, Joan received from Cauchon permission, unprecedented for a lapsed heretic, to make her confession and receive Holy Communion.

Accompanied by two Dominicans, she was then led to the Place du Vieux-Marche (Square of the Old Market) and placed on a high platform where she had to endure one more sermon. Guillaume Érard preached a sermon on the text, "As the branch cannot bear fruit of itself, except it abide in the vine."

In the middle of his sermon, with wretched taste he ventured to exclaim:"Ah! noble house of France, which has ever been a defender of the faith, hast thou been so misguided as to hold with a heretic and a schismatic! The pity of it is great."

Whereupon Joan pluckily broke in: "By my faith, sir, saving your reverence, I make bold to say to you and to swear to you, under penalty of my life, that King Charles is the most noble Christian of all Christians, and the one who best loves the faith and the Church."

## A Moving Tribute

Such a moving tribute rendered by a martyr to the king, who had forsaken her, enraged Cauchon.

"Make her hold her tongue," he shouted to the guards.

When the sermon was finished, a final exhortation to submit herself to the Church was addressed to the pitiful prisoner.

"As to submission to the Church," she replied, "it is a point upon which I have spoken. Let everything which I have said be sent to Rome and laid before the Sovereign Pontiff, to whom and to God first of all I appeal. But in regard to what I have said and done, it has all been by God's command."

"Are you ready to condemn all the words and actions which the clergy condemn?" asked Cauchon.

"I appeal to God and to our Holy Father the Pope."

"That is not sufficient, we cannot go all that distance to find the Pope. The bishops are judges in matter of faith, each in his own diocese."

## Joan at the Stake

Joan was bidden to consider the salvation of her soul by the preaching friars ministering to her. They dwelt upon "her crimes, her abjuration, her vain-glorious retraction, and finally declared her to be a heretic and backslider, excommunicated from the Church and abandoned to the secular authorities, with the request that they would deal mercifully with her and moderate her sentence, not going to the length of death or mutilation." This was sheer mockery, meaningless mumbo-jumbo, for turning one over to the secular arm meant only one thing—death at the stake.

Then an atrocious and monstrous illegal thing took place. The bailiff, a secular judge named Jean le Bouteiller, was present with his assistant judges, and it devolved upon him to decide the fate of the girl whom the Church had abandoned. This tool of the English party was in such a hurry to get the job done that he forgot to make some pretense of judging or at least condemning Joan before burning her, but merely said to the executioner: "Proceed with your duties." Thus Joan was burned without any explicit death sentence being passed upon her.[7]

The executioner seized her and led her to the stake, lighting the pyre. One of the Dominicans, Martin Lavenu, consoled Joan, who requested him to hold high a crucifix for her to see and to shout the assurance of salvation so loudly that she should hear him above the roar of the flames. As the flames were consuming her, she cried out continuously the name Jesus. "Until the last," reported Manchon, the recorder at the trial, "she declared that her voices came from God and had not deceived her." After death her ashes were thrown into the Seine.

## CHAPTER XIII

# Savonarola: A Heretic?

In a great cause: the block may soak their gore;
Their heads may sodden in the sun; their limbs
Be strung to city gates and castle walls—
But still their spirit walks abroad.

LORD BYRON

S CARCELY LESS FAMOUS than the trial of Joan of Arc is that of
Girolamo Savonarola, the Dominican reformer and prophet of
Florence, Italy. Both had marked similarities and differences.
Both felt they were called by God to lead their respective
countries out of the moral and religious wilderness and both were
willing to stake their lives for that cause. But Savonarola was a
scholar and an orator of exceptional ability, while the Maid of
Orléans was illiterate.

The Inquisition to which each was subject was quite different.
It was a court of thirty-seven Inquisitorial judges which condemned Joan as a lapsed heretic and sentenced her to the stake,
while it was the pope himself who played the leading Inquisitorial
role in having Savonarola sentenced to the flames as a heretic.
Both have dramatic elements which have caused their names to
be linked together in the respective histories not only of their two
countries but also of the world at large. Both have lessons to
teach us.

Born at Ferrara, Italy, September 21, 1452, Savonarola early displayed marked intellectual talents, especially in philosophy and
medicine. He was tutored by his paternal grandfather, Michele,
a distinguished physician and a man of rigid moral and religious

principles. He exercised a marked influence upon his grandson.

In 1474, while on a journey to Faenza, Girolamo heard a forceful sermon by an Augustinian and resolved to renounce the world. He carried out his decision at once and entered the Dominican novitiate at Bologna without first informing his parents. Four years later his studies brought him back to Ferrara where he formed a friendship with the noted humanist, Pico della Mirandola.

In 1482 he was assigned, as lecturer in theology, to the priory of San Marco, Florence. Here he gained a great reputation for his learning and asceticism, At Brescia in 1486 Savonarola explained the Book of Revelation and from that time became more and more absorbed in apocalyptic ideas concerning his own era, the judgment of God which threatened it, and the regeneration of the Church that was to follow. In 1490, at the insistence of the city's ruler, Lorenzo de Medici, he was recalled to Florence where he became prior of San Marco. This was to be the scene of his future labors and triumphs as well as his tragic fall.

## Pulpit Rules City

During this year Savonarola delivered his first sermons to ever increasing audiences in the Duomo, combining vigorous onslaughts on vice with sharp criticism of the Medici regime. All Florence thronged to hear him so that from his sermons at the cathedral he acquired a constantly growing influence over the people. Indeed, he virtually ruled the city from the pulpit.

His moral leadership was facilitated by the following political events: the fall of the Medici government, the Italian expedition of the French king, Charles VIII, in 1494, and the death of Lorenzo. The widely circulated rumor that Savonarola had refused him absolution on his deathbed has been proven by documentary evidence to be unfounded.

In autumn 1494 the French invaded Italy and were soon at the gates of Florence. Piero de Medici fled, and the whole city turned for guidance to Savonarola. He perceived in this invasion a fulfillment of the prophecies of a divine chastisement that was to fall upon Italy. In his judgment Charles VIII was the "sword of God." This identification was destined to have disastrous and ultimately fatal consequences for Savonarola. For some years he had formed the conviction, due in part to his absorption with the prophetical books of the Bible, that he was a prophet inspired to proclaim God's judgments upon Italy and the Church.

It was not this claim, however, but his support of the French invader that brought him into conflict with the reigning pope. In 1493 Alexander VI had entered into an alliance with Milan and Naples against the French and in 1495 the league included Venice, Spain and the Emperor Maximilian I. Florence, kept loyal to Charles by Savonarola, was a serious obstacle to the pope's plans. Even apart from the moral issues, it was inevitable that Alexander should come to consider Savonarola as a political nuisance and should attempt either to silence him or to remove him from Florence.

After the departure of King Charles a novel, unique and theocratic constitution, based on the social and political doctrines of the Dominican monk, was set up in Florence. Christ was proclaimed the king of Florence and the protector of its liberties. The moral life of its citizens was regenerated. Many persons brought articles of luxury, ornaments, dice, playing cards, the writings of pagans and lewd pictures of beautiful women to the monastery of San Marco, where they were publicly burned.

## Pope Summons Friar

A brotherhood, founded by Savonarola for young people, fostered a devout Christian life among its members. On Sunday some members of this brotherhood went from house to house and along the streets to exhort luxuriously dressed married and single women to lay aside frivolous ornament. The principles of the fiery prophet and severe judge of morals were carried out in too extreme a manner.

Success encouraged Savonarola to speak with ever increasing daring. Without regard to consequences, he lashed out at the pleasure-seeking, worldly and immoral life of the Florentines, so that a very large part of the citizens became temporarily contrite and returned to the practice of Christian virtue. From 1493 Savonarola spoke with increasing vehemence against the immoral life of many of the clergy, especially of the members of the

Roman Curia, even of the wearer of the tiara, Alexander VI, and against the wickedness of princes and courtiers.

On July 21, 1495, the pope sent to Savonarola a brief, in which he commended the miraculous fruits of Savonarola's work and summoned him to Rome to pronounce his prophecies from his own lips. Savonarola saw the trap prepared for him. Accordingly he asked to be permitted to delay his journey, pleading illness as an excuse. He mentioned that he "might be killed on the road," and he promised to send Alexander a book he had recently composed, which would give the pope all the necessary information.

The pope seemed to be satisfied, but on September 8 he sent a second brief in which praises now turned to curses and vituperation. He commanded Savonarola to go to Bologna under pain of excommunication. With respectful firmness Savonarola replied, pointing out no fewer than eighteen errors in the document. The brief was replaced by another of October 16, in which Savonarola was forbidden to preach.

A few months later, when Lent was drawing near, Florentine ambassadors called on the pope and requested him to revoke the ban. While refusing a formal revocation of the ban, the pope conceded it orally. This enabled Savonarola to deliver his sermons on Amos, in which he attacked the Roman court with renewed vigor. It seemed that some parts of it might be interpreted as referring to the pope's scandalous private life, and this increased the pope's ire and kindled his desire for vengeance. A college of theologians, however, found nothing to criticize in what the friar had said. Consequently he was able to begin, with no further remonstrances from Rome, his sermons on the prophet Micah.

## A Cardinal's Hat

At this juncture the wily pontiff tried a new tack. He would win over the friar by offering him a cardinal's hat. "A red hat?" he replied to Alexander's agent. "I want no hat but that of martyrdom, reddened with my own blood." [1]

In a brief of November 7, 1496, Alexander incorporated the Congregation of San Marco, of which Savonarola was vicar, with another, in which he would have lost all authority. Savonarola faced a difficult dilemma. If he obeyed, his reforms would be lost. If he disobeyed, he would be excommunicated. While protesting vigorously, Savonarola did not disobey because no one came forward to put the brief into force. Consequently he went on unperturbed in Advent 1496 and the following Lent with his series of sermons on Ezekiel.

During the carnival season that year his authority received a symbolic tribute in the "burning of the vanities" when personal ornaments, gaming tables and lewd pictures were burned. Events now turned against Savonarola, however, and even in Florence his power was lessened by unfavorable economic and political developments.

A plague prevented all preaching in Florence during the summer of 1497. But on October 13 Savonarola wrote to Alexander, asking his pardon but without declaring his submission on any specific point. The pope did not reply. Desperate, Savonarola then pushed his defiance to the point of celebrating Mass publicly on Christmas day and of recommencing his preaching in the Duomo. In his first sermon, February 11, he declared that whoever accepted his excommunication as valid was a heretic.

Fearing that Alexander was about to lay an interdict on the city, the city council (Signoria) earnestly requested Savonarola to stop preaching, and he did. He took, however, the further and fatal step of sending letters to the sovereigns of Europe, calling on them to summon a council to reform the church and to depose Alexander. The die was now cast and there would be no retreating by either party.

Clerical friends reminded Savonarola of the dangerous course on which he embarked in calling upon lay rulers to appoint a new pope. They pointed out that this would place supreme authority in the hands of secular sovereigns and thus destroy the independence of the Church—a goal for which she had so long struggled. Savonarola acknowledged the danger, but contended that he was not attacking the papacy itself but merely its scandalous present occupant.

Furthermore, he declared that all efforts at reform of the Church were doomed to failure because of the example of Alexander. "How can the Church discipline its priests for living with mistresses," he asked, "when the pope does the same and flaunts his illegitimate offspring before the public? How can we exalt holy poverty when the pope flagrantly sells benefices and other offices to the highest bidder?"

There seems little doubt that Savonarola's opposition to Alexander VI stemmed primarily from the burning conviction that the notorious and scandalous personal life of the pontiff not only rendered impossible any reform in the Church but would spread its contagion throughout every phase of the Church's ministry and life. Since this, in Savonarola's judgment, was the central issue, let us look briefly at the personal life of the man who is generally acknowledged to have been the most immoral prelate ever to sit upon the papal throne. It is a painful task, but any treatment of Savonarola is sadly incomplete if it is shirked under the pretext of not wishing to scandalize the "little ones."

An impartial appraisal of the career of Alexander must distinguish between the man and the office. Respect and reverence for the papal office do not necessarily require the same sentiments toward its human occupants. Hence there is no reason to presuppose worthiness, merits and holiness when they are actually lacking in the minister, be he a humble missionary in an African jungle or the wearer of the papal tiara in St. Peter's Cathedral. Human weaknesses may be cheerfully acknowledged without disturbing our joyous appreciation of divinely revealed truth. Accordingly we undertake a brief sketch of Rodrigo Borgia to help us appraise his character.

## Alexander: A Renaissance Product

Rodrigo Borgia was born at Xativa, near Valencia, Spain, in January, 1431. His mother's brother was Cardinal Alfonso Borgia, who later became Pope Callistus III. The young Rodrigo had not chosen his profession when the elevation of his uncle to the papacy opened up new prospects. He was immediately adopted into the family of Callistus with no consideration of the question as to whether or not he had a vocation to the priesthood.

In 1456, at the youthful age of twenty-five, he was made cardinal-deacon of St. Nicolo and held that title until 1471, when he was appointed cardinal-bishop of Albano. Five years later he was made cardinal-bishop of Porta and dean of the Sacred College of

Cardinals. His official position in the Curia after 1457 was that of vice-chancellor, an enormously lucrative office which he held until 1492.

In June, 1460, in his twenty-ninth year, he received the following scathing letter of rebuke from Pope Pius II for his scandalous misconduct in Siena, which shocked the whole town and the court:

Beloved Son, We have heard that, four days ago, several ladies of Siena—women entirely given over to worldly frivolities—were assembled in the gardens of Giovanni di Bichis and that you, quite forgetful of the high office with which you are invested, were with them from the seventeenth to the twenty-second hour. With you was one of your colleagues whose age alone, if not the dignity of his office, ought to have recalled him to his duty. We have heard that the most licentious dances were indulged in, none of the allurements of love were lacking and you conducted yourself in a wholly worldly manner. Shame forbids mention of all that took place—not only the acts themselves but their very names are unworthy of your position. In order that your lusts might be given free rein the husbands, fathers, brothers and kinsmen of the young women were not admitted. . . . All Siena is talking about this orgy. . . . Our displeasure is beyond words. . . . A cardinal should be beyond reproach. . . [2]

This was a period of European history comprising approximately the fourteenth, fifteenth and sixteenth centuries, which is called the Renaissance. It marked the gradual ending of the Middle Ages and the advent of the modern world. It was ushered in with a glorification of the learning, art and culture of Greece and Rome. The glorification came ultimately to include not only the classical works but also the hedonistic and humanistic ideals which permeated the writings and the art of pagan times.

The Renaissance rendered skepticism fashionable and weakened the sanctions of religion without supplying another basis for morality. After describing the deeper degradation in both the moral and the spiritual condition of society brought about by the Renaissance in Italy, Lea concludes: "The world has probably never seen a more total disregard of all law, human and divine, than that displayed by both the Church and the laity during the pontificates of Sixtus IV, Innocent VIII and Alexander VI. Increase of culture and wealth seemed only to afford new attractions and enlarged opportunities for luxury and vice, and from the highest to the lowest there was indulgence of unbridled appetites, with a cynical disregard even of hypocrisy." [3]

As vice-chancellor of the Roman Church, Cardinal Rodrigo Borgia was in an excellent position to amass great wealth. This was increased by revenues from his abbeys in Italy and Spain, and his three bishoprics of Valencia, Porto and Cartagena. It is no wonder that a contemporary Roman chronicler wrote: "It is believed that he possessed more gold and riches of every sort than all the cardinals put together, excepting only Estouteville." [4]

## Borgia Buys Papal Tiara

Following the death of Pope Innocent VIII in 1492, a conclave of cardinals met on August 6 to elect a successor. The first four days Borgia bargained incessantly and "lined up" many supporters. Chief among these was Cardinal Ascanio Sforza of Milan, who proved to be a good bargainer and extracted from Borgia not only the lucrative office of vice-chancellor but also a huge cash payment as well.

By the evening of August 10, Borgia had bought the votes of thirteen cardinals, including members of the oldest and noblest Roman families. He needed but one more vote and he bought it from the ninety-six-year-old Cardinal of Venice for the modest sum of 5,000 ducats. The conclave went through the gestures of election, praying to the Holy Spirit for guidance, and early in the morning of August 11 the name of Cardinal Rodrigo Borgia was taken from the urn.

"I am pope! I am pope!" exclaimed Borgia excitedly as he hurried to robe himself in papal vestments. Burchard, the master of ceremonies, was instructed to prepare slips of paper, bearing the legend, "We have for pope, Alexander VI, Rodrigo Borgia of Valencia," and to scatter them among the crowd outside. It is not without significance that he chose for his name not the Piuses, nor the Clements, nor the Innocents, but the name of the mightiest pagan conqueror of antiquity.

Heard on the tongues of many Romans on the days following the election was the saying: "Alexander sells the keys, the altar and Christ himself. He has a right to do so for he *bought* them." [5]

When someone criticized his wholesale distribution of pardons, even for the most monstrous crimes, one of which included the murder of a daughter by the father, Alexander retorted: "It is not God's wish that a sinner should die, but that he should live—and *pay*."

## Alexander's Family Life

Along about the year 1460 the young Rodrigo Borgia had begun an association with Vannozza Catanei, a thrice-married member of one of the lesser noble families of Rome. Over the ensuing twenty years Vannozza bore him four children: Giovanni, Cesare, Lucrezia and Joffre. Before he met Vannozza, Borgia had fathered at least four other children by other women. For one of these, his eldest son Pedro, he secured the dukedom of Gandia in Spain; but the young man died before his father became pope, and his title was passed on to the next in line, the fourteen-year-old Giovanni.

Not much is known of Vannozza, but obviously she must have possessed some special qualities of both character and charm to hold such an important lover for decades. Upon her Borgia lavished both his love and protection even after her beauty had faded, at least in part, and a younger woman had at last taken her place in his bed.

Borgia considerately supplied her with three successive husbands, each of whom gave her his name in return for the comfortable living provided by her secret lover. She must have felt her anomalous situation, for in her letters to her daughter she was in the habit of signing them "your fortunate and unfortunate mother." In 1486 when she was in her mid-forties, she married for the third and last time, giving her a total of six husbands.

It was at this point that Borgia terminated a relationship that had endured for almost a quarter of a century. The two older children, Giovanni and Cesare, had long since left the maternal home, and now the six-year-old Lucrezia and her young brother were removed from Vannozza's care and placed in the home of Borgia's cousin and lifelong confidante, Madonna Adriana.

Here it was, three years later, that Borgia met the beautiful

Giulia Farnese, who came to Adriana's house as her future daughter-in-law. In 1489, when Giulia was about sixteen, she was married to Adriana's only son, and about the same time was added to the lengthy list of Borgia's mistresses. As Adriana was a widow, there was no husband to raise difficulties about the unconventional situation.

The Farnese family, who might have objected to the debauching of a daughter, was evidently not only satisfied but even pleased with the flow of gifts from the papal cornucopia. Shortly after ascending the papal throne as Alexander VI, the pope made Alessandro Farnese, Giulia's brother, a cardinal. The Romans joshingly called him the "Petticoat Cardinal" and he bore the title until he too became pope in his turn, as Paul III.

"Borgia," observes E. R. Chamberlin, "was forty years his mistress' senior, but it was not the obvious story of a family pandering their daughter to an elderly roué for the sake of gain. Giulia was a willing partner even after she matured and could, within limits, make her own decisions, for her lover was an immensely attractive man." [6] Carte Strozziane echoes the same thought in a somewhat different way: "He was a comely person of cheerful countenance full of honeyed discourse, who gains the affection of all women he admires and attracts them as the lodestone attracts the iron." [7]

## Alexander's Unrestrained Nepotism

Alexander's efforts to place his sons in high positions of church and state and to have them as well as his daughters marry into wealthy and powerful families brought him many headaches and endless embarrassment. Like a stern Nemesis, his nepotism pursued him to the grave. While still a cardinal, he married one daughter, Girolama, to a Spanish nobleman. For his son, Pedro Luis, he had bought from the Spanish monarch the Duchy of Gandia. When Pedro died soon afterward, he secured it for Juan, his oldest surviving son by Vannozza.

Perhaps the greatest mistake was his selection of his boy Cesare as the ecclesiastical representative of the Borgias. In 1480 Pope Innocent VIII made the boy eligible for Orders by absolving him from the ecclesiastical irregularity that followed his birth from the union of a cardinal-bishop and a married woman. The pope conferred several Spanish benefices on him, the last being the bishopric of Pompeluna, in the neighborhood of which, by a strange fatality, he eventually met his death.

A week after his coronation Alexander appointed Cesare, now eighteen years old, to the archbishopric of Valencia; but Cesare neither went to Spain nor did he ever take Orders. He followed this by creating Cesare a cardinal. Neither did His Holiness neglect his favorite daughter Lucrezia. When in her thirteenth year, she was a married woman of six months' standing. Legally speaking, it was her third marriage, for nuptial contracts had been exchanged on her behalf twice before, with noblemen in her father's native country.

But when Cardinal Rodrigo Borgia became Pope Alexander VI, Lucrezia's value increased astronomically and Alexander repudiated both contracts and sought a more suitable husband. He turned to the man who was second in influence only to the pope: Cardinal Ascanio Sforza, who had so powerfully helped Rodrigo Borgia to reach the papal throne and who was now vice-chancellor of the Roman Church. The cardinal proposed his cousin Giovanni, who was most acceptable to the pope.

## A Vatican Wedding

Giovanni was delighted at the prospect of becoming the pope's son-in-law and the deal was finalized. The wedding was celebrated in the Vatican on June 12, 1493, in the presence of the pope, ten cardinals and the chief nobles of Rome with their ladies. No precedent was being established, for Pope Innocent VIII had celebrated his son's marriage in the same place.

Burchard, the meticulous papal master of ceremonies, describes the gala scene: "Don Juan Borgia, Duke of Gandia, the pope's son and Donna Lucrezia's elder brother, was commanded by His Holiness to escort Lucrezia. He brought her in as far as the last room, a Negro girl carrying her train, and she was followed by Donna Battistina—the granddaughter of Pope Innocent VIII of unblessed memory—and her train too was borne by a Negress. Donna Giulia Farnese, the pope's concubine, and many other

Roman ladies, numbering in all about one hundred and fifty, followed Lucrezia and Battistina."

It seems that in their excitement, to the horror of Burchard, the ladies failed to genuflect as they passed the pope on his great throne, "except Lucrezia and a few beside her." This despite Burchard's admonitions. The festivities continued all night. The ubiquitous ambassador from Ferrara thus depicts the festivities briefly in a letter to his master:

When the banquet was over the ladies danced and, as an interlude, we had an excellent play with much singing and music. The pope and all the others were there. What more can I say? My letter would never end were I to describe it all. Thus we spent the whole night, whether for good or ill I will leave Your Highness to determine.[8]

## No Happy Ending

What was the outcome of this marriage, performed with such pomp and ceremony? Unfortunately we cannot say of it what novelists are fond of saying of many newly wedded couples, "And they lived happily ever afterward." Pope Alexander's daughter was married for the second time, as the first stage of a complex plan to place her brother Cesare upon the throne of Naples. But how could this be, since she had been validly married by the head of Christendom and the couple had lived together for three and a half years?

Giovanni was asked to agree to a divorce. He refused and pressure was at once put on him. An obedient papal commission accepted Lucrezia's statement that she was still a virgin and that Giovanni Sforza was impotent. If true, this afforded canonical grounds for a declaration of nullity. Observers were quick to point out, however, how curious it was that there had not been the slightest hint of impotency previous to Alexander's expressed wish of using his daughter again as a pawn for the purpose indicated.

Actually Lucrezia may have saved Giovanni's life, unless she and her brother had planned together to give him a stern warning. Cesare came to her suite when Sforza's chamberlain was with her. She instructed the chamberlain to hide and he heard Cesare's declaration that he would get rid of Sforza by murder. After

Cesare had left, Lucrezia instructed the chamberlain to tell his master what he had heard. This he did, and Giovanni immediately fled.

In July, 1498, Lucrezia was next given in marriage to Alfonso of Aragon, duke of Bisceglia, an illegitimate son of Alfonso II of Naples. The following year, however, the papal-Neapolitan alliance collapsed when Alexander and Cesare came to an understanding with Louis XII of France, and in August, 1499, Alfonso fled from Rome. In October he returned with Lucrezia. Then on July 15, 1500, as he was leaving the Vatican, he was attacked by assassins. On August 18, as he was recovering from his wounds, he was murdered in his house, apparently at Cesare's orders.

The early years of Alexander VI's reign on the papal throne sounded the authentic note of his whole pontificate. Despite occasional outbursts of penitence and shame, he continued his worldly and immoral life to the end. Cesare outdid him in villainy and wickedness and his name has become a symbol of unscrupulous, treacherous and scandalous conduct and casts shame upon his father. Lucrezia, who seems to have been more sinned against than sinning, suffers from having been the pawn of her unscrupulous father and her name has not escaped tarnishment from his notorious immorality and the still worse deeds of her brother Cesare.

It is hoped that this brief glimpse of the life, time and character of Pope Alexander VI will give the reader a better understanding of the reasons why Savonarola was convinced in conscience that he must, for the good of the Church, speak out, not against the papacy, but against its occupant, cost what it may.

## Pope's Example

When the church has been threatened with widespread disaster, there have not been wanting saintly men and women to warn the church and to urge her to adopt reform which would lessen the likelihood of such calamities. For centuries a succession of such prophets—Joachim of Flora, St. Catherine of Siena, St. Birgitta of Sweden, Tommasino of Foligno and the monk Telesforo—had arisen with predictions which were received with respect and reverence.

Savonarola saw himself called to play a similar role. His absorption with the prophets of the Old Testament deepened that conviction, which was further strengthened when he looked at the widespread corruption in both the head and members of the Church.

A census of prostitutes disclosed that 680 were plying their trade unmolested each night in Rome. "When the vicar of the city," reports Lea, "issued a decree ordering all ecclesiastics to dismiss their concubines, Innocent VIII sent for him and ordered its withdrawal, saying that all priests and members of the curia kept them, and that it was no sin."[9]

While such a degradation of morals greatly disturbed Savonarola, he was even more upset and agonized over the scandalous example of Pope Alexander's private life, in which concubines played so important and conspicuous a role during virtually all his adult life. Often did Savonarola reflect upon the scene in the scriptures, where Christ is depicted carrying his cross to Calvary and some women bewailed and lamented him.

Turning to them he said: "Daughters of Jerusalem, weep not over me; but weep for yourselves and for your children. For behold the days shall come wherein they will say: 'Blessed are the barren and the wombs that have not borne and the paps that have not given suck. Then shall they begin to say to the mountains: "Fall upon us; and to the hills: Cover us. For if in the green wood they do these things, what shall be done in the dry?" ' " [10]

The Savior does not reject their sympathy, but warns them of the terrible chastisements that shall befall Jerusalem. The meaning of this figurative language is, "If the Romans who know that I am innocent, treat me so severely, how much more severely will they treat you as a rebellious nation." The figure is taken from the fact that dry wood burns more easily than green wood. So the Florentines, who know of the innocence and holiness of Savonarola, can expect to receive more severe punishment than the other Christians of Italy, who do not know of the dedication and holiness of the Dominican prophet.

## Appeal to Sovereigns

After giving Alexander fair warning on March 13, 1497, to look to his safety because there could no longer be a truce between them, the Dominican friar appealed to the sovereigns of Christendom, in letters purporting to be written under the mandate of God. It called upon them to convene a general council for the reformation of the Church in its head and members. It was diseased, he declared, and because of its intolerable stench, God had not permitted it to have a lawful head.

"The moment of decision has arrived," wrote Savonarola in his *Letter to the Princes.* "The Lord commands me to reveal new secrets, and make known to the world the peril by which the bark of St. Peter is threatened owing to your long neglect. The Church is teeming with abominations from the crown of her head to the soles of her feet. Yet, not only do you apply no remedy, but you do homage to the cause of the woes by which she is defiled. . . ."

Continuing, he said: "Now, I testify, God being my witness, that *this Alexander is no Pope*, nor can he be held as one. Leaving aside the mortal sin of simony by which he obtained the papal chair and daily sells the benefices of the Church to the highest bidder, and also leaving aside his other evident vices, I declare solemnly that *he is no Christian and believes in no God.* Infidelity can go no further." [11]

It was at this point, February, 1498, that Savonarola committed a fatal blunder. It was due doubtless to his inexperience in matters of statecraft, and it was to send him flying headlong to an ignominious and horrible death at the flaming stake a scant two months later. What was his mistake? Instead of dispatching the letters directly to the sovereigns, he first sent copies to supposedly trusted friends, requesting them to back him in the gigantic task of ousting the supreme pontiff of the Universal Church.

Some of these fell into hostile hands and were forwarded to the pope. Other copies were sent to ambassadors who were urged to request their sovereigns to express to the pope their full agreement with Savonarola's denunciations and proposals.

With the exception of the king of France, apparently none of the other monarchs received Savonarola's missives. Although the ambassadors did, they not only took no action but did not even acknowledge receipt of the friar's letters. A copy fell into the hands of Cardinal Ascanio Sforza in Rome, who hastened with it to the pope. His rage can easily be imagined.

## *Threat of Council*

Since the Councils of Constance and Basel, the convocation of a council had been the cry of every reformer and the terror of the incumbent pope. In 1482, Ferdinand and Isabella, by the threat of calling a council, brought Pope Sixtus to renounce his alleged right to fill the sees of Spain with his own favorites. In 1495 a rumor circulated throughout Europe that the Emperor was about to cite the pope to a general council to be held in Florence. Because of the discontent throughout Christendom the prospect of a council was enough to terrify Alexander.

The chips were down. Now not words, but actions were called for. The last thing Alexander wanted was an investigation of his private life, focused especially upon his practice of maintaining concubines. While celibacy was required by canon law, it was honored more in the breach than in the observance in many countries of Europe. Realizing that he was peculiarly vulnerable here, Alexander strove desperately to prevent the convocation of a general council which might well result in his expulsion from the papal office.

By long hours of prayer, Scripture reading and meditation Savonarola sought to strengthen himself for the approaching climax. In the social revolution which he had effected in Florence, he neither strove for his own personal advancement nor permitted any of his colleagues to make personal profit. He fortified himself by recalling often the words of the saintly and scholarly Jean Gerson, acclaimed by many as the greatest churchman of that century: "We must show humility and meekness to the sovereign pontiff, but, when humility fails, then we must assume a courageous freedom."

On May 12, 1497, Alexander announced the excommunication of Savonarola, and on June 19 the latter published a letter against the excommunication as being fraudulently obtained, and he sought to show that the judgment against him was null and void.

The Florentine ambassadors endeavored to prevent any further measures against him, but their hopes were dimmed when Savonarola became more defiant and resumed preaching in the Duomo.

## Ordeal of Fire

In Florence itself the opposition to Savonarola increased, especially when the pope threatened to put the city under interdict. Frightened by that threat, the city council requested Savonarola to cease his preaching. One of his Dominican colleagues, Dominico de Pescia, offered to prove the truth of his master's cause by throwing himself from the roof of the Palazzo della Signoria or by entering fire.

A Franciscan adversary, Francesco della Puglia, took it up and offered to share the ordeal with Savonarola. The latter refused, however, unless a papal legate and ambassadors from all Christian princes could be present so that it might be made the commencement of a general reform in the Church. Frà Dominico accepted the challenge and offered to establish, by argument or miracle, these propositions:

1. The Church of God requires renovation. 2. The Church is to be scourged. 3. The Church will be renovated. 4. After chastisement Florence will be renovated and will prosper. 5. The infidel will be converted. 6. The excommunication of Frà Girolamo is void. 7. There is no sin in not observing the excommunication.

This statement was affixed to the door of the Church of Santa Croce. Passions were inflamed on both sides, and partisans kept the city in an uproar. In 1215 the Council of Lateran had prohibited all ordeals of all kinds, and they were definitely under the ban of the Universal Church. Francesco declared that he had no personal quarrel with Dominico and, if Savonarola would undergo the trial, he would only produce an adversary. This he did in the person of Frà Rondinelli, a Franciscan.

On the other side, the friars of San Marco, numbering nearly three hundred, pledged to submit themselves to the ordeal and Savonarola declared that in such a cause anyone could do so without risk. So enormous was the enthusiasm that when, on the day before the trial, he preached on the subject in San Marco, all the audience rose and offered to take Dominico's place in vindicating the truth.

On April 7 in the Piazza della Signoria a large pile of dry wood was built to the height of a man's eyes, with a central gangway through which the contestants were to pass. An enormous crowd turned out to witness the strange contest. The people waited patiently through torrents of rain and, late in the day when the contestants could not agree on the terms of the ordeal, they felt cheated out of the promised spectacle and were furious. Savonarola had confidently promised them a miracle and their faith in him as a spokesman of God was badly shaken.

## Savonarola Tortured

Savonarola and his two disciples, Domenico Buonvicini and Silvestro Maruffi, were taken prisoners and subjected to torture, especially that of the *strappado*. With their wrists tied behind them, they were raised to a great height and then dropped to within a few inches or feet of the floor. This was repeated so often that the pain became unbearable and the pathetic victim, driven out of his mind, would thus be compelled to admit virtually any charge which the papal Inquisitorial commissioners, sent from Rome, desired to make against him.

Savonarola was obliged to endure not merely one trial but three so that his enemies could inflict the maximum of torture upon him. His case had been already prejudged in Rome, as Romolino, the leader of the papal commissioners or Inquisitors, openly boasted: "We shall have a fine bonfire, for I bring the sentence with me." [12] The whole proceedings were a barefaced mockery of justice.

A notary was hired to garble the report of the trial. One of the examiners admitted these falsifications in later years; another at that time threw up his office, declaring he wanted no share in this homicide. Even after eleven days of torture the commissioners were obliged to send word to the pope: "By many and assiduous tortures, after many days, we extorted scarce anything from him by force."

Finally when driven virtually senseless, he involved himself in all sorts of contradictions as to his visions and prophecies as a result of the same unfair interrogatories that the Inquisitors had employed with Joan of Arc. After similar tortures and questioning the commissioners condemned his two Dominican colleagues to the same fate. They too endured the same cruel tortures and rejoiced in remaining with their master to the bitter end.

## Alexander's Glee

In Rome Alexander was beaming with joy. He had silenced the voice in Christendom that had called out most clearly and valiantly for his removal from the papal throne and for the house-cleaning so desperately needed by the Church. Now he could continue his philandering with greater ease and comfort.

Hence it was that in his glee he showered plenary indulgences upon all who had striven against Savonarola, "regardless of the crimes and even murders which they might have committed for this purpose." [13] This was a flat contradiction of Catholic doctrine that indulgences can be gained only by persons free from mortal sin, and murder would surely be one of the greatest of these.

One of the tortures inflicted by the bailiffs was to hang Savonarola upside down and to ply him with questions. This would continue until the victim was incoherent and his answers could be twisted into self-incriminations. The shrieks of pain could be heard outside the torture chamber and naturally terrified the other two Dominicans, but the tortures provoked not curses from Savonarola but prayers for the forgiveness of his torturers.

"There are but few if any parallels," observes Pierre Van Paassen, "in the history of Christian martyrdom to be placed alongside the almost incredible demonstration of fortitude, love of souls, and forgiveness with which Savonarola confronted his tormentors in the last weeks of his life. There he lay on the bare stone floor of a prison cell without bed, chair or blankets and the most elementary hygienic facilities. When he asked his jailer for water he was given to drink from a bowl which was first purposely befouled. He suffered excruciating pain in the abdomen. His whole body was bruised and crushed by the hideous brutality. It is almost inconceivable that he did not succumb or was driven insane." [14]

## Savonarola's One Request

The one request which Savonarola made when he recovered the power of rational speech was that they spare his right arm and hand so that he might be able to write. This they did. Lying on the floor of the Alberghettino prison, he wrote his *Meditation on Psalm 51*, which is a heart-searing lament, consisting of prayers in praise of God and pleadings for his mercy and love. Published in many languages, it is among the most widely circulated spiritual works in world literature—second only to the Bible and *The Imitation of Christ* by Thomas à Kempis—and one of the most moving, as the following paragraphs show:

Where shall I turn, to whom shall I flee, I who have no one left in all the world to give me aid or solace? Who will take pity on me? I dare not lift my eyes to heaven for I have grievously sinned. On earth I find no refuge for I have become an object of scandal and offense to men. What then shall I do? Shall I give myself over to despair? No, this I must not, for God abundantly pardons, my redeemer is full of mercy. God alone is my refuge, He will not abandon the work of his hands and the human being made in his image. I approach thee, therefore, O Lord, my God, as a beaten and defeated soul. In thee alone is my hope. In thee alone seek I refuge. But what words shall I speak? I will plead for thy commiseration, for thy pardon and forgiveness. . . .

O dear Lord, my God, have mercy on me! O hidden God, O God who canst not be understood by human intelligence, nor expressed with the words of man or of angels, O incomprehensible God, O unseizable God, to thee I call because thou art reality, the sole reality, the source and cause of all reality. Thou canst not change thine own essence and nature. Thou must carry out thy work which is to create, to love, to forgive, to redeem, to bless. . . . Look down upon my miserable state. My misery is great because of my sins. I have sinned against thee, against thee who so loved me that thou camest down from heaven to be crucified for me. O Lord, my God, my Rock and my Redeemer, forgive my sins! . . . Deep calls unto deep, the abyss of misery calls to the abyss of divine mercy. The abyss of sin calls to the abyss of grace. May thine abyss of mercy devour my abyss of sin and blot it out. . . . [15]

Frà Girolamo began to write a treatise, *In God Is My Trust*. But some of his enemies, fearful of the growing sympathy for him, saw to it that quills, ink and writing paper were removed from his cell. The Signoria received a letter from Louis XII, king of France, urging cessation of any further disciplinary action against Savonarola. Among the papal Inquisitors were G. Turriano, an eighty-four-year-old Dominican who covered his face with his hands during most of the trial, and Francesco Romolino, bishop of Ilerda. He was one of the most profligate members of the Roman Court, and a tutor of Cesare, of the same savage and murderous disposition as his pupil. He informed the other Inquisitors that Pope Alexander's instructions to take the friar's life were irrevocable, and quoted him as saying, "Even if Savonarola is a saint like John the Baptist, he must die."

After Girolamo had been suspended for a long time by his one bruised and swollen arm, he was dropped. When he was loosened, he lay on the floor in a dead faint. Upon recovering consciousness, he was informed that unless he signed a confession, drawn up by Ser Francisco Ceccone, appointed as notary by Romolino, the torture would be renewed. Scarcely had he signed it, when to the surprise of all present, he rose to his feet and put on his Dominican robe.

## Revokes Confession

"I signed," he said, "because I was afraid of being tortured anew. I revoke my confession entirely. If I am to die, I will die for the truth. The truth is that God did speak through me to the people of Florence. I speak the truth now. I deny all your accusations. The Church of God will be purified. Florence too after the scourging, will be purified and will prosper."[16]

In that moment his grandeur of soul and awesome moral superiority shone forth like a flash of lightning in his dark and loathsome torture chamber. How he could stand on his feet after such wracking physical torture and speak with such fearlessness bore witness to the unimpeachable purity and consistency of his holy life.

Early in the morning of May 22, 1498, Frà Girolamo Savonarola, with his legs chained together, was carried back to the Signoria tower. Along with him Domenico Buonvicini and Silvestro Maruffi were condemned to be defrocked on the morrow and to be handed over to the secular arm for execution "as heretics and schismatics and for the teaching of novelties." The trial was a travesty of justice, for there was not found the slightest evidence of heresy or schism in any of the three Dominicans.

A scaffold was erected in the Piazza della Signoria in approximately the same spot where the structure for the ordeal by fire stood a month before, and where today lies the bronze memorial slab in front of Ammannati's fountain. Fagots were piled up to the height of a man's shoulder. Three separate tribunals were erected, one for the lay commissioners, one for the papal Inquisitors and one for the members of the city council. The square was filled with people eager for the spectacle.

At dawn on May 23, the turnkey awakened Frà Girolamo who had fallen asleep with his head resting on the knees of the Benedictine monk, Jacopo Niccolini, to whom he had gone to confession. He celebrated Mass, at which his two Dominican brethren assisted. Bailiffs led the three downstairs, where two Dominicans divested them of their white Dominican robes and black mantles.

Kissing his old tattered robe, Frà Girolamo said: "Oh, sacred gown, how ardently I desired you. God gave you to me and I can say with all my heart that I have kept you unsullied and holy. I still hold you pure in my hands and I would willingly always hold you. But you are taken away from me."

## *"I Separate You"*

The three were divested, piece by piece, of their Mass vestments by Bishop Paganotti, a former pupil of Girolamo's, to signify their desecration. At one point in the rite, the bishop said: "I separate you from the Church Militant," whereupon Savonarola gently interrupted him: "Not from the Church Triumphant in heaven, for that is beyond your power." Overcome with emotion, the bishop corrected himself and then broke into a fit of sobbing.

Bishop Romolino read the entire minutes of the trial, including the so-called confessions and the verdict. Then, departing from the written text, he spoke these strange and surprising words: "I have received word from His Holiness Alexander VI this very day that he grants you a plenary indulgence in the moment of death with release from all canonical censures and excommunications. His Holiness sets you back into your original state of sinlessness. . . . You will not undergo the punishment of purgatory. . . . Do you accept?"[17] All three bowed in assent.

The formalities had begun at eight in the morning, and it was now three o'clock. Frà Silvestro, the first to be hanged, climbed up the ladder. At the top an executioner fastened an iron collar around his neck, which would strangle him. The executioner pushed him off the ladder and the body swung free. Those near the scaffold heard the few muffled cries, "Jesus have mercy! Christ have mercy!" Then there was a silence that gripped the vast multitude which packed the square and gazed in awe at the spectacle.

Next came Domenico. Ascending the ladder, he called out: "The Church will be purified. The Holy Spirit will send his heavenly fire." The bodies of the two friars hung at the two extremities of the crossbeam. The middle, the place of honor, was reserved for the "arch criminal and heresiarch," as the verdict called Frà Girolamo.

As he walked to the ladder, some of his most bitter enemies, called Compagnacci, broke through the police lines and slashed at him with their knives and daggers and spit upon him. When he reached the top rung, he turned and faced the awe-stricken crowd. Then he tugged at the rope around his hands, as if he was trying to free his right hand to raise it in blessing, as he had always done when facing a congregation. Whereupon the executioner struck him a hard blow on the back of the head, sending him careening from the ladder into immortality.

At precisely 3:30 in the afternoon the vast pile of fagots was kindled and smoke rose in a thick column hiding the bodies from view. But soon a strong breeze blew into the Piazza, dispersing the smoke, and the bodies of the three friars were visible again. Great care was taken to see that the bodies were completely consumed and that every bit of ashes was scrupulously gathered up and thrown into the Arno River to prevent the preservation of relics.

Yet at the risk of their lives, some of his disciples secretly managed to secure a few relics which were treasured and honored even to recent times. For more than two centuries the place of execution was secretly covered with flowers on the night of the anniversary, May 23. The life which Girolamo, as a young Dominican novice, had offered to his Creator, he now surrendered in its entirety.

## An Uncrowned Saint

Centuries ago a great Teacher in ancient Galilee summed up his message to mankind when he said: "This is my commandment, that you love one another as I have loved you. Greater love than this no one has, that one lay down his life for his friends." [18] Frà Girolamo gave his life not only for his friends but for his enemies as well. More than this no man can do.

Writing about Savonarola, Van Paassen says that "his life was one of the greatest. We cannot lament his fate. His body they could kill, but not his soul. The martyr's death suffered by Savonarola was a proper and fitting climax to his life as a prophet. He ran his course as by special providential arrangement. His belief that the world and all men in it are at the disposal of a transcendent power was never shaken. What he desired most ardently, and also clearly foresaw, the renewal of the Church of God, became a glorious reality a few decades later." [19]

Antonio Lupi, O.P., also pays tribute to the life, achievement and holiness of the great Florentine: "His doctrine, as the Church was to declare later, is untainted by heresy; the legitimacy of his conduct has been demonstrated. . . . His voice has outlived his own day; it belongs to the Church immortal. Witness his veneration by so many saints since his time and the steady growth of a general appreciation of his achievement. . . . He remains for us a model of dauntless and unshakeable integrity: a sign that is contradicted, but a sign of salvation for many." [20]

Hanging from the infamous gibbet in the Piazza della Signoria in Florence on that May day, Savonarola gave mute but eloquent testimony to the awesome reality that the path to truth, holiness and progress leads from gallows to gallows and from stake to stake. In canonizing Savonarola, the Church would be honoring herself. Long after the names of the papal Inquisitors who condemned him are either forgotten or recalled with odium, the name of Frà Girolamo Savonarola will be remembered. It will be treasured not only by the Church and her members but also by people of all faiths, who admire honesty, reverence for truth, and a willingness to die in the battle of decency against indecency, debauchery and corruption.

## CHAPTER XIV

# Galileo Faces the Inquisition

Some day, after mastering the winds, the waves, the tides and gravity, we shall harness for God the energies of love and then, for the second time in the history of the world, man will discover fire.

TEILHARD DE CHARDIN

ONE OF THE MOST FAMOUS TRIALS conducted by the Roman Inquisition was that of the Italian mathematician, inventor, astronomer and physicist, Galileo Galilei, commonly known by his first name. While his scientific discoveries and inventions have contributed to his fame, it is his condemnation by the Inquisition which most people remember. Instead of dispatching him into obscurity, the Roman Inquisitors conferred immortal renown upon him, while making themselves the symbol of unwarranted and outmoded opposition to the findings of science.

Incidentally, the Inquisition, Index and Holy Office are all parts of the organization to protect the purity of doctrine and to suppress heresy. They all have much the same ethos, spirit and climate, and the three work hand in hand for the purpose mentioned.

Born at Pisa in February, 1564, Galileo belonged to a noble family of straitened fortune. His father, Vincenzio, had gained some distinction as a musician and mathematician. At the age of twelve, Galileo was enrolled in the monastery school at Vallombrosa, and it seems that he entered the Vallombrosan order as a novice. He was withdrawn by his father, however, before he completed his novitiate and in 1581 he entered the University of Pisa to pursue the liberal arts course as a prerequisite for entering the school of medicine.

After four years he was compelled by lack of funds to leave the university without graduating. His formal education was thus completed when he was just twenty-one. He continued to study privately and began to write. In 1586 he wrote a treatise on the hydrostatic balance and two years later he published a work on the center of gravity in solids, thus showing clearly that his interest and talent were in mathematics and physics.

He was fortunate enough to attract the attention of a wealthy patron, the Marchese del Monte, who had him appointed in 1589 as a lecturer in mathematics at the University of Pisa. In 1592 his patron secured an appointment for him at the nearby Venetian University of Padua, where he remained for eighteen years, the most industrious and happy period of his life. This appointment enabled him to follow his native bent, which soon placed him in the first rank of natural philosophers.

## Storm of Protest

It was to the great merit of Galileo that he combined experiment with calculation and thus went counter to the prevailing system which held that the laws and processes of nature were best learned by going not directly to nature, but to Aristotle. The latter was deemed to have spoken the last word upon all such matters. Setting himself resolutely and emphatically against such superstition, Galileo soon discredited many beliefs which had long been regarded as indisputable as the revealed truths of scripture.

This stirred a storm of protest and indignation among those whose opinions Galileo had discredited. Moreover he was a fierce controversialist who not only refuted his opponents but confounded them as well. This naturally exasperated his adversaries and did much to bring him the intense and bitter opposition with which his name has long been associated. "The boldness," observes Sir David Brewster, "may we not say the recklessness, with which Galileo insisted on making proselytes of his enemies, served but to alienate them from the truth."[1]

Although the general public regards Galileo chiefly as an astronomer, scientists consider his contributions in the field of mechanics, and especially of dynamics, as by far the most significant. While in the Pisa cathedral during his first year as a student at the university, Galileo is said to have noticed a lamp swinging and found that the lamp always required the same amount of time to complete an oscillation, no matter how large the range of the swing. Galileo verified this observation experimentally in life, and pointed out that the principle of the pendulum might be applied in the regulation of clocks.

## Galileo's Greatest Invention

Early in 1609 Galileo heard that a Dutch optician, named Lippershey, had produced an instrument by which the apparent size of distant objects was magnified. At once Galileo realized the principle by which such a result could be obtained. After a single night devoted to the study of refraction, he managed to construct a telescope which magnified three times, and he soon increased it to thirty-two. Not a few scholars regard this as the greatest of his inventions and perhaps even of his achievements.

As the first man in history to use the telescope to study the skies, Galileo accumulated new evidence that tends to prove that the earth revolves around the sun and is not the center of the universe as had been believed. He discovered the surface of the moon to be irregular and not smooth as had been supposed. He saw that the Milky Way was a collection of distant stars. He discovered the satellites of Jupiter and named them Sidera Medicea in honor of his former pupil and future employer, Cosimo II, grand duke of Tuscany.

Galileo published these startling discoveries in 1610 in *Sidereus nuncius (Starry Messenger)* and their discoverer was acclaimed the greatest astronomer of the age, if not the greatest who ever lived. Coming to Rome in 1611, Galileo was received in triumph; all the world, clerical and lay, turned out en masse to greet him. Setting up his telescope in the Quirinal Garden belonging to Cardinal Bandini, he showed the sunspots and other celestial objects to an admiring throng.

Through the ages people considered the earth as the center of the universe, and it was known as the geocentric or Ptolemaic system. It had received its doctrinal formulation in the writings of Aristotle (384-322 B.C.) and Ptolemy (ff. 150 B.C.). Both considered the earth as the fixed and immovable center of the universe. It was not until Nicolaus Copernicus (1473-1543) that a different system was sufficiently well formulated to challenge the Aristotelian-Ptolemaic position.

In his epochal work *De revolutionibus orbium coelestium* (*The Revolutions of Celestial Bodies*, 1543), Copernicus advanced the idea of a sun-centered universe in which the earth was a planet that revolved on its axis and around the sun. It is virtually certain that Copernicus belived that his system described the real motions of the heavens. But chiefly because of a misleading preface inserted in *De revolutionibus* by a Lutheran minister, Andreas Osiander, to avoid religious opposition to the new system, the reader is left with the impression that the system is only a mathematical hypothesis—an indulgence of the imagination.

This statement caused Galileo and other upholders of the Copernican viewpoint all kinds of difficulty. It was being constantly quoted against them and it was not easy to explain how a combination of circumstances was responsible for the book expressing a conclusion which was in direct conflict with the central truth that Copernicus hoped to leave as his chief legacy to mankind.

## Greatest Roadblock

After studying *De revolutionibus*, Galileo wrote to Johann Kepler in 1597 that he had discarded the Ptolemaic position several years ago and believed in the reality of the Copernican system. To demonstrate the truth of the new astronomy was soon to become the ambition and passion of his life. The greatest roadblock in his way was to be the explicit words of Scripture which contradicted some of the teachings of Copernicus.

Against his teaching that the sun, and not the earth, was the center of our world, his adversaries wanted to know why Joshua would command the sun to "stand still" if it never moved anyway (Josh. 10:12-13). They also wondered how a moving earth could be reconciled with the statement that God "fixed the earth upon its foundations, not to be moved forever" (Ps. 103:5). They also believed that the sun must be in motion, for the Book of Ecclesiastes states that "the sun rises and the sun goes down: then it presses on to the place where it rises" (Eccl. 1:5).

In December, 1613, Galileo learned from Father Benedetto Castelli that these and other texts from the Bible were being cited against the Copernican system. It was a common practice for the preachers of that day to spread the notion that the earth was the center of the universe precisely because it was the abode of man, who was the particular object of God's concern. Moreover, it was to this earth that his only begotten Son came to redeem mankind. Furthermore, the removal of man from the center seemed to minimize his cosmic significance—booting him heartlessly from the throne of all creation.

## Disturb Divine Plan?

Theologians and ecclesiastics were fearful that the radical innovations implicit in Galileo's astronomical writings would destroy the traditional conception of their whole cosmography. This was based not only on the framework of the crude science of their day but also upon a generous scaffolding of scriptural texts and theological considerations. These in the course of centuries had become so twined about the framework until the whole structure appeared as a single organic whole. Astronomy, the Bible and theology seemed to the people at the time of Galileo to stand or fall together.

The geocentric and anthropocentric view of the world had become embedded in the matrix of a religious faith as part and parcel of a divine plan. To disturb it would appear, therefore, to be disturbing the whole scheme of eternal salvation. Let us look more closely at a few of the details of their cosmography which they had arranged so neatly and with such orderly precision.[2]

The earth is the center of the universe. Surrounding it are successive transparent spheres moved by angels about the earth and each bearing one or more heavenly bodies along with it. Enclosing all is the empyrean, or tenth heaven. This is immovable and constitutes the boundary between creation and the vast outer void, wherein the Triune God sits enthroned in light, inaccessible, and with the "music of the spheres" rising to him as they course along.

Just beneath the earth is a literal hell of never-ceasing fire and brimstone. It is tenanted chiefly by the angels who rebelled under the lead of Lucifer, prince of the seraphim. Some of the rebellious angels rove among the planetary spheres causing trouble to the good angels. Others roam about the atmosphere of the earth bringing storms, lightning, drought and hail. Still others move unseen among human society, luring men to sin.

Dante gives a vivid picture of the cosmography of the medieval mind, portraying the empyrean and the concentric heavens, paradise, purgatory and hell, with the occupants of each presented as vividly as the historian of his day might describe the classifications of the feudal system in western Europe. It all seemed very real to the medieval mind. It was enshrined in all their religious symbolism and imagery, and was entwined in their thinking for centuries.

Their religious outlook had thus become so intimately interwoven into the Ptolemaic cosmography through the use of biblical texts and theological considerations that the resultant world-view was considered impregnable and final. To assail it was scarcely less than blasphemy. Such was the world-view, geocentric and anthropocentric, enshrined in the poetry and prose, in the beliefs and the yearnings, in the hopes and the fears of Christendom down to the middle of the seventeenth century.

## Bible and Science

It was against this background that Galileo wrote a letter to Castelli in which he presented his views on the relation between the Bible and science. Copies of it were widely circulated and this further stimulated discussion. Now the dispute was in the open. In December, 1614, a Dominican, Tommaso Caccini, preached a sermon at St. Maria Novella in Florence, in which he vehemently condemned the new astronomy.

Whereupon a copy of Galileo's letter on the Bible and science was forwarded to the Holy Office for examination. Its officials found nothing contrary to faith in it. A Carmelite, Paolo Foscarini, published a book that attempted to reconcile the Copernican system with scripture. He forwarded a copy of the book to Cardinal Robert Bellarmine, the leading theologian in Rome, and asked his opinion of it. In his reply Bellarmine voiced the unofficial but definite attitude of theologians toward the new astronomy.

He frankly acknowledged that the Copernican system saved the appearances better than the Ptolemaic and consequently could be considered a superior and more plausible hypothesis. But with equal candor, he pointed out that it was still not established as a fact. Furthermore, the prelate explained that no one is permitted to interpret the Scriptures contrary to the common agreement of the Fathers of the Church, and they seem to interpret the relevant texts literally.

To go contrary to their exegesis was to oppose the truth of the Scriptures themselves. In case of doubt there could be no deviation from the interpretation of the Fathers, and a doubt would always remain unless Galileo could produce a clear and unmistakable demonstration of his theory. Curiously enough, Bellarmine's opinion was erroneous on three distinct points.

## Three Errors

First, such outstanding leaders among the Fathers as St. Augustine and St. Thomas Aquinas had declared centuries previously that the Bible was not intended to teach science and consequently its authority should not be invoked in scientific disputes.

Second, although most of the Fathers, like most people generally, did believe that the earth was fixed and immovable, and that the sun moved, not a single one of them held that this had to be believed as a revealed truth.

Third, while it is true that the common interpretation of a text, whose meaning is not defined, renders that exegesis highly probable, there is still room for an alternative, if less probable, interpretation. Bellarmine insisted, however, upon a physical demonstration before he would permit any other interpretation. It is a bit surprising that a churchman of such eminence as Cardinal Bellarmine should have deviated so decisively from the common teaching of theologians on all three points.

Much more relevant was the statement he made in the letter to the Carmelite, Paolo Foscarini: "I say that if real proof be found that the sun is fixed and does not revolve around the earth, but the earth around the sun, then it will be necessary very carefully to proceed to the explanation of the passages of Scripture which appear to be contrary, and we should rather say that we have misunderstood these than pronounce that to be false which is demonstrated."

## Galileo's Views

What were the views of Galileo on Scripture and science, or what many call nature? He expressed them in his letter to Castelli and revised them in his *Letter to the Grand Duchess Christina*, who was uncertain what she should believe on this subject. Lofty and solemn, the letter has rightly become famous, as it contains passages which are among Galileo's most beautiful. It shows how Galileo's faith in nature and its laws went side by side with his faith in God.

"I think in the first place," Galileo wrote, "that it is very pious to say and prudent to affirm that the holy Bible can never speak untruth—whenever its true meaning is understood. But I believe nobody will deny that it is often very abstruse, and may say things which are quite different from what its bare words signify."

Later on he continues:

Nature . . . is inexorable and immutable; she never transgresses the laws imposed upon her, or cares a whit whether her abstruse reasons and methods of operation are understandable to men. For that reason it appears that nothing physical which sense-experience sets before our eyes, or which necessary demonstrations prove to us, ought to be called in question (much less condemned) upon the testimony of biblical passages which may have some different meaning beneath their words. For the Bible is not chained in every expression to conditions as strict as those which govern all physical effects; nor is God any less excellently revealed in Nature's actions than in the sacred statements of the Bible. . . .

But I do not feel obliged to believe that that same God who has endowed us with senses, reason, and intellect has intended to forgo their use and by some other means to give us knowledge which we can attain by them. He would not require us to deny sense and reason in physical matters which are set before our eyes and minds by direct experience or necessary demonstrations.

Galileo made one unfortunate slip, however, in his otherwise

logical and well-reasoned exposition of the relations of Scripture
and science, conceding to Scripture superior authority even in
science, unless contrary physical arguments were demonstrative.
"As to the [physical] propositions which are stated but not rigorously demonstrated," he wrote, "anything contrary to the Bible
involved in them must be considered undoubtedly false and should
be proved so by every possible means." By thus granting biblical
texts precedence over probable physical arguments to the contrary
and by his failure to prove the truth of the Copernican system,
Galileo was caught in what J. J. Langford rightly calls a "logical
snare." This was to cause him all kinds of trouble, approaching
a veritable nightmare. It was a snare that could have been avoided
if Galileo had simply reaffirmed what he had previously stated
in his *Letter to the Grand Duchess Christina* that the Bible was
not meant to teach astronomy and consequently was not admissible
as evidence in astronomy.

## Galileo in Rome

Hearing that quite a number of ecclesiastics were denouncing
his new astronomical system as antiscriptural, Galileo went to
Rome, arriving there on December 7, 1615, and was courteously
received. With incredible boldness he set about the task of convincing theologians and churchmen and even his avowed adversaries of the truth of the Copernican system of astronomy.
Describing Galileo's campaign in a letter to the Grand Duke, his
ambassador at Rome, Piero Guicciardini, wrote:

He is passionately involved in this fight of his, and he does not see
or sense what it involves, with the result that he will be tripped up and
will get himself into trouble, together with anyone who supports his
views. For he is vehement and stubborn and very worked up in this
matter and it is impossible, when he is around, to escape from his
hands. And this business is not a joke, but may become of great consequence, and the man is here under our protection and responsibility.[3]

Galileo sought to carry his campaign to the pope himself. He
obtained a letter from the Grand Duke to Cardinal Orsini. He
explained to the Cardinal that he now had conclusive proof of
the heliocentric system. Would the cardinal present the new argument to Pope Paul V for him? Orsini agreed. Reading between

the lines of the letter written by Guicciardini to the Grand Duke, one would judge that Orsini's urging of Galileo's new proof was the last straw needed to convince the pope that the whole matter had gotten badly out of hand.

On February 19, 1616, the theological consultors of the Holy Office were summoned to give a formal decision on the Copernican system. Two propositions representing Galileo's doctrine were submitted to the consultors for their opinion.

1. The sun is the center of the world and completely immovable by local motion. 2. The earth is not the center of the world, nor immovable, but moves according to the whole of itself, and also with diurnal motion.[4]

The consultors met on February 23 and decided upon the following censures: The first proposition was declared unanimously to be foolish and absurd in philosophy and formally heretical inasmuch as it expressly contradicts the doctrine of Holy Scripture in many passages, both in their literal meaning and according to the general interpretation of the Fathers and Doctors.

With regard to the second proposition, all were agreed that it merited the same censure in philosophy, and that, from a theological standpoint, it was at least erroneous in the faith.

"Both opinions," points out Langford, "were completely wrong. No Church historian can defend them. But it is legitimate to point out that the error had a number of causes, which, though they do not justify it, do help to explain how it could happen. The blame must fall chiefly on the eleven consultors. They were not mere rubber stamps. Many of them were eminent theologians who were far from afraid to speak out in defense of their opinions."[5]

What was particularly unfortunate and militated strongly against the likelihood of a fair verdict was the fact that there was not a single scientist—astronomer or mathematician—among them. They were all theologians and hence were completely out of their field of scholarship and competence. But one still wonders why, instead of paying attention to Augustine, Aquinas, Campanella or even Galileo, they adopted without any discussion Cardinal Bellarmine's faulty exegetical procedure.

"This," as Langford points out, "was nobody's fault but their own. They are the ones who actually judged that the new astronomy contradicted sacred Scripture. Pope Paul V is also partly responsible for the error. He had called for a hasty and premature decision." Neither can Galileo be held completely blameless. Profoundly convinced of the physical proof of Copernicanism, he was confident that it would eventually be recognized by all mankind. But he wanted this done almost overnight and thereby antagonized all who wanted visible, physical facts and completely demonstrable evidence, which unfortunately were not available at that time.

## Galileo before Cardinal Bellarmine

Galileo was directed to appear before Cardinal Bellarmine and was admonished not to hold or defend the Copernican astronomy any longer. Then, it would appear, the commissary-general of the Holy Office, in an excess of zeal, stepped forward and gave the astronomer an absolute order not to hold, teach or defend his opinion in any way, either verbally or in writing. Since Galileo had accepted the decision, there was no reason for the official to give Galileo such an absolute injunction. Such would have been called for only if Galileo had refused to accept the decision.

The report of this meeting, found in the files of the Holy Office under date of February 26, 1616, has been the subject of prolonged controversy. It is quite possible, points out Langford, that the commissary-general did serve such an absolute injunction upon the astronomer, but that Cardinal Bellarmine, conscious that it had not been called for, informed Galileo that he was not bound by it. Lacking the required signature and notarization, it was defective in form and therefore invalid. At any rate, with Galileo's promise to comply with the instructions, the case was closed before the Holy Office.

It was against such a background that on March 5, 1616, the Congregation of the Index issued a decree placing Copernicus' book, *De revolutionibus orbium coelestium,* and any others upholding that viewpoint upon the list of forbidden books. The decree states:

Inasmuch as it has come to the notice of the said Congregation, that false Pythagorian doctrine, directly contrary to the Holy Scripture, about the mobility of the earth and the immobility of the sun, taught by Nicolaus Copernicus in his book *De revolutionibus orbium coelestium*, and by Didacus a Stunica in his *Commentary on Job*, has now become widespread and is received by many, . . . therefore, lest such an opinion should creep further to the destruction of Catholic truth, the Congregation has decreed that the said books of Copernicus and Stunica be suspended until they are corrected, . . . and that all other books teaching the same doctrine be prohibited; and in the present decree the Congregation prohibits, condemns, and suspends them all.

In this decree no mention is made of Galileo or any of his books. Neither is the name of the pope introduced, though there is no doubt that he thoroughly approved the action, since he presided at the session of the Inquisition wherein the matter was fully discussed.

## A Deplorable Error

"In thus acting," says *The Catholic Encyclopedia*, "it is undeniable that the ecclesiastical authorities commited a grave and deplorable error, and sanctioned an altogether false principle as to the proper use of Scripture. Galileo and Foscarini rightly urged that Holy Writ is intended to teach men how to go to heaven not how the heavens go."[6]

It should be mentioned, however, that the decree of the Index received papal approval only in "common form" and consequently was only the fallible decision of a Roman Congregation. Nevertheless it still bound Catholics, but permission could easily be secured by scholars and others doing research in this special field.

The publication of the Index decree afforded Galileo's adversaries abundant material for speculation about the theological orthodoxy of the Florentine astronomer. This prompted Galileo to appeal to Cardinal Bellarmine for a written statement that he could use in self-defense. In response to Galileo's appeal, the prelate issued the following statement:

We, Robert Cardinal Bellarmine, having heard that it is calumniously reported that Galileo Galilei has in our hand abjured, and has also been punished with salutary penance, and being requested to state the truth as to this, declare that the said Signor Galileo Galilei has not abjured, either in our hand or the hand of any other person here in Rome, or anywhere else, so far as we know, any opinion or doctrine held by him; neither has any salutary penance been imposed upon him, but only the declaration made by the Holy Father, and published by the Sacred Congregation of the Index, has been intimated to him, wherein it is set forth that the doctrine attributed to Copernicus—that the earth moves round the sun, and that the sun is stationary in the centre of the world, and does not move from east to west—is contrary to the Holy Scriptures, and therefore cannot be defended or held. In witness whereof, we have written and subscribed these presents with our hand this 26th day of May, 1616.[7]

In 1623 Pope Gregory XV died and Cardinal Maffeo Barberini, a good friend of Galileo, was elected pope, taking the name of Urban VIII. To him Galileo dedicated his book *Saggiatore* (*The Assayer*), a polemic against the Jesuit Grassi. A year later Galileo went to Rome where he had six lengthy audiences with the pope. Although he refused to lift the ban on "realist" Copernican writings, he seems to have assured the Florentine scientist that as long as he discussed the subject hypothetically and did not attempt to prove the Copernican system, he was free to go ahead, write and carry on his experiments.

## Galileo Risks Everything

Galileo decided, however, to risk everything in the hope he could demonstrate his theory by convincing physical facts. Most of the succeeding six years Galileo spent on what he thought would be the conclusive proof of the Copernican system. He embodied his findings in a book, *Dialogo dei Massimi Sisteme* (*Dialogue on the Two Great World Systems*), which was published with an imprimatur in 1632. Unfortunately the main argument of the book was based on the faulty motion of sunspots.

Widespread criticism broke out over the clear implication of the book that the geocentric explanation is the one that best fits the findings of science. Urban VIII stressed again the necessity of emphasizing the hypothetical character of the book's conclusion. In addition it must carry—what the pope regarded as an unanswerable argument—the following line of reasoning: "God is all-powerful. All things are therefore possible for him. Therefore the tides cannot be adduced as a *necessary* proof of the double motion of the earth without limiting God's omniscience, which is absurd."

The conversation is carried on among three gentlemen: Salviati, who represents the scientist, and through whom Galileo speaks; Sagredo, who represents the intelligent and cultivated layman interested in science; and Simplicio, who represents the Aristotelian philosopher who stands for authority and does not admit arguments that he cannot deduce from texts. Unfortunately the name Simplicio commonly contains the implication of a simpleton, and readers immediately thought of him as the dunce who was always on the weak or wrong side of the argument. To make matters worse, Galileo has Simplicio mouth the "weighty" argument inserted into the book at the insistence of the pope. Hence it was not difficult for Galileo's enemies to convince Urban VIII that the Florentine scientist was making a laughingstock out of him.

His Holiness was furious and was not slow in venting his ire. Why was Simplicio brought into the picture? It seems incredible that Galileo would purposely seek to insult the pope and thus alienate the one man whose good will he wanted and needed more than that of any other human being. This is one of the mysteries in the life of Galileo which historians are unable to solve or even to throw any light upon.

## Storm of Protest

The *Dialogue* provoked a storm of protest. Ecclesiastics and laymen declared it was now obvious that Galileo had attempted to prove the Copernican system. The modified introductory and closing paragraphs could not disguise that patent fact. Instead of heeding the pope's instructions, the Florentine scientist had made the pontiff look ridiculous. Urban appointed a special commission of theologians to investigate. Once again Galileo was in trouble up to his neck.

The special commission made two principal charges against the astronomer. First, he had presented the Copernican system as an established fact. This was in direct opposition to the decree of the Index and of Bellarmine's admonition of 1616.

Second, he had been dishonestly silent about an order given to him in 1616 by the commissary-general during the audience with Bellarmine not to "hold, teach or defend" the new astronomy in any way, either verbally or in writing. The commission found a record of this rigorous injunction in the files of the Holy Office, and news of it came as a surprise, even to the pope. This is the document which we have already discussed and about whose authenticity scholars have recently raised serious questions.

Thus Georgio D. Santillano, professor of the history and philosophy of science at the Massachusetts Institute of Technology, writes in the *Encyclopaedia Britannica:* "The consensus of historians, based on evidence made available when the file was published in 1877, has been that the document was a plant and that Galileo was never so enjoined."[8]

On September 23, 1632, Pope Urban VIII sent word to the Inquisitor at Florence to notify Galileo that he was to appear during October before the commissary-general in Rome. As Galileo was then nearing seventy and had been failing in health for several years, he pleaded incapacity for travel and procured a medical certificate to that effect. On December 30 a papal order arrived informing the astronomer that, if he did not soon come voluntarily, Roman authorities would bring him in iron manacles.

## A Radical Shift

Accordingly Galileo, accompanied by a physician and full of forebodings, set out for Rome on January 20, 1633, and arrived there on February 13. He was kindly received and was allowed to accept lodging at the home of the Tuscan ambassador instead of in the prison of the Inquisition. Galileo had planned to fight the charge of teaching Copernican astronomy, but on the advice of friends and in view of the strong bias against him, finally gave up all idea of opposition and resolved on complete submission.

This must be regarded as a radical shift due to the strong official pressure put upon him and justifiable in the technical sense of the plea "not guilty." The second examination took place on April 30. Instead of repeating his previous denials, he now spontaneously acknowledged that he had defended those views. Why this about-face?

The explanation is that the commissary-general visited Galileo privately and persuaded him to make a clean breast of his "fault" as the only chance of appealing to the mercy of the court. Looming up too was the realization of the horrendous capacity of the Inquisitors for torture and burning victims at the stake. The prospect of being turned over to the torture-hungry hands of these monsters was enough to cause any man to shudder. Large portions of Europe were then resounding with the fearful screams of their pitiable victims. Accordingly, when asked what he had to say, the elderly astronomer made the following abject and humiliating confession:

In the course of some days' continuous and attentive reflection on the interrogations put to me on the 12th of the present month, and in particular as to whether sixteen years ago an injunction was intimated to me by order of the Holy Office forbidding me to hold, defend, or teach, in any manner, the opinion that had just been condemned—of the motion of the earth and the stability of the sun—it occurred to me to reperuse my printed *Dialogues* (which for three years I had not seen), in order carefully to note whether, contrary to my most sincere intention, there had by any inadvertence fallen from my pen anything from which a reader or the authorities might infer not only some taint of disobedience on my part, but also other particulars which might induce the belief that I had contravened the orders of Holy Church.

And being by the kind permission of the authorities at liberty to send about my servant, I succeeded in procuring a copy of my book, and having procured it I applied myself with the utmost diligence to its perusal and to a most minute consideration thereof. And, owing to my not having seen it for so long, it presented itself to me as if it were a new writing and by another author. I freely confess that in several places it seemed to me to set forth in such a form that a reader ignorant of my real purpose might have had reason to suppose that the arguments adduced on the false side, and which it was my intention to refute, were so expressed as to be calculated rather to compel conviction by their cogency than to be easy of refutation.

Two arguments there are in particular—the one taken from the sunspots, the other from the ebb and flow of the tide—which in truth come to the ear of the reader with far greater show of force and power than ought to have been imparted to them by one who regarded them as inconclusive and who intended to refute them; as, indeed, I truly and sincerely held and do hold them to be inconclusive and admitting of refutation. And as excuse to myself for having fallen into an error so foreign to my intention, not contenting myself merely with saying that when a man recites the arguments of the opposite side with the object of refuting them he should, especially if writing in the form of dialogue, state them in their strictest form, and should not cloak them to the disadvantage of his opponent.

Not contenting myself with saying this, I now see I was misled by that natural complacency which every man feels with regard to his own subtleties, and in showing himself more skilful than the generality of men in devising, even in favor of false propositions, ingenious and plausible arguments. However, although with Cicero *avidior sim gloriae quam satis est* (I may be more avid of glory than I should be), if I had now to set forth the same reasonings, without doubt I should so weaken them that they should not be able to make an apparent show of force of which they are really and essentially devoid. My error, then, has been—and I confess it—one of vainglorious ambition and of pure ignorance and inadvertence. This is what occurs to me to say with reference to this particular, and what suggested itself to me during the reperusal of my book.

## Not Far Enough?

Galileo was permitted to withdraw after completing this self-debasing statement and no questions were put to him. He must have concluded from this silence or from other signs that he had not gone far enough in the denial of his inmost convictions. Perhaps the Inquisitors would be conciliated by the resolution publicly to correct his error. Whatever prompted the impulse, Galileo returned immediately to the court and spoke as follows:

And in confirmation of my assertion, that I have not held and do not hold as true the opinion which has been condemned, if there shall be granted to me, as I desire, means and time to make a clearer demonstration thereof, I am ready to do so; and there is a favorable opportunity for this, seeing that in the work the interlocutors agree to meet again after a certain time, to discuss several distinct problems of nature connected with the matter discussed at their meetings.

As this affords me an opportunity of adding one or two other "days," I promise to take up the arguments already adduced in favour of the said opinion, which is false and has been condemned, and to confute them in such most effectual manner as by the blessing of God will be possible to me. I pray, therefore, this sacred tribunal to aid me in this good resolution, and to enable me to put it into effect.

Before returning to the Tuscan embassy, Galileo was required
to take an oath to remain there, to discuss the matter with nobody,
and to present himself to the Holy Office when summoned. On
May 10 Galileo appeared before the Inquisition for the third time.
He handed in a written statement in which among other admis-
sions, obviously made under strong moral pressure, he acknowledged that he had a strict injunction in 1616. He explained why
he had not mentioned it in applying for the imprimatur in 1630.
The document concludes as follows:

Lastly, it remains for me to pray you to take into consideration
my pitiable state of bodily indisposition, to which at the age of seventy
years I have been reduced by ten months of constant mental anxiety,
and the fatigue of a long and tiresome journey at the most inclement
season, together with the loss of the greater part of the years of which,
from my previous condition of health, I had the prospect. I am encouraged to ask this indulgence by the clemency and goodness of the
most eminent lords, my judges, and hope that they will be pleased
to remit what may appear good to their entire justice, and to consider
my sufferings as adequate punishment.

It is obvious that Galileo's attitude in this matter had changed
to one of yielding, against his own profound convictions, to
forces utterly beyond his power to resist. He gives one the impression of a man fighting for his life, struggling desperately to
escape the flaming fagots at the stake or the cold dark dungeons
where he would be chained to pillars, unable to walk. Such
threatened tortures can break the independent spirit of virtually
any man.

On June 16, 1633, at a private meeting of the Inquisition, over
which the pope presided, it was decided to try Galileo as to his
intention under threat of torture. If this failed, he was then to
be called upon to recant before a full assembly of the Holy Office.
There he could be sentenced to imprisonment at their pleasure,
and be forbidden to discuss, either in writing or speaking, the
opinion that the earth moves and the sun is stationary, or even the
contrary opinion, under the pain of further punishment.

Furthermore, the *Dialogues* were to be prohibited, and copies
of the sentence were to be sent to all papal envoys and Inquisitors,
the same being read publicly in Florence. Accordingly, on June
21 Galileo was summoned once more. In response to questions

put three times, Galileo replied on oath: "I do not hold and have not held this opinion of Copernicus since the command was given me that I must abandon it. For the rest I am here in your hands. Do with me as you please."

## Galileo Sentenced

Following this session, Galileo was lodged in a comfortable apartment in the Holy Office awaiting the official sentence. Finally, on June 22, 1633, he was led to the hall of the Dominican Convent of S. Maria sopra Minerva, where before a full assembly his sentence was read to him. The document begins: "We the undersigned," then the names of 10 cardinals and their respective churches are listed, and then it continues:

By the grace of God, Cardinals of the Roman Church, Inquisitors General throughout the whole Christian Republic, Special Deputies of the Holy Apostolical Chair against heretical depravity:

Whereas you, Galileo, son of the late Vincenzio Galilei, of Florence, aged 70 years, were denounced, in 1615, to this Holy Office, for holding as true a false doctrine taught by many, namely, that the sun is immovable in the centre of the world, and that the earth moves, and also with a diurnal motion; also for having pupils whom you instructed in the same opinions; also for maintaining a correspondence with the same with some German mathematicians; also for publishing certain letters on the sun-spots, in which you developed the same doctrine as true; also for answering the objections which were continually produced from the Holy Scriptures, by glozing the said Scriptures according to your own meaning; and whereas thereupon was produced the copy of a writing, in form of a letter, professedly written by you to a person formerly your pupil, in which, following the hypothesis of Copernicus, you include several propositions contrary to the true sense and authority of the Holy Scriptures.

Therefore (this Holy Tribunal being desirous of providing against the disorder and mischief which were thence proceeding and increasing to the detriment of the Holy Faith), by the desire of his Holiness and of the Most Eminent Lords, Cardinals of this supreme and universal Inquisition, the two propositions of the stability of the sun and the motion of the earth were qualified by the Theological Qualifiers as follows:

1. The proposition that the sun is the centre of the world and im-

movable from its place is absurd, philosophically false, and formally heretical; because it is expressly contrary to the Holy Scriptures.

2. The proposition that the earth is not the centre of the world, nor immovable, but that it moves, and also with diurnal motion, is also absurd, philosophically false, and, theologically considered, at least erroneous in faith.

But whereas, being pleased at that time to deal mildly with you, it was decreed in the Holy Congregation, held before his Holiness on the twenty-fifth day of February 1616, that his Eminence the Lord Cardinal Bellarmine should enjoin you to give up altogether the said false doctrine; and, if you should refuse, that you should be ordered by the Commissary of the Holy Office to relinquish it, not to teach it to others, nor to defend it; and in default of acquiescence, that you should be imprisoned; and whereas in execution of this decree, on the following day, at the Palace, in presence of his Eminence the said Lord Cardinal Bellarmine, after you had been mildly admonished by the said Lord Cardinal, you were commanded by the Commissary of the Holy Office, before a notary and witnesses, to relinquish altogether the said false opinion, and, in future, neither to defend nor teach it in any manner, neither verbally nor in writing, and upon promising obedience you were dismissed.

## A "Pernicious" Doctrine

And, in order that so pernicious a doctrine might be altogether rooted out, nor insinuate itself further to the heavy detriment of the Catholic truth, a decree emanated from the Holy Congregation of the Index prohibiting the books which treat of this doctrine, declaring it false and altogether contrary to the Holy and Divine Scripture.

And whereas a book has since appeared, published at Florence last year, the title of which showed that you were the author, which title is *The Dialogue of Galileo Galilei, on the Two Principle Systems of the World—the Ptolemaic and Copernican;* and whereas the Holy Congregation has heard that, in consequence of printing the said book, the false opinion of the earth's motion and stability of the sun is daily gaining ground, the said book has been taken into careful consideration, and in it has been detected a glaring violation of the said order, which had been intimated to you; inasmuch as in this book you have defended the said opinion, already, and in your presence, condemned; although, in the same book, you labor with many circumlocutions to induce the belief that it is left by you undecided and merely probable, which is equally a very grave error, since an opinion can in no way be probable which has been already declared and finally determined contrary to the Divine Scripture.

Therefore, by Our order, you have been cited to this Holy Office, where, on your examination upon oath, you have acknowledged the said book as written and printed by you. You also confessed that you began to write the said book ten or twelve years ago, after the order aforesaid had been given. Also that you had demanded licence to publish it, without signifying to those who granted you this permission that you had been commanded not to hold, defend, or teach the said doctrine in any manner. You also confessed that the style of the said book was, in many places, so composed that the reader might think the arguments adduced on the false side to be so worded as more effectually to compel conviction than to be easily refutable, alleging, in excuse, that you had thus run into an error, foreign (as you say) to your intention, from writing in the form of a dialogue, and in consequence of the natural complacency which every one feels with regard to his own subtleties, and in showing himself more skilful than the generality of mankind in contriving, even in favor of false propositions, ingenious and plausible arguments.

And upon a convenient time being given you for making your defence, you produced a certificate in the handwriting of his Eminence the Lord Cardinal Bellarmine, procured, as you said, by yourself, that you might defend yourself against the calumnies of your enemies, who reported that you had abjured your opinions, and had been punished by the Holy Office; in which certificate it is declared that you had not abjured nor had been punished, but merely that the declaration made by his Holiness, and promulgated by the Holy Congregation of the Index, had been announced to you, which declares that the opinion of the motion of the earth and stability of the sun is contrary to the Holy Scriptures, and, therefore, cannot be held or defended.

Wherefore, since no mention is there made of two articles of the order, to wit, the order "not to teach" and "in any manner," you argued that We ought to believe that in lapse of fourteen or sixteen years they had escaped your memory, and that this was also the reason why you were silent as to the order when you sought permission to publish your book, and that this is said by you, not to excuse your error, but that it may be attributed to vainglorious ambition rather than to malice. But this very certificate, produced on your behalf, has greatly aggravated your offence, since it is therein declared that the said opinion is contrary to the Holy Scriptures, and yet you have dared to treat of it, and to argue that it is probable.

Nor is there any extenuation in the licence, artfully and cunningly extorted by you, since you did not intimate the command imposed upon you. But whereas it appeared to Us that you had not disclosed the whole truth with regard to your intention, We thought it necessary to proceed to the rigorous examination of you, in which (without any prejudice to what you had confessed, and which is above detailed against you, with regard to your said intention) you answered like a good Catholic.

## Final Sentence

Therefore, having seen and maturely considered the merits of your cause, with your said confessions and excuses, and everything else which ought to be seen and considered, We have come to the underwritten final sentence against you:

Invoking, therefore, the Most Holy Name of our Lord Jesus Christ, and of His Most Glorious Virgin Mother, Mary, We pronounce this Our final sentence, which sitting in council and judgment with the Reverend Masters of Sacred Theology and Doctors of both Laws, Our Assessors, We put forth in this writing in regard to the matters and controversies between the Magnificent Carlo Sincero, Doctor of both Laws, Fiscal Proctor of the Holy Office, of the one part: and you, Galileo Galilei, defendant, tried and confessed as above, of the other part.

We pronounce, judge, and declare, that you, the said Galileo, by reason of these things which have been detailed in the course of this writing, and which, as above, you have confessed, have rendered yourself vehemently suspected by this Holy Office of heresy, that is, of having believed and held the doctrine (which is false and contrary to the Holy and Divine Scriputres) that the sun is the centre of the world and that it does not move from east to west, and that the earth does move, and is not the centre of the world; also that an opinion can be held and supported as probable after it has been declared and finally decreed contrary to the Holy Scripture; and, consequently, that you have incurred all the censures and penalties enjoined and promulgated in the sacred canons and other general and particular constitutions against delinquents of this descriptions. From which it is Our pleasure that you be absolved, provided that with a sincere heart and unfeigned faith, in Our presence, you abjure, curse, and detest the said errors and heresies, and every other error and heresy contrary to the Catholic and Apostolic Church of Rome, in the form now shown you.

But that your grievous and pernicious error and transgression may not go altogether unpunished, and that you may be made more cautious in future, and may be a warning to others to abstain from delinquencies of this sort, We decree that the book *Dialogues of Galileo Galilei* be prohibited by a public edict,[9] and We condemn you to the formal prison of this Holy Office for a period determinable at Our pleasure; and by way of salutary penance We order you during the next three years to recite, once a week, the seven penitential psalms, reserving to Ourselves the power of moderating, commuting, or taking off the whole or part of the said punishment or penance.

And so We say, pronounce, and by Our sentence declare, decree, and reserve, in this and in every other better form and manner, which lawfully We may and can use. So We, the subscribing Cardinals, pronounce.

## Abjuration on Knees

In conformity with the preceding sentence, Galileo was required to kneel before the Inquisition, and make the following abjuration:

I, Galileo Galilei, son of the late Vincenzio Galilei of Florence, aged seventy years, being brought personally to judgment, and kneeling before you, Most Eminent and Most Reverend Lords, Cardinals, General Inquisitors of the Universal Christian Republic against heretical depravity, having before my eyes the Holy Gospels which I touch with my own hands, swear that I have always believed, and, with the help of God, will in future believe, every article which the Holy Catholic and Apostolic Church of Rome holds, teaches, and preaches.

But because I have been enjoined, by this Holy Office, altogether to abandon the false opinion which maintains that the sun is the centre and immovable, and forbidden to hold, defend, or teach the said false doctrine in any manner; and because, after it had been signified to me that the said doctrine is repugnant to the Holy Scripture, I have written and printed a book, in which I treat of the same condemned doctrine, and adduce reasons with great force in support of the same, without giving any solution, and therefore have been judged grievously suspected of heresy.

That is to say, that I held and believed that the sun is the centre of the world and immovable, and that the earth is not the centre and movable, I am willingly to remove from the minds of your Eminences, and of every Catholic Christian, this vehement suspicion rightly entertained towards me, therefore, with a sincere heart and unfeigned faith, I abjure, curse, and detest the said errors and heresies, and generally every other error and sect contrary to the said Holy Church; and I swear that I will nevermore in future say or assert anything, verbally or in writing, which may give rise to a similar suspicion of me; but that if I shall know any heretic, or anyone suspected of heresy, I will denounce him to this Holy Office, or to the Inquisitor and Ordinary of the place in which I may be.

I swear, moreover, and promise that I will fulfil and observe fully all the penances which have been or shall be laid on me by this Holy Office. But if it shall happen that I violate any of my said promises, oaths, and protestations (which God avert!), I subject myself to all the pains and punishments which have been decreed and promulgated by the sacred canons and other general and particular constitutions and against delinquents of this description. So, may God help me, and His Holy Gospels, which I touch with my own hands, I, the above-named Galileo Galilei, have abjured, sworn, promised, and bound myself as above; and in witness thereof, with my own hand have sub-scribed this present writing of my abjuration, which I have recited word for word.

At Rome, in the convent of Minerva, 22nd June, 1633, I Galileo Galilei have abjured as above with my own hand.

The prison sentence was never imposed, though Galileo re-mained under house arrest in Florence for the remainder of his life. Back in Florence, Galileo plunged into the study of dynamics and in 1636 he finished *Two New Sciences*, probably his greatest work. Not wishing to go through the trouble incurred in seeking an imprimatur for a previous work of his, he arranged for its publication in Amsterdam which was beyond the jurisdiction of the Inquisitors. A second edition, with corrections dictated by the blind scientist, followed in 1641.

In 1637, shortly after discovering the moon's libration, Galileo lost the sight of his right eye and a year later he was completely blind. Writing to a friend about his misfortune, he said: "Your dear friend and servant Galileo is irreparably and completely blind; in such a way that that sky, that world and that universe, which with my wondrous observations and clear demonstrations I amplified a hundred and thousand times over what was believed most commonly by the learned of all past centuries, is for me now so diminished and narrowed that it is no greater than what my body occupies."[10]

With the help of two disciples Galileo continued his scientific research until the end. Galileo had a son, Vincenzio, a bright and intelligent youth; and two daughters, both of whom became nuns at the age of sixteen. The younger took the name of Sister Arcangela and the elder the name of Sister Maria Celeste who developed outstanding qualities of mind and heart.

She poured out her affection and tender care upon her father and was a great comfort to him in his many trials with the Inquisitors. Galileo died on January 8, 1642, fortified by the last rites of the Church and the benediction of Urban VIII, and was buried in the Church of Santa Croce in Florence. The hostility and vengeance of the Church authorities, which so often plagued Galileo in life, pursued him even in death.

## Dawn of New Day

The Grand Duke sought permission to place a fitting monument over the tomb of the great scientist who opened up new worlds for mankind. He was refused permission on the grounds that it would not be fitting, since Galileo had given rise to the "greatest scandal in Christendom." Probably the tragic conflict between Galileo and his Church merits that title. But who will deny that the blame rests overwhelmingly upon the array of ecclesiastics who stubbornly refused to admit the world-shaking truths laid before them by the immortal Florentine scientist?

It was not until 1737, almost a century after his death, that ecclesiastical authorities finally granted permission for the erection of a monument over Galileo's tomb. In spite of the progressive and complete verification of the fundamental truths of Copernican astronomy, the congregation of the Index was incredibly slow in removing books teaching such truths from the Index.

As late as 1746, Boscovich, the noted Jesuit scientist, wishing to publish a work reflecting the heliocentric system of astronomy, asserted: "As for me, full of respect for the Holy Scriptures and the decree of the Holy Inquisition, I regard the earth as immovable; nevertheless for simplicity in argumentation I will argue as if the earth moves, for it is proven that of the two hypotheses the appearances favor this idea."[11]

The edition of the Index published in 1819 still listed the works of Copernicus and Galileo as inexorably as had all its predecessors since 1616. But in 1820 the matter came to a head. Canon Settele, professor of astronomy at Rome, had prepared an elementary book in which the Copernican astronomy was taken for granted. The master of the sacred palace, Anfossi, who acted as censor of the press, declined to permit the book to be printed unless Settele revised the volume and treated the Copernican system as a mere hypothesis.

Settele appealed from the decision of the censor to the pope, Pius VII, who referred the question to the Congregation of the Holy Office. On August 16, 1820, the Congregation decided to permit Settele to teach the Copernican system as established, and the pope confirmed this decision. The decision provoked considerable discussion, but finally on September 11, 1822, the cardinals of the Holy Inquisition agreed that "the printing and publication of works treating of the motion of the earth and the stability of the sun, in accordance with the general opinion of modern astronomers, is permitted at Rome."

Thus it was more than two centuries after that fateful night on January 11, 1610, when Galileo swept the heavens with his crude telescope and secured striking confirmation of the revolutionary astronomical theory of the great Copernicus, that the Church officially permitted the publication of works presenting the system as an established scientific fact. But it was not until 1835 that there was issued an edition of the Index from which was omitted the condemnation of works affirming the double motion of the earth. This was almost three centuries after the appearance of the epochal work of Copernicus on the revolutions of the heavenly bodies, *De revolutionibus orbium coelestium*, which had long ago changed mankind's whole conception of the world in which he lived.

Much of the animosity toward the Church is traceable to its historic tendency to hold on to conceptions of the universe which science has long outmoded and to use the Bible as a textbook of science—a use for which it never was intended. Surely the name Galileo will be a constant reminder of this truth. Leo Joseph Cardinal Suenens of Belgium sounded this warning to the thousands of prelates at Vatican Council II in Rome, on October 29, 1964, when he said: "Venerable Brethren, one Galileo case is enough."

That sentiment for the clearing of Galileo's name of guilt for teaching that the earth is not the fixed and immovable center of the world but revolves around the sun is widespread throughout the Church and especially among its leaders would seem to be evidenced by the proposal of another cardinal. In an address at a meeting of Noble Prize winners at Lindau, Germany, in July, 1968, Francis Cardinal Koenig of Vienna stated that the Vatican may appoint a commission to retry the Galileo case. The cardinal expressed the hope that clearing Galileo's name would "heal one of the deepest wounds between science and religion." Though such vindiction of Galileo's name would be more than three centuries late, it would shine like a rainbow in the sky and herald the dawning of a new and brighter day in the relations between science and religion within the Church.

## CHAPTER XV

# A New Era

When men are animated by the charity of Christ they feel united, and the needs, sufferings and joys of others are felt as their own.

POPE JOHN XXIII

THE PURPOSE OF THIS FRANK AND HONEST DISCLOSURE of the harsh, cruel and inhuman treatment of deviates from the Catholic faith by the medieval Inquisitors has not been to revive old animosities. On the contrary, it endeavors to show the utter futility of seeking to coerce, through violence and torture, doctrinal deviates into conformity with the official Catholic viewpoint. Faith is a matter of the intellect. In consequence it is, as we have previously pointed out, unamenable to physical force or torture of any kind.

Even though the accused may appear to conform, it will be only an outward conformity. Conscience is an impregnable fortress which opens only from within. Hence the Inquisition faced an impossible task, as the infliction of pain and torture remain forever fruitless.

This is the important truth which the history of the Inquisition brings out and it is worth stressing, for the temptation to resort to pressure on the part of those in power seems always to remain. Ecclesiastical authorities have learned this lesson and they have put it into practice on a worldwide scale.

In fact, there is the dawning of a new era in the relations of Catholics with Protestants, Jews and other non-Christian religious organizations. This era of ecumenism was brought about largely by Pope John XXIII and Vatican Council II which he convoked. One of the most remarkable in the long line of prelates who have sat upon the chair of Peter, Pope John brought to his task a great simplicity, a transparent compassion and a warmth of affection which won the hearts of people everywhere.

After announcing his intention to convoke an ecumenical, or general, council, he astonished members of other Christian Churches by inviting the larger denominations to send representatives to the Council. This they did, and their attendance and informal participation gave to the Council an ecumenical aspect never previously witnessed.

He met with these delegates, gave them choice seats at the Council, provided them with copies of all relevant documents and special interpreters to enable them to follow the proceedings which were in Latin. Many of the Council Fathers acknowledged that they too would have welcomed that service.

In addition, he requested the representatives to favor the Council with their thoughts, suggestions and criticisms. Mingling freely with the bishops, they entered into discussions with them, and their observations were genuinely welcomed. Taking cognizance of their active presence, the speakers began to address them along with the Council Fathers, calling the Protestant representatives *Carissimi Osservatores* (Dearest Observers).

## *"Let Us Come Together"*

Passing up his throne at St. Peter's Cathedral, Pope John took a seat among the Council Fathers and said: "We do not intend to conduct a trial of the past; we do not want to prove who was right or who was wrong. The blame is on both sides. All we want is to say: 'Let us come together. Let us make an end of our divisions.' "

Speaking with similar warmth and affection, his successor, Pope Paul VI, said to them: "After so many years of separation, after such polemics, what else can we do but again love one another, listen to one another and pray for one another?"

Vatican II issued no single condemnation. It was entirely constructive, seeking to enlarge areas of common agreement. It changed the whole climate of the Christian world, and replaced suspicion and aloofness with understanding, brotherhood and love—a climate that was the exact reverse of the Inquisition with its flaming hostility, vengeance and torture.

The Fathers of Vatican II showed similar concern to eradicate the anti-Semitism which has so often disgraced the relation of Christians toward their Jewish neighbors. Pointing out the great debt which the Christian world owes to the people of Israel, the Council sought to replace anti-Semitism with brotherhood and love.

In its *Declaration on the Relationship of the Church to Non-Christian Religions,* the Council states that the blame for the death of Christ cannot be placed upon all the Jews then living, without distinction, nor upon the Jewish people today. It states that Jews are not to be presented as repudiated or cursed by God as if such views followed from Holy Scripture.

While the Church, observed the Council, repudiates persecution against any man, it is especially mindful of its common patrimony with Jews and consequently it "deplores the hatred, persecutions, and displays of anti-Semitism directed against the Jews at any time and from any source." In short, if the injunctions of the Council concerning the relations of Christians with Jews were put into practice, the Anti-Defamation League of B'nai B'rith could close up shop.

The Declaration also refers with great warmth and kindness to members of other non-Christian religions. We shall present briefly its chief highlights. Pointing out that every day people are being drawn closer together by numerous ties, the document declares that all peoples comprise a single community and have a single origin, since God made the whole race of men. God, his providence, manifestations, goodness and saving designs extend to all men.

From ancient times down to the present, there has existed among different peoples a perception of that hidden power which hovers over the course of things and over the vicissitudes of human life. Recognition of a Supreme Divinity and a Supreme Father can be discerned and such a recognition invests the lives of these people with a deep religious sense.

Thus in Hinduism people contemplate the divine mystery and express it in various ways. They seek release from the anguish of their condition through ascetical practices, or deep meditation, or a loving trustful flight toward God.

Similarly in its multiple forms Buddhism acknowledges the radical insufficiency of this shifting world. It points to a path by which persons in a devout and confident spirit can either reach a state of absolute freedom or attain supreme enlightenment by their own efforts or by assistance from on high.

The Catholic Church, points out the document, rejects nothing which is true and holy in these and other religions. Accordingly, she exhorts her sons "prudently and lovingly, through dialogue and collaboration with the followers of other religions, and in witness of Christian faith and life, to acknowledge, preserve, and promote the spiritual and moral good found among these men, as well as the values in their society and culture."

One of the Council's other great achievements was the issuance of *The Declaration on Religious Freedom*, in which the right of the person and of communities to social and civil freedom in religious matters is continually stressed. It emphasizes the dignity of the human person and his right to a responsible freedom, not driven by coercion but motivated by a sense of duty.

The document develops the doctrine of recent popes on the inviolable rights of the human person and on the constitutional order of society. In brief, it replaces the horrible and shameful violence of the Inquisitors with religious freedom and recognizes the civil right of the citizen to follow his conscience in faith and worship. One can well imagine the surprise, chagrin and horror of Inquisitors such as Bernard Gui, Nicolas Eymeric and especially of the Spanish Inquisitor General, Tomas de Torquemado, with some two thousand victims to his discredit, if they were to read this Declaration of Vatican II on religious freedom.

## Trailblazing Steps

One of the most remarkable of all the documents issued by Vatican II is the *Decree on Ecumenism*. It takes unprecedented steps toward the achievement of Christian unity. The decree cites the moving prayer of Christ at the paschal meal in the upper room the night before his death on Calvary's cross: "Holy Father, keep in thy name those whom thou hast given me, that they may be one even as we are . . . that they also may be one in us, that the world may believe that thou hast sent me . . . that they may be perfected in unity" (John 17:11-23).

After referring to the great religious upheaval of the sixteenth century which shattered Christian unity, the document frankly acknowledges that men on both sides were to blame. Then it points out that persons born and reared in the separated Christian communities cannot be charged with the sin of separation. On the contrary, the Church accepts them with respect and affection as brothers.

Persons who believe in Christ and have been properly baptized are brought into a certain, though imperfect, communion with the Church. True enough, differences in doctrine, discipline, and in regard to the structure of the Church create obstacles, sometimes serious ones, to full ecclesiastical union. But the ecumenical movement has brought a new spirit of understanding, good will, respect and love into the relations of all Christians and is striving with the guidance and assistance of the Holy Spirit to remove those obstacles.

Hence in spite of all the difficulties and roadblocks, there is the great comforting truth, more clearly recognized now than ever before, that all who have been justified by faith in baptism are incorporated into Christ. Therefore they "have a right to be called Christian, and so are correctly accepted as brothers by the children of the Catholic Church."

Equally trailblazing is the frank acknowledgment by the Council that many of the most significant elements and endowments, which together build up and give life to the Church itself, can and do exist outside the visible boundaries of the Catholic Church. Among the most important of these vitalizing elements are the written word of God, the life of Grace, faith, hope, and charity along with the other interior gifts of the Holy Spirit, as well as visible elements. Furthermore, our separated brethren also carry out many liturgical actions of the Christian religion. These certainly engender and foster a life of Grace and hence can aptly give access to the communion of salvation.

Thus the documents of Vatican II show vividly the giant steps which the Church has taken since the days of the medieval Inquisition. Indeed the distance between the two is so great that in can only be expressed in terms of light-years.

# Notes

## CHAPTER I

### Understanding the Inquisition

1. *Sacramentum Mundi*: An Encyclopedia of Theology, Ed. Karl Rahner et al., General Editor: Adolf Darlap, 6 vols. (New York: Herder & Herder, 1968–1970) 3:139-140.
2. *The Catholic Encyclopedia for School and Home*, 12 vols. (New York: McGraw-Hill, 1965) 5:475.
3. *Encyclopædia Britannica*, 24 vols. (Chicago: Encyclopaedia Britannica, 1971) 12:270.
4. Hoffman Nickerson, *The Inquistion: A Political and Military Study of its Establishment*, 2nd ed. (London: John Bale Sons and Danielsson, 1932) p. xxxix.
5. Leo XIII; *Brief on Historical Studies*, Aug. 18, 1893.
6. John Henry Newman, *Historical Sketches*, 3 vols. (New York: Longmans, Green and Co., 1903) 2:231.
7. Paul Fredericq, *Historiographie de l'Inquisition*, the preface to Reinach's French translation of Lea's *History of the Inquisition in the Middle Ages*, p. xiv.
8. Elphège Vacandard, *The Inquisition: A critical and historical study of the coercive power of the Church*, trans. Bertrand L. Conway, C. S. P. from the 2nd ed. (New York: Longmans, Green and Co., 1907) p. vii.
9. G. G. Coulton, *Inquisition and Liberty* (Boston: Beacon Press, 1938).
10. Vacandard, *op. cit.*, p. viii.
11. Henry Charles Lea, *A History of the Inquisition of the Middle Ages*, 3 vols. (New York: Macmillan Co., 1887) 1:iii.
12. G. Pelhisse, *Chronique* (1230-1237), Ed. Douhais (Paris, 1882) pp. 97-98; L. Tanon, *Histoire Des Tribunaux De l'Inquisition en France* (Paris, 1893) pp. 54-55.

## CHAPTER II

### Establishment of the Inquisition

1. *New Catholic Encyclopedia*, 15 vols. (New York: McGraw-Hill, 1967) s. v. "Inquisition," 7:536.
2. Coulton, *op. cit.*, p. 113.
3. Vacandard, *op. cit.*, p. 118–119.
4. Barnardus Guidonis, *Practica inquisitionis heretice pravitatis*, ed. Celestin Douais (Paris: A. Picard, 1886) pp. 232–233.
5. Coulton, *op. cit.*, 108–109.

CHAPTER III

## The Inquisition in Operation

1. Bull *Prae Cunctis*, July 28, 1262 in Ripoll, *Bullarium ordinis franciscani Praedicatorum*, (Paris: Bibliotheque Nationale) 1:428
2. Vacandard, *op. cit.*, p. 167
3. Lea, *op. cit.*, 1:364
4. *Ibid.*, 1:406. Cf. Louis de Paranio, *De origine et progressu officii sanctae Inquisitionis ejusque utilitate et dignitate.* (Madrid, 1598) pp. 32–33.
5. Yves Dossat, *Les crises de l'inquisition toulousaine au xiii^e siècle (1233-1273)* (Bordeaux, Imprimerie Biere, 1959) pp. 249–259.
6. Vacandard, *op. cit.*, p. 196.
7. *Ibid.*, p. 184.
8. D. Vaissete, *Histoire generale du Languedoc*, 10 vols. (Toulouse, J. B. Paya, 1840–1845) 10:c. 273.
9. Celestin Douais, *Documents pour servir à l'histoire de l'Inquisition dans le Languedoc*, 2 vols. (Paris: Renouard, 1900) 2:307.
10. Cf. J. M. Vidal, "Le tribunal de l'Inquisition de Pamiers," Annales de Saint-Louis-des-francais (Rome and Paris, Oct. 1905) p. 5.
11. Cf. J. Hulillard-Bréholles, *Historia diplomatica Frederici II*, 7 vols. in 12 (Paris, 1852–1861) 4:462; also 4:435 and 444.
12. Lea, *op. cit.*, 1:487.
13. *Ibid.*
14. *Ibid.*, 1:487, footnote.


CHAPTER IV

## Extortion of Confession

1. Arch. de l'Inquis. de Carcassonne (Doat, xxxi: 5, 103); Zanchini, *Tract. de Haeret.*, c. ix. Cf. Lea, *op. cit.*, 1:399.
2. Lea, *op. cit.*, 1:401.
3. Muratori, *Antiquitat. Ital. Dissert.*, 60; Zanchini, *op. cit.*, cc. xxiv and xl; Lami, *Antichità Toscane* p. 497. Cf. Lea, *op. cit.*, 1:405.
4. Guidonis, *op. cit.*, c. iv–v (Doat, xxx). Cf. Lea, *op. cit.*, 1:409.
5. Lea, *op. cit.*, 1:410.
6. Chassaing, *Spicilegium Brivatense* (Paris, 1886) p. 92. Cf. Lea, *op. cit.*, 1:408.
7. Guidonis, *op. cit.*, c. v; "Modus examinandi Haereticos," *Mag. Bib. Pat.*, xiii: 342. cf. Lea, *op. cit.*, 1:411.
8. Lea, *op. cit.*, 1:414.

CHAPTER V

## The Use of Torture

1. Coulton, *op. cit.*, p. 1.
2. For Glaber see Jacques Paul Migne, *Patrologiae cursus completus, Series Latina,* 221 Vols. (Paris 1844–1864) 142: 632–698. Specifically, Liber iv, Caput iv, col. 676 & 677.
3. Ferdinand Lot, *The End of the Ancient World* (New York: A. Knopf, 1931) p. 392.
4. Vacandard, *op. cit.*, p. 153.
5. Lea, *op. cit.*, 1:421-423.
6. *Superstition and Force,* 3rd ed. (1878) pp. 419-420; *Lib. Civ. Verone,* Ann. 1228, c. 75; *Constit. Sicular Lib.,* I, Tit. 27; *Frid. II. Edict.* 1220, c. 5. Cf. Lea, *op. cit.*, 1:422.
7. Jean Guiraud, *The Medieval Inquisition,* trans. E. C. Messenger (London: Burns Oates and Washbourne, 1929) pp. 86-87.
8. Nicolas Eymeric, *Directorium Inquisitorum* (1376) pp. 480, 592, 614; Zanchini, *Tract. De Haeret.,* c. ix; Bernard Comens, *Lucerna Inquis.* (Rome 1584) S.V.V. "Indicium," "Torturae," no. 19, 25. Cf. Lea, *op. cit.*, 1:426.
9. Lea. *op. cit.*, 1:429.
10. Vacandard, *op. cit.*, p. 147.
11. *Ibid.*, p. 158.
12. Christopher Hollis in *European Civilization,* ed. Eyre, 4:692-693; quoted by Coulton, *op. cit.*, p. 152.

CHAPTER VI

## The Cathar Threat

1. *Catholic Encyclopedia.* 15 vols. (New York: Robert Appleton Co., 1908) s. v. "Cathari," 3:435.
2. Lea, *op. cit.*, 1:89.
3. Coulton, *op. cit.*, p. 73-74.
4. *Ibid.*, p. 74-76.
5. *Ibid.*, p. 76
6. *Ibid.*, p. 77.
7. Vacandard, *op. cit.*, p. 99.
8. Coulton, *op. cit.*, p. 79-80.
9. A. L. Maycock, *The Inquisition: From Its Establishment to the Great Schism* (London: Harper and Brothers, 1927) p. 42.
10. *Ibid.*, p. 42.
11. Coulton, *op. cit.*, p. 81.
12. Guiraud, *op. cit.*, p. 25.
13. *Ibid.*, p. 29.

14. *Ibid.*, p. 29.
15. *Ibid.*, p. 128.
16. *Enc. Brit.*, 1971. s. v. "Cathari," 5:72.

CHAPTER VII

*The Confiscation Policy*

1. Guidonis, *Practica*, pars 3, p. 185.
2. E. Langlois, *L'Inquisition d'Après les travaux recents* (Paris, 1902). Cf. Vacandard, *op. cit.*, p. 204.
3. Lea, *op. cit.*, 1:501-524.
4. *Ibid.*, 1:480-481.
5. *Ibid.*, 1:502 f.
6. Coulton, *op. cit.*, p. 132.
7. Douais, I, 226. Cf. Coulton, *op. cit.*, p. 133.
8. Lea, *op. cit.*, 1:517.
9. *Archives de l'Évêché d'Albi* (Doat, xxxv, 83); *Les Olim*, I, 556. Cf. Lea, *op. cit.*, 1:517-518.
10. Alvarus Pelagius, *De Planctu Ecclesiae*, (1517) lib. II, c. 77, f. 219, b.
11. *Archives de l'Évêché d'Albi* (Doat, xxxiii, 207-272). Cf. Lea, *op. cit.*, 1:519-520.
12. *Les Olim*, II, 247 (Doat, xxvi, 253). Cf. Lea, *op. cit.*, l: 521.
13. *Archives Générales de Belgique, Papiers d'État*, v., 405; *Memoires de Jacques du Clerq*, Liv. IV, ch. 4, 14. Cf. Lea, *op. cit.*, 1:521-522.
14. Lami, *Antichità Toscane*, pp. 497, 536-537. Cf. Lea *op. cit.*, 1:523.
15. *Ibid.*, p. 593.
16. C. Molinier, *L'Inquisition dans le midi de la France Aux XIIIᵉ et au XIVᵉ Siècle. Étude sur les Sources de son Histoire* (Paris, 1880) p. 308. Cf. Lea, *op. cit.*, 1:528.
17. Lea, *op. cit.*, 1:529.
18. Lea, *op. cit.*, 1:532-533.

CHAPTER VIII

*The Spanish Inquisition*

1. Guidonis, *op. cit.*, 1:353.
2. A. S. Turberville, *Medieval Heresy and the Inquisition* (London, 1920) p. 173.
3. Vancandard, *op. cit.*, p. 189.
4. Quoted by Coulton, *op. cit.*, p. 288.
5. Lea, *op. cit.*, 2:174.

## CHAPTER IX

### Expulsions from Spain

1. W. E. H. Lecky, *History of the Rise and Influence of the Spirit of Rationalism in Europe*, 2 vols. (New York: D. Appleton and Co., 1872) 1:331; also 1:328-329.
2. H. C. Lea, *A History of the Inquisition of Spain*, 4 vols. (New York: Macmillan Co., 1907) 3:18, 28f. Hereafter referred to as *Inq. Sp.*
3. *Ibid.*, 3:24-26
4. C. J. Cadoux, *Philip of Spain and the Netherlands* (London: Lutterworth Press, 1947), p. 61.
5. J. L. Motley, *History of the United Netherlands*, 4 vols. (London: John Murray, 1875-1876) 3:419.
6. Lecky, *op. cit.*, 2:33-34.
7. Langlois, *op. cit.*, pp. 105-106.
8. K. J. von Hefele, *Le Cardinal Ximenes*, (Paris, 1850), p. 291.
9. Lea, *Inq. Sp.*, 1:189-211.
10. Coulton, *op. cit.*, p. 297.
11. Lea, *Inq. Sp.*, 1:139.
12. Henry Kamen, *The Spanish Inquisition* (New York: New American Library, 1965) p. 215.
13. *Lettres Ec., de R. Soc. de l'Hist. de France*, (1853) 1:333n.
14. Lea, *Inq. Sp.*, 3:389-390.
15. Vacandard, *op. cit.*, p. 199.
16. *Ibid.*, p. 199.
17. Coulton, *op. cit.*, p. 300.
18. Quoted by Coulton, *op. cit.*, p. 300.

## CHAPTER X

### The Witch-Hunt Mania

1. *Catholic Encyclopedia*, s. v. "Witchcraft," 15:674.
2. Gratian *Decretum*, Part II, C. 26, q. 5, c. 12 "Episcopi"; *Corpus Iuris Canonici*, ed. E. Friedberg (Leipzig, 1879) 1: cols. 1030-1031. Eng. trans. H. C. Lea in *Materials toward a History of Witchcraft*, 3 vols. (Univ. of Pennsylvania Press, 1939) 1:178-180.
3. de Cauzons, *La Magie en France*, 4 vols. (Paris, 1909) 2:217; *Catholic Encyclopedia*, 15:675.
4. Latin text in J. Hansen, *Quellen und Untersuchungen zur Geschichte des Hexenwahns* (Bonn: C. Georgi, 1901) pp. 25-27. Eng. trans. G. L. Burr, *The Witch Persecutions*, (Philadelphia: Dept. of History of the Univ. of Pennsylvania, 1897) pp. 7-10.
5. *Catholic Encyclopedia*, 15:676.
6. Vacandard, *op. cit.*, p. 200, note 1.

7. *The Table Talk of Martin Luther*, trans. William Hazlitt (London: David Bogue, 1848) p. 251.
8. Martin Luther, *A Commentary on St. Paul's Epistle to the Galatians* (Philadelphia, 1875) pp. 287; 590.
9. John Calvin, *Institutes of the Christian Religion*, ed. John T. McNeill, trans. Ford Lewis Battles, *Library of Christian Classics*, vol. XX (Philadelphia: Westminister Press, 1960) Book I, ch. XIV, 13-14, pp. 172-174.
10. Alan C. Kors and Edward Peters, eds., *Witchcraft in Europe, 1100-1700*, (Philadelphia: Univ. of Pennsylvania Press, 1972), p. 13.
11. Norman Cohn, "The Myth of Satan and his Human Servants" in *Witchcraft: Confessions and Accusations*, ed. Mary Douglas (London: Tavistock Publications, 1970) p. 12.
12. Lea, *Inq. Mid. Ages*, 3:549.

## CHAPTER XI

## The Sabat: Heart of Witchcraft

1. Ponzinibii, *de Lamiis*, c. 65; Bartolomeo de Spina (Rome, 1575) p. 175. Cf. Lea, *Inq. Mid. Ages*, 3:499.
2. Lea, *Inq. Mid. Ages*, p. 500.
3. Bartolomeo de Spina, O. P. *Tractatus de Strigibus et Lamiis* (Venice 1523).
4. Montague Summers, *The History of Witchcraft and Demonology* (London: K. Paul, Trench, Trubner & Co.; New York: A. A. Knopf, 1926) p. 119.
5. *Ibid., p.* 133.
6. Quoted by Summers, *op. cit.*, p. 134.
7. Quoted by Summers, *op. cit., p.* 143.
8. *De Sortilegiis*, Liber II, c. III, n. 6. Cf. Summers, *op. cit.*, p. 146.
9. Cotton Mather, "*The Wonders of the Invisible World: A Hortatory Address*," p. 81. Quoted by Summers, *op. cit.*, p. 146.
10. Calmeil, *De la folie*, 1:344. Cf. Summers, *op. cit.*, p. 149.
11. Memoires de Jacques du Clerq, Lib. IV, c. 4. Cf. Lea, *Inq. Mid. Ages*, 3:501.
12. Ord. Vital., *Hist. Eccles.*, Lib. VIII, e. 17. Cr. Migne, *P. L.*, CLXXXVIII, 607; also Lea, *Materials*, 1:171.
13. Hansen, *Quellen*, pp. 99-104. Cf. Lea, *Materials*, 1:177.
14. Desmarest, *Histoire de Magdelaine Bavent*, 4 vols. (Paris, 1652). Cf. Summers, *op. cit.*, p. 149-150.
15. *Malleus Maleficarum*, P. II, Q. 1, c. 2, 4, 11, 15; Q. 2, c. 4. Cf Lea, *Inq. Mid. Ages*, 3:502.
16. H. Boguet, *Discours*, c. XXII, p. 137. Cf. Summers, *op. cit.*, p. 157.
17. Summers, *op. cit.*, p. 157.
18. T. Wright, ed., *Dame Alice Kyteler*, (Camden Society, 1843) pp. 1-2. Cf. Summers, *op cit.*, p. 158.

19. *Mall. Malefic.*, Pars I, q. XI.
20. F. Ravaisson-Mollien, *Archives de la Bastille* (Paris, A. Durand et Pedone-Lauriel, 1866-1904) VI, p. 295. Cf. Summers, *op. cit.*, p. 160.
21. *Encyclopedia of Witchcraft and Demonology*, 1959, s. v. "Inquisition."
22. Lynn Thorndike, "Magic, Witchcraft, Astrology and Alchemy" in *The Close of the Middle Ages, Cambridge Medieval History* (New York: Macmillan Co., 1936) 8:686-687.
23. Summers, *op. cit.*, pp. 163-164.
24. Lea, *Inq. Mid. Ages*, 3:508-509.
25. *Cath. Enc.*, 15:677.
26. Cohn, *op. cit.*, pp. 11-12.

## CHAPTER XII

## Joan of Arc

1. Coulton, *op. cit.*, p. 263.
2. *Cath. Enc.*, s. v. "Joan of Arc," 8:410.
3. *Enc. Brit.*, 1971, s.v. "Joan, Saint," 13:4.
3ᵃ. Coulton, *op. cit.*, p. 259.
4. Coulton, *op. cit.*, p. 259.
5. L. Petit de Julleville, *Joan of Arc* (London: Duckworth & Co., 1901) p. 113.
6. Coulton, *op. cit.*, pp. 254-255.
7. Petit de Julleville, *op. cit.*, p. 158 f.

## CHAPTER XIII

## Savonarola: A Heretic?

1. Lea, *Inq. Mid. Ages*, 3:215.
2. Caesar Baronius, *Annales Ecclesiastici;* continued by Raynaldus (Lucca, 1738-1756) An. 1460, 31. Cf. E. R. Chamberlin, *The Bad Popes* (New York: Dial Press, 1969) pp.161; 298, 295, 291.
3. Lea, *op. cit.*, 3:209-210.
4. Jacopo da Volterra, *Diario Romano 1479-1484*, ed. E. Carusi in R. I. S., n.s. XXIII, Part III, p. 130. Cf. Chamberlin, *op. cit.*, pp. 166-167.
5. Stefano Infessura, *Diario della Citta di Roma*, ed. Oreste Tommasini in R. I. S. (1890) III, 2, ch. 14. Cf. Chamberlin, *op. cit.*, p. 170.
6. Chamberlin, *op. cit.*, p. 175.
7. Carte Strozziane, quoted in Ferdinand Gregorovius, *Lucretia Borgia: According to Original Documents and Correspondence of Her Day*, trans. John Leslie Garnet (London, 1903), p. 61. Cf. Chamberlin, *op. cit.*, p. 175.
8. Gregorovius, *op. cit.*, p. 59. Cf. Chamberlin, *op. cit.*, p. 178.

9. Alvarus Pelagius, *De Planctu Ecolesiae*, Lib. II, Art. I, II. Cf. Lea, *Inq. Mid. Ages*, 3:644.

10. Luke 23:28-31.

11. Pierre Van Paassen, *A Crown of Fire* (New York: Charles Scribner's Sons, 1960) p. 267.

12. Lea, *Inq. Mid. Ages*, 3:233.

13. Coulton, *op. cit.*, p. 261.

14. Van Paassen, *op. cit.*, p. 296.

15. *Ibid.*, pp. 296-297.

16. *Ibid.*, p. 304.

17. *Ibid.*, p. 312.

18. John 15: 12-13.

19. Van Paassen, *op. cit.*, p. 315.

20. Antonio Lupi, O. P., "Did Savonarola Disobey?" *Blackfriars* 33 (1952) p. 504.

CHAPTER XIV

## Galileo Faces the Inquisition

1. *Cath. Enc.*, s. v. "Galilei, Galileo," 6:342.

2. For a statement of the theological view of the geocentric universe, the antipodes, etc., see Heinrich von Eicken, *Geschichte und System der mittelalterlichen Weltanschaung.* (Aalen: Scientia Verlag, 1964) pp. 618ff.

3. Galileo Galilei, *Le Opere di Galileo Galilei*, 20 vols. (Florence, 1929-1939) 12:243. Cf. Jerome J. Langford, O. P., *Galileo, Science and the Church* (New York: Desclee Company, 1966) pp. 86-87.

4. *Ibid.*, 19:321. Cf. Langford, *op. cit.*, p. 89.

5. Langford, *op. cit.*, pp. 90-91.

6. *Cath. Enc.*, 6:344.

7. This and all the following documentary statements concerning the Inquisition process are to be found in an excellent work, *Galileo and his Condemnation* by Ernest R. Hull, S. J. (London: Catholic Truth Society, 1913).

8. *Enc. Brit.*, 1971, s. v. "Galileo Galilei," 9:1089.

9. A decree of the Index to this effect was published on August 23, 1634.

10. Laura Fermi and Gilberto Bernadini, *Galileo and the Scientfic Revolution* (New York: Basic Books, Inc., 1961) p. 109.

11. Joseph Bertrand, *Les Fondateurs de L'Astronomie moderne* (Paris: Hetzel, n. d.) p. 59-60.

# Bibliography

*The following is a brief and practical bibliography of works in English that will be of interest and help to the general reader. Most of these books contain extensive bibliographies that will be of interest to the specialist.*

### GENERAL

Coulton, G. G. *Inquisition and Liberty*. Boston: Beacon Press, 1938.

De Julleville, Louis Petit. *Joan of Arc*. Trans. Hester Davenport. London: Duckworth & Co., 1901.

Emery, Richard Wilder. *Heresy and Inquisition in Narbonne*. New York: Columbia University Press, 1941.

Foch, Ferdinand, et al. *For Joan of Arc:* An act of homage from nine members of the French Academy. London: Sheed and Ward, 1930.

Kamen, Henry. *The Spanish Inquisition*. New York: New American Library, 1965.

Lea, Henry Charles. *A History of the Inquisition of Spain*. 4 vols. New York: Macmillan Co., 1906-1907.

———. *A History of the Inquisition of the Middle Ages*. 3 vols. New York: Harper & Brothers, 1887.

———. *Materials Toward a History of Witchcraft*. 3 vols. New York: T. Yoseloff, 1957 (©1939).

Pratt, Sister Antoinette Marie. *The Attitude of the Catholic Church Towards Witchcraft and the Allied Practices of Sorcery and Magic*. Washington, D. C.: National Capitol Press, 1915.

Russell, Jeffrey Burton. *Religious Dissent in the Middle Ages*. New York: Wiley, 1971.

———. *Witchcraft in the Middle Ages*. Ithaca, N. Y.: Cornell University Press, 1972.

Shannon, Albert Clement. *The Popes and Heresy in the Thirteenth Century*. Villanova, Pa.: Augustinian Press, 1949.

Summers, Montague. *The History of Witchcraft and Demonology*. 2nd ed. London: Kegan Paul & Co., 1926.

Vacandard, Elphège. *The Inquisition: A critical and historical study of the coercive power of the Church*. Trans. from the 2nd ed. Bertrand L. Conway, C.S.P. New York: Longmans, Green & Co., 1907.

Van Paassen, Pierre. *A Crown of Fire: The Life and Times of Giro-lamo Savonarola.* New York: Scribner, 1960.

Wagenknecht, Edward Charles. *Joan of Arc: An Anthology of History and Literature.* New York: Creative Age Press, 1948.

Walsh, William Thomas. *Characters of the Inquisition.* New York: P. J. Kenedy & Sons, 1940.

#### THE SPANISH INQUISITION

Adler, E. N. *Auto-da-fe and Jews.* New York: H. Frowde, 1908.

Jacobs, Joseph. *An Inquiry into the Sources of the History of the Jews in Spain.* New York: Macmillan, 1894.

Kamen, Henry. *The Spanish Inquisition.* New York: New American Library, 1965.

Lea, Henry Charles. *A History of the Inquisition of Spain.* 4 vols. New York: Macmillan Co., 1906-1907.

Llorca, Bernardino. *La Inquisición Española: Estudio Crítico.* Comillas: Universidad Pontifica, 1953.

Plaidy, Jean (pseudonym for Eleanor Hibbert). *The Spanish Inquisition: Its Rise, Growth and End.* New York: Citadel Press, 1967.

Turberville, A. S. *The Spanish Inquisition.* London: Butterworth, 1920.

#### JOAN OF ARC

Barrett, W. P. (ed. and trans.) *The Trial of Jeanne d'Arc.* London: G. Routledge & Sons, 1931.

De Julleville, Louis Petit. *Jeanne d'Arc.* Paris, 1901.

France, Anatole. *Vie de Jeanne d'Arc.* 2 vols. Paris, Calmann-Levy: n.d.

Lanery, P. *Le Livre d'or de Jeanne d'Arc.* Paris, 1894.

Lang, Andrew. *The Maid of France.* New ed. London: Longmans, Green & Co., 1924.

Pernoud, Régine. *The Retrial of Joan of Arc: The Evidence at the Trial for Her Rehabilitation, 1450-1456.* Trans. J. M. Cohen. New York: Harcourt, Brace & Co., 1955.

Quicherat, Jules Etienne. *Procès De Condemnation et de Rehabilitation de Jeanne d'Arc.* 5 vols. Paris: J. Renouard & Co., 1841-1849.

Sackville-West, Victoria Mary. *Saint Joan of Arc.* New York: Stackpole Sons, 1938.

Shaw, George Bernard. *Saint Joan* (preface). New York: Brentano's, 1924.

Twain, Mark. *Personal Recollections of Joan of Arc.* New York: Harper & Brothers, 1896.

## GIROLAMO SAVONAROLA

Bellonci, Maria. *Lucrezia Borgia: La sua vita e i suoi tempi.* Milan: A. Mondadori, 1967.

Ferrara, Mario. *Bibliografia Savonaroliana Bibliografia Ragionata degli Scritti Editi dal Principio del Secolo XIX ad Oggi.* Florence: L. S. Olschki, 1958.

Ridolfi, Roberto. *The Life of Girolamo Savonarola.* Trans. C. Grayson. New York: A. A. Knopf, 1959.

*La Storoa Di Girolamo Savonarola.* 2 vols. New ed. Florence: Le Monnier, 1887.

Schnitzer, J. *Savonarola.* 2 vols. Munich: E. Reinhardt, 1924.

Soranzo, Giovanni. *Il Tempo di Alessandro VI Papa e di Fra Girolamo Savonarola.* Milan: Società Editrice Vita e Pensiero, 1960.

Van Paassen, Pierre. *A Crown of Fire: The Life and Times of Girolamo Savonarola.* New York: Scribner, 1960.

Villari, Pasquale. *Life and Times of Girolamo Savonarola.* Trans. Linda Villari. London: T. F. Unwin, 1918.


## GALILEO GALILEI

Brophy, James and Paolucci, Henry (eds.). *The Achievement of Galileo.* New York: Twayne Publishers, 1962.

Clagett, Marshall. *The Science of Mechanics in the Middle Ages.* Madison: University of Wisconsin Press, 1959.

De Santillana, George. *The Crime of Galileo.* Chicago: University of Chicago Press, 1955.

Fahie, John Joseph. *Galileo: His Life and Work.* London: J. Murray, 1903.

Fermi, Laura and Bernadini, Gilberto. *Galileo and the Scientific Revolution.* New York: Basic Books, 1961.

Galilei, Galileo, et al. *The Controversy of the Comets of 1618.* Trans. Stillman Drake and C. D. O'Malley. Philadelphia: University of Pennsylvania Press, 1960.

———. *Dialogues Concerning Two New Sciences.* Trans. Henry Crew and Alfonso de Salvio. New York: Dover Publications, 1914.

———. *Discoveries and Opinions of Galileo.* Trans. Stillman Drake. Garden City, N. Y.: Doubleday, 1957.

Hull, Ernest R. *Galileo and His Condemnation.* London: Catholic Truth Society, 1913.

Koestler, Arthur. *The Sleepwalkers: A History of Man's Changing Vision of the Universe.* New York: Macmillan, 1959.

Langford, Jerome J. *Galileo, Science and the Church.* New York: Desclee Co., 1966.

Randall, John Herman. *The School of Padua and the Emergence of Modern Science.* Padua: Editrice Antenore, 1961.

Taylor, Frank Sherwood. *Galileo and the Freedom of Thought.* London: Watts & Co., 1938.

# INDEX

# *Index*

Accusation, 28
Albigensian Crusade, 70-71
Alexander III (pope), 9, 76
Alexander IV (pope), 14, 15, 46, 117
Alexander VI (pope), 161, 162-71,
    172, 173, 177, 180-81
Alphonse of Poitiers, 33, 79-80, 84,
    86-87
Arnaud, William, 12
Augustus of Saxony, 122
Auto-da-fé, 30, 43

Baniol, Hugues de, 118
Bavent, Madeleine, 137
Belegnego, Jean de, 46

Bellarmine, Robert Cardinal, 188-90,
    192, 193, 194-95, 196, 197, 202,
    203
Benedict XI (pope), 46
Bernard, Saint, 3, 66-67
Bodin, Jean, 138
Boguet, Henri, 138
Bonaccorsi, Frà Filippo, 69
Bonaparte, Joseph, 104
Boniface VIII (pope), 80, 134
Bruno, Giordano, 127
Burning at the stake, 21-22, 30, 113,
    122, 126

Cadreyta, Fray Pedro de, 97, 98
Calmet, Dom Augustin, 133

Calvin, John, 7, 122, 123-24, 125
Caspan, Fra Paolo de, 133
Cathar heresy
collapse, 71-72
doctrines, 56-59, 60, 61-63 64-65, 66
Inquisition and, 59-61, 63
Cauchon, Pierre, 149, 153, 156, 157
Caux, Bernard de, 20, 24, 28
Chapelle, Taillefer Cardinal de la, 23
Charles V (emperor of Spain), 102, 109
Charles VIII (king of France), 160, 161
Chastelain, Georges, 148
Clement IV (pope), 85-86
Clement V (pope), 23, 43-44, 47, 80-81, 95
Clement VI (pope), 25, 96
Clement VII (pope), 109
Colonico, Fray Guillen, 97
Como, Bernardo di, 49
Concorezzo, Lorenzo du, 136
Confessions, 18, 19, 24, 31-32, 48-49, 51, 117-18
Confiscation
application, 73-74, 78, 81-82
financial support of Inquisition, 85-87
fines, 80-81, 85, 86
medieval law, 78
pecuniary penances, 74, 80, 85, 86
prescription of time, 83-84
prosecution of the dead, 29-30, 73, 74-75, 83-84
responsibility of the Church, 76-77
Spanish Inquisition, 91-92, 105, 106, 107

Conrad of Marburg, 3, 10, 12, 22
Conversions, 31-32

D'Ablis, Geoffroi, 24
D'Arsis, Jean, 79
D'Aversa, Frà Tomaso, 46
David of Augsburg, 59
Denunciation, 28

Elich, Philip Ludwig, 134-35
Excommunication, 29, 50-51, 53
Eymeric, Nicolas, 22, 49, 50, 75, 88, 98, 100, 213

Felgar, Bishop Raymond du, 8
Ferdinand and Isabella, 88, 89, 92, 95, 96, 104-5, 106-7, 108, 174
Ferris, Miguel, 99
Florente, Juan Antonio, 104
Fortescue, Sir John, 52-53
Fossato, Giovanni da, 136
Franc, Martin de, 136
Fraserii, Pedro, 99
Frederick I Barbarossa (emperor), 59
Frederick II (emperor), 21, 23, 29, 68-69
Fredol, Cardinal Berenger de, 23
Frias, Alonso Salazar y, 127

Galand, Jean, 14, 22, 24
Galileo Galilei
confession, 197-99, 200
early life, 183
scientist, 184-85, 186, 206
sentenced, 201-5, 206
views on Scripture and science, 186-87, 190-91

Garcias, Pierre, 63-64
Gatine, Etienne de, 16
Gerson, Jean, 174
Glaber, Ralph, 41-42
Gregory IX (pope), 9, 10-11, 13, 23, 63, 68, 97
Gregory XV (pope), 128
Grillard, Paul, 135
Grimaldo, Frà, 30, 84
Gui, Bernard, 11, 20, 21, 22, 32, 33, 43, 47, 52, 59-61, 65-66, 74, 77, 88, 213
Guibourg, Abbé, 139

*Hammer of Witches, The (Malleus maleficarum)*, 121-22, 125, 139
Henry II (king of Castile), 95
Henry VII (king of Germany), 117
Heresies, 9, 39, 56, 66-71, 99, 113
Heribert, Archbishop of Milan, 67
Holy Office, 183, 200, 201, 203, 204, 205
Homate, Bartolomeo de, 136
Honorius IV (pope), 22
Hopkins, Matthew, 125-26

Index, 183, 193, 194, 196, 202, 207-8
Innocent III (pope), 70, 76
Innocent IV (pope), 12, 14, 45, 80, 97
Innocent VIII (pope), 118, 165, 166, 168-69, 172
Inquisition
establishment, 9-10
Inquisition Tribunal, 11-12
judgment, 1-3, 7, 40
and medieval Christendom, 6-7, 41-42, 53-54

Monastic, 10
opposition, 12
Papal, 10, 16
procedure, 12-14, 28, 30-31
secular rulers, 23-24, 68-69
spread of, 10-11, 12, 21, 90
*see also* Spanish Inquisition and specific topics
Inquisitor
ideal, 11, 22, 98
interrogation, 33-37
irregularities, 46
role, 26-28, 30-31, 33
Institoris, Henry, 118, 120, 121
Interrogation, 33-37

Jacquerius, Nicholas, 130
Jayme II (king of Spain), 97, 98
Jews, 89, 94, 95-97, 102, 105, 107-8, 110, 212
Joan of Arc
early life, 144
execution, 157-58
trial, 140-50, 151, 152-57
John XXII (pope), 23, 44, 46, 47, 49
John XXIII (pope), 211-12

Koenig, Francis Cardinal, 209

La Voisin, 139
LeBourge, Robert, 3
Ledrede, Richard de, 138
Leo XIII (pope), 4
Louis IX (king of France), 71
Louis, Saint, 84-85, 86
Loyola, Saint Ignatius, 91
Lucero, 105-6

Lucius III (pope), 59, 76
Luther, Martin, 122-23

Manichaean heresy, 55, 56, 61, 76
Marsollier, Jacques, 44
Martin IV (pope), 85
Martin V (pope), 99
Mather, Cotton, 135
Michaelis, Sebastian, 138
Moors of Spain, 89, 94, 95, 96, 102,
    108, 109-10
Moranis, Bishop, 22
Mozzolino, Silvestro, 131

Nicholas I (pope), 117
Nicholas III (pope), 12
Nicholas IV (pope), 70

Odilo of Cluny, 41

Paramo, Louis de, 19
Pastor, Ludwig, 121
Paul V (pope), 191, 193, 194
Paul VI (pope), 211
Pelagius, Alvarus, 81
Pelisso, Guillaume, 63.
Penal code, 6-7
Penances, 17, 74, 80, 85, 86
Peter of Verona, 12
Philip the Fair (king of France),
    22-23, 46
Philip the Good (king of Bur-
    gundy), 83
Philip II (king of Spain), 91, 92,
    108-9
Pius IV (pope), 91

Pius V (pope), 91
Pius VII (pope), 208
Ponzinibio, Gianfrancesco, 131
Poyet, Pons de, 86
Presumption of guilt, 28-29, 31
Prosecution of the dead, 29-30, 73,
    74-75, 83-84, 97
Psychological pressure, 47-48
Puigerios, Fray Bernardo, 98

Raymond V (count of Toulouse),
    67
Raymond VI (count of Toulouse),
    76
Raymond VII (count of Toulouse),
    84
Retraction, 51, 52
Ribera, Juan de, 111
Robert the Dominican, 22
Rois, Gilles de, 139

Sabbat
    canon law and, 129-30, 131-32
    descriptions, 129, 130, 132-33, 134-
        37, 138, 140-42
    sacrifices, 138-39
    see also Witchcraft
Saint-Pierre, Jean de, 29
Salazo, Fray Pedro, 98-99
Santillano, Georgio D., 197
Savonarola, Frà Girolamo
    early life, 159-60
    execution, 180-82
    torture, 176-79
    trial, 179-80
Scala, Albert della, 69
Scaliger, 69, 70
Secular rulers, 23-24, 68-69

Sentences, 17-18, 20-22
Servitus, 7
Sixtus IV (pope), 89, 105, 106, 165, 174
Spanish Inquisition
  background, 94-95, 105
  confiscation, 91-92, 105, 106, 107
  ecclesiastical complexion, 93-94
  motivation of Inquisitors, 102-3, 106
  organization, 90-91, 111
  pecuniary aspect, 106
  persecution of Jews, 89, 94, 95-97, 102, 105, 107-8, 110
  persecution of Moors, 89, 94, 95, 96, 102, 108, 109-10
  persecution of witches, 125, 127
  political character, 91-93, 105
  torture, 100-6
  *see also* Ferdinand and Isabella, Tomas Torquemado
Spee, Friederich von, 128
Spina, Bartolomeo de, 131, 132
Sprenger, James, 118, 120, 121, 130, 138
Stephen of Narbonne, 12
*Strappado*, 44, 176
Strozziane, Carte, 168
Suenens, Cardinal Leo Joseph, 208

Talavera, Hernando de, 105
Theodore, Saint, 133-34
Thomas of Cantimpre, 130
Tinnidio, Friar, 69
Tonenes, Fray Pedro de, 97
Torquemado, Tomas, 89-90, 97, 105, 213
Torture, 1, 7, 8, 22-23
  application, 50-52
  methods, 44-45, 46

papal investigation, 43-47
Spanish Inquisition, 100-6
and system of punishments, 14-15, 40, 49-50
for witchcraft, 117, 118
of witnesses, 49, 112
Trilles, Martin, 99
Truce of God, 42

Urban IV (pope), 19
Urban VIII (pope), 195, 196, 197, 207

Vatican Council II, 2, 211-14
Verdict, 15-16
Vincent de Paul, Saint, 127
Vitalis, Ordericus, 136

William of Dijon, 41
Witchcraft
  and the Bible, 114-15
  canon law, 115-16, 129-30, 131-32
  confessions, 117-18
  defined, 113-14, 137-38
  in New England, 126, 135
  papal bull, 118-20, 134-35
  persecution of, 117, 121, 125-28
  responsibility, 139-42
  Spanish Inquisition, 125, 127
  torture, 117, 118
  *see also* Sabbat
Witnesses, 13, 18, 31, 49, 112

Ximenes, Cardinal, 92, 106

Zanghino, 49, 52